CONRAD WEISER
AND THE INDIAN POLICY OF COLONIAL PENNSYLVANIA

CONRAD WEISER
From a sketch found in York, Pa., by H. Diffenderfer, member of the Pennsylvania German Society

CONRAD WEISER
and the Indian Policy of Colonial Pennsylvania

JOSEPH S. WALTON

an imprint of Sunbury Press, Inc.
Mechanicsburg, PA USA

an imprint of Sunbury Press, Inc.
Mechanicsburg, PA USA

Copyright © 1900, 2022 by Joseph S. Walton.
Cover Copyright © 2022 by Sunbury Press, Inc.

Sunbury Press supports copyright. Copyright fuels creativity, encourages diverse voices, promotes free speech, and creates a vibrant culture. Thank you for buying an authorized edition of this book and for complying with copyright laws. Except for the quotation of short passages for the purpose of criticism and review, no part of this publication may be reproduced, scanned, or distributed in any form without permission. You are supporting writers and allowing Sunbury Press to continue to publish books for every reader. For information contact Sunbury Press, Inc., Subsidiary Rights Dept., PO Box 548, Boiling Springs, PA 17007 USA or legal@sunburypress.com.

For information about special discounts for bulk purchases, please contact Sunbury Press Orders Dept. at (855) 338-8359 or orders@sunburypress.com.

To request one of our authors for speaking engagements or book signings, please contact Sunbury Press Publicity Dept. at publicity@sunburypress.com.

FIRST DISTELFINK PRESS EDITION: November 2022

Set in Adobe Garamond | Interior design by Crystal Devine | Cover by Lawrence Knorr | Edited by Lawrence Knorr.

Publisher's Cataloging-in-Publication Data
Names: Walton, Joseph S., author.
Title: Conrad Weiser and the Indian Policy of Colonial Pennsylvania / Joseph S. Walton.
Description: First trade paperback edition. | Mechanicsburg, PA : Distelfink Press, 2022.
Summary: Quaker scholar Joseph Walton compiled an excellent record of the discourse between the colonists and the various native nations during the colonial period in the Mid-Atlantic from primary sources. Conrad Weiser's interactions are the focus as the proprietors sought westward movement while maintaining the peace.
Identifiers: ISBN : 978-1-934597-87-3 (softcover).
Subjects: BIOGRAPHY & AUTOBIOGRAPHY / Adventurers & Explorers | HISTORY / United States / Colonial Period (1600-1775) | HISTORY / US History / Mid-Atlantic.

Product of the United States of America
0 1 1 2 3 5 8 13 21 34 55

Continue the Enlightenment!

To
Dr. Nathan C. Schaeffer,
Superintendent of Public Instruction in Philadelphia.

CONTENTS

Foreword..xi
Preface..xiii

CHAPTER I
Indian Affairs in the Middle and Southern Colonies,
1720–1731...1

CHAPTER II
The Treaty of 1736.......................................13

CHAPTER III
The Onondaga Journey.....................................20

CHAPTER IV
Religious Revivals at Ephrata Temporarily Win Weiser
Away from Indian Affairs................................27

CHAPTER V
The Alienation of the Delawares..........................38

CHAPTER VI
The Virginia Trouble of 1743.............................52

CHAPTER VII
The Lancaster Treaty.....................................64

CHAPTER VIII
The Iroquois Struggle for Neutrality.....................85

CHAPTER IX
The First Winning of the West...........................106

CHAPTER X
The Ohio Mission 126

CHAPTER XI
Turning the People Off 138

CHAPTER XII
Rival English Traders 151

CHAPTER XIII
The French Traders in the Ohio Valley 159

CHAPTER XIV
Who Shall Take the Initiative? 175

CHAPTER XV
The Ohio Indians Go Over to the French 192

CHAPTER XVI
Weiser and the Pennsylvania Efforts for Defense 212

CHAPTER XVII
Reconciliation 232

CHAPTER XVIII
Peace 257

Conclusion 274
Index 281

Illustrations

Conrad Weiser . . . . frontispiece
Sir William Keith 3
Conrad Weiser's Wife 6
Stenton 15
The Cloisters at Ephrata 28
Bethania, Brothers' House, Ephrata 33
Count Zinzendorf 36
Shikellamy 74
Colonel George Croghan 109
Governor James Hamilton 143
George Washington 189
Washington and the Indians 203
Autograph and Letter of Conrad Weiser 216
John Harris' Ferry [Harrisburg, Pa.] 221
The Beginnings of Bethlehem 226
Teedyuscung 237
Charles Thomson 251
Conrad Weiser's House in Reading 261
Weiser's Money Box and Lock 271
Weiser's Burial Place 277

Foreword

BY the time William Penn had been granted his claim to Penn's Woods in the New World in 1681, colonies in Massachusetts and Virginia had been operating for over sixty years. This Mid-Atlantic wilderness had been explored and settled sparsely by Dutch and Swede traders but was largely the purview of the Lenni Lenape or Delaware Indians in the region surrounding what is now Philadelphia. To the west were the Susquehannocks, and to the north, the Five Nations of the Iroquois, soon to be Six.

Penn's promise to his colonists of a more open society based on the non-violence dictum of the Quakers attracted many Protestant colonists from Great Britain, Alsace-Lorraine, and the Rhine Valley. Among them were Quakers, Huguenots, Scotch-Irish Presbyterians, and thousands of German speakers of varied faiths, including Mennonites, Dunkards, Lutherans, Reformed, Moravians, Seventh-Day Adventists, and others. They found a rapidly growing town in Philadelphia and fertile farmlands all around.

Quickly it was clear the natives were to be bargained with. For many decades before Penn's charter, the indigenous peoples of North America had been decimated by the silent killer of disease, potentially killing up to ninety percent of their population over many years. This great decline caused stress and collapse. In some cases, there was a consolidation of tribes and the domination of the weak by the strong. The Iroquois based in what is now northern New York State were strong and dominated the discourse in the coming decades.

As the colonists landed and sought opportunity, William Penn and his sons sought to expand the colony ever westward. While doing so, they required an Indian agent who knew the language and customs of the tribes involved. That man was the German Conrad Weiser, who had moved with other settlers from Schoharie in New York to the Tulpehocken Valley in what is now western Berks County, Pennsylvania. Weiser had been raised among the Iroquois and knew them well.

Over the coming years, Weiser deftly handled the competing interests of the tribes and the wishes of his employer, the proprietor of Pennsylvania. Along the way, he made a lasting friendship with Chief Shikellamy, cementing the peace for over twenty years. After the chief's passing, and as Weiser aged, he found it more difficult to influence events as in the past.

Other colonies also had competing interests. In the north, Connecticut claimed substantial territory that overlapped with Pennsylvania. In the south, an ongoing border dispute with Catholic Maryland would put Philadelphia in that colony or Baltimore in Pennsylvania. In the west, Virginia sought to expand into the Ohio Country. And in the north, the French in Canada sought to expand their influence into western Pennsylvania and the fur trade.

As Weiser faded from the scene, others who were less respectful of the natives gained influence. Rum was traded, and squatters took land without permission. Then came the war with the French, which redefined the structure of the region.

Joseph Walton has compiled a classic history of the interactions of Weiser and others and the various native leaders during this formative stage of this region's history. While late in coming, Philadelphia rapidly grew into the largest city in North America and became the hub for trade, commerce, and revolutionaries. Conrad Weiser helped set the stage by negotiating honestly, without personal gain in mind, unlike those who followed. Weiser is an oft-overlooked figure in American history. Without him, the path forward would have been more difficult and the colony could not have been as stable during its formative time, when liberty and freedom were gaining a foothold.

Lawrence Knorr
November 2022

Preface

DURING colonial times, the French greatly excelled the English in their ability to secure the friendship and the trade of the Indians.

The eagerness which characterized the men of New France, as they explored the watercourses searching for new scenes and new lands, was in marked contrast with the conservative English who clustered near the coast and despised Indian affiliations.

The French quickly absorbed the Indians' customs and language and reveled in their metaphorical phrases.

The typical Englishman despised these things; consequently, his intercourse with the Indians was unfortunate and disastrous. The French captured the friendship and the trade of the natives.

The Germans and Dutch, on the contrary, were signally successful in the Indian trade, not merely because they were honest but largely because they grasped with skill the spirit of the Indian language. In this respect, none excelled Conrad Weiser, the champion of the English among the Indians. He enlarged the trade facilities of Pennsylvania, Virginia, and Maryland, while he jealously guarded the encroachments of the French.

Weiser's skill in guiding and controlling the Indian policy of Colonial Pennsylvania, and the South, postponed the threatened rupture with the Six Nations until the English Colonies were prepared to cope with their French enemies.

A history of this man was suggested to the author by Dr. Nathan C. Schaeffer, Superintendent of Public Instruction in Pennsylvania. As the work grew, the late Dr. Frederick Stone, Librarian of the Pennsylvania Historical Society, recommended that it assume its present size and purpose.

The manuscript correspondence of Conrad Weiser, and Richard Peters, has been especially helpful in preparing the work.

The author is under obligation to Dr. M. G. Brumbaugh, Prof. W. W. Deatrick, E. W. Zeigler, and a number of Weiser's descendants for material and aid so cheerfully furnished.

I

Indian Affairs in the Middle and Southern Colonies, 1720–1731

STATUS OF INDIAN AFFAIRS IN THE MIDDLE AND SOUTHERN COLONIES PREVIOUS TO THE PUBLIC APPEARANCE OF CONRAD WEISER—THE TULPEHOCKEN SETTLEMENT—THEIR LAND TITLES—THEIR LAND FINALLY PURCHASED FROM THE INDIANS—IROQUOIS REVISE THEIR ESTIMATE OF LAND VALUES—THE TUSCARORA WAR—SHALL CAROLINA AID THE CATAWBA INDIANS?—PEACE DESIRED BETWEEN THE NORTHERN AND SOUTHERN INDIAN CONFEDERACIES—VIRGINIA'S TROUBLE WITH THE IROQUOIS INDIANS—CONRAD WEISER—HIS EDUCATION—HE COMES TO PENNSYLVANIA—SHIKELLAMY SENT BY THE ONANDAGO COUNCIL TO SUPERVISE INDIAN AFFAIRS IN PENNSYLVANIA—THE LIQUOR TRAFFIC WITH THE INDIANS—ASSEMBLY AND GOVERNOR DIFFER UPON THE COURSE TO PURSUE—SHIKELLAMY SENT TO ONANDAGO—JAMES LOGAN'S EXPLANATION—SHIKELLAMY RETURNS AND BRINGS CONRAD WEISER—THE IROQUOIS CONFERENCE OF 1732—FRUITLESS EFFORTS TO INDUCE THE SHAWANESE TO RETURN—THOMAS PENN GIVES THE INDIANS ADVICE.

CONRAD WEISER came into service of the province of Pennsylvania in about 1738. At that time, a radical change in the management of Indian affairs was taking place. The Delaware tribes were losing their former prestige, and the powerful confederacy of the Six Nations were claiming more and more attention from the Pennsylvania authorities. While the province was under the personal control of William Penn, unusual care had been taken to placate the Delaware Indians. A broad belt of purchased land had been kept between the frontier settlers and the Indians' eastern claims. Penn's heirs, on the other hand, were indifferent in this matter, and as a result, misunderstandings arose, not only between the Indians and the settlers but between the proprietors and the governors.

The sufferings of the German Palatines in the Schoharie Valley were related to Governor Keith at Albany. His interest and sympathy were at once aroused. He offered them a home in Pennsylvania, where their titles could be clear and their land free from Indian claims.

A number of these Germans, led by Conrad Weiser's father, cut a road from the Schoharie Valley through the forests into the headwaters of the Susquehanna. Down this rock-strewn river, these hardy pioneers floated their precious freight until they reached the mouth of the Swatara Creek. They ascended this stream, crossing the divide between the Susquehanna and the Schuylkill, and entered the fertile valley of the Tulpehocken. Their cabins were scarcely built, and their little patches of corn ground were planted until the Indians informed them that the government had never purchased this land. Immediately petitions were sent to the governor from these long-suffering and oppressed Germans, praying that their lands might be relieved from any Indian claims. They insisted that Governor Keith had given them this promise before they left the Schoharie. Long delegations of Delaware Indians came down to Philadelphia demanding an explanation. Surely, they said, brother Onas would never have permitted such things to happen. Allummappees, their chief, said he could not believe that William Penn's people would do this, and he did not believe it until he went there and viewed the Tulpehocken lands with his own eyes. James Logan, the land agent, explained that these settlements were made without his knowledge, that Governor Keith had acted entirely on his authority, and contrary to the well-known desire of the former proprietary William Penn. Governor Gordon was now in office, Keith having, in various ways, deferred consideration of these things during his administration. The new Governor suggested that the disputed lands might have been included in one of the former purchases. The Indians immediately informed Gordon that no lands had ever been sold northwest of the Blue Ridge, then known as the Lehigh Hills. In the face of this evidence, the claims of the Delaware Indians in the Tulpehocken remained unsatisfied for nine years after the first German settlement. The purchase was finally made in 1732.[1] It included all the land drained by the Schuylkill River between the Blue Mountains and the Blue Ridge. This reluctant recognition of Indian rights, together with the well-known Walking Purchase in Bucks County in 1737, combined to alienate the Delaware Indians from the Pennsylvania government.

---

1. *Penna. Archives*, vol. 1., pp. 344-7.

SIR WILLIAM KEITH, GOVERNOR OF PENNSYLVANIA

The exodus of the Schoharie Germans to the Tulpehocken Valley seems to have first opened the eyes of the Six Nation Indians to the value of land in Pennsylvania. After that time, they denied the right of the Delaware Indians to sell any territory and pressed their own claims with diplomatic skill. The Iroquois quickly learned that the French and English were rival powers and claimants for the same colonial possessions. These Indians realized it was possible to hold the balance of power by skillful use of confederated strength. In 1711 the Tuscarora nation, then located south of the Ohio River and west of the Allegheny Mountains, entered into a conspiracy with several neighboring tribes to fall upon the Carolina settlers. The white men immediately availed themselves of the ancient feud between the Northern and Southern Indians and formed an alliance with the Catawba and other Muskokee Indians. After some severe fighting, fifty Carolinians and 1000 Indians drove the Tuscaroras out of their hunting grounds. The broken remnant of this once-famous nation retired to Pennsylvania and New York, becoming a part of the great Iroquois Confederacy. Thus in 1713, the Five Nations became the Six Nations. From that hour, the Iroquois hatred of the Catawba Indians became relentless.

Scarcely a season passed, but several roving bands of painted warriors followed the mountain valleys toward the South, where they might satiate their revenge with Southern scalps. The Catawba Indians demanded protection from the men of Carolina. It was a well-known fact that if the white men, while aiding the Catawbas, should injure any of the Six Nation Indians, it would precipitate an Iroquois war, in which event it was feared that the Six Nations would form an alliance with the French, and jeopardize the very existence of the American colonies. The English crown, before whom the Six Nations had already been represented by able deputies, counseled peace at all hazards. New York and Pennsylvania colonies were decidedly opposed to war with the Iroquois. Accordingly, Carolina's purpose was to effect peace between the Northern and the Southern Indians. For over thirty years, this subject was pending. In these negotiations, Carolina appealed to Virginia, and Virginia, in turn, to Pennsylvania and New York. There was one man who, during these difficulties, retained the confidence of both the Iroquois and the Southern Indians, and that man was Conrad Weiser. Although a lasting peace was never made between the Indian confederacies, Conrad Weiser managed the Six Nations to reduce hostilities to a minimum. He guided not only the Indian policy of Pennsylvania but also Virginia and Carolina. In this affair, the influence of Colonel Johnson in New York stopped with the Mohawks, but Conrad Weiser operated upon all the remaining nations of the confederacy and for twenty-five years held the Iroquois aloof from the French with one hand, while with the other, he prevented Virginia and Carolina from bringing on a war with this powerful confederation. And all these years were needed to enable the English to win the victory which swept French dominion from North America in 1763.

When the Virginia settlements began encroaching upon Iroquois war trails to the South, these bands of Northern warriors annoyed the settlers by picking up a living as they passed. The Virginians would not submit to this and passed their famous ranger law,[2] which provided for a body of rangers or lieutenants, who were authorized to arrest all armed bands of roving Indians and take them before the nearest magistrate for further examination, and until said Indians could give a satisfactory account of themselves, they were to be lodged in the county jail. This law further provided that if any Indians resisted or ran away, it would be entirely legal for the officers to kill them. The effects of such legislation, as executed by the frontier magistrate, plunged Virginia into endless trouble with the Iroquois, and had it not been for Conrad Weiser, the results might have been serious. Pennsylvania, on the other hand, followed a different course. When the settlers lost any of their stock through the thieving propensities of some of the Indians, the matter was laid before the nearest magistrate, and certification of the amount of damage was sent to the governor, who paid the bill out of sums of money appropriated for Indian affairs; and at the next council, these things were all charged to the Indians and deducted from the value of their presents, or the purchase money for land. As a result, the Iroquois warriors were extremely careful of their behavior while passing through Pennsylvania, but when they reached Virginia, they took every opportunity to annoy the settlers. Such was the condition of Indian affairs when Conrad Weiser entered public life in 1731.

This sturdy, honest, strong-willed man of frontier diplomacy was born at Afsteadt, in Herrenberg, near Wurtemberg, Germany, in 1696. When thirteen years old, he came with his father to America and assisted his people for three years in a vain effort to make tar and raise hemp on the Livingston Manor in New York. Then these long-suffering people revolted and looked around for other lands. The Weisers spent the winter of 1713–14 with a chief of the Iroquois Indians at Schenectady. Here, doubtless, young Weiser secured his first lessons in the Maqua tongue; he followed his father in the spring to Schoharie and suffered want and privation to the verge of starvation among his people for a year. "Our hunger," he wrote, "was hardly endurable; many of our feasts were wild potatoes and ground beans, which grew in abundance. We cut mallows

---

2. *Virginia State Papers*, vol. I., p. 153.

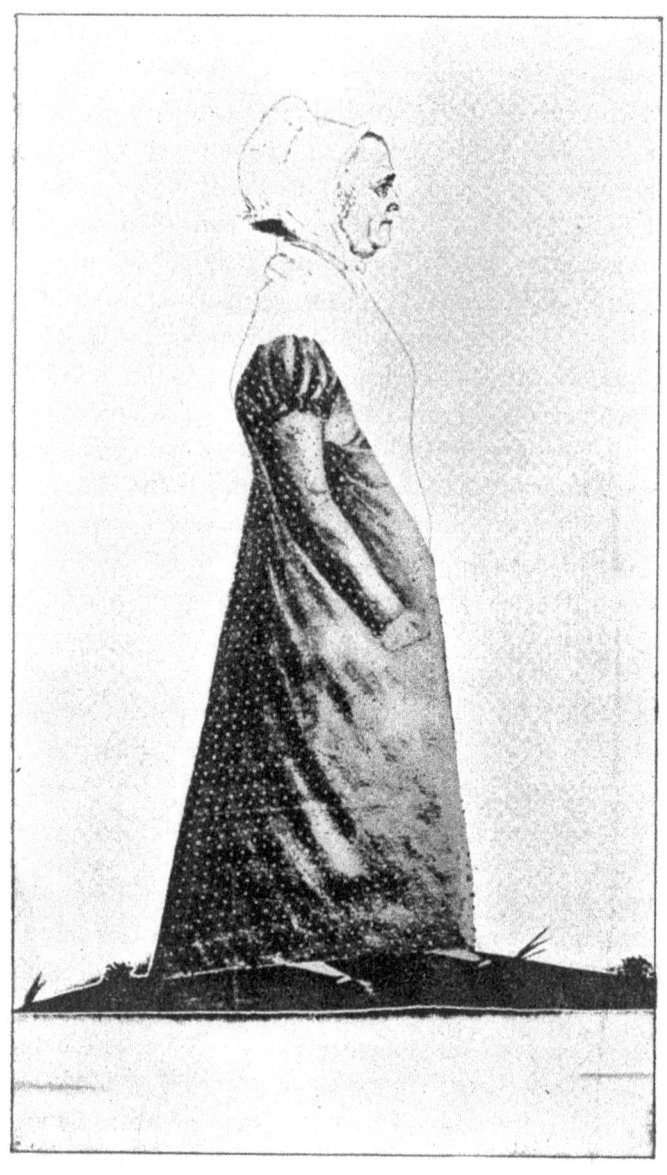

CONRAD WEISER'S WIFE
From a sketch found in York, Pa., by H. Diffenderfer, member of the Pennsylvania German Society

and picked juniper berries. . . . If we were in need of meal, we were obliged to travel from thirty-five to forty miles and beg it on trust."

When Conrad was seventeen, he went to live with Quagnant, a prominent Indian chief. "I went," said Weiser, "on my father's request, I endured a great deal of cold in my situation, and by spring, my hunger surpassed the cold by much." After eight months, Conrad returned to his father's house. Here he did good service as an interpreter between "the high mettled Dutch and the tawny nation . . . There was plenty of business and no pay." Doubtless, Conrad was a stubborn boy; at any rate, the father's discipline was not lax. "I had frequently . . . determined to desert from my father," he said, "but the bit of the bridle had been laid so tight in my mouth that I gave up this resolution. I was tied with a cord to prevent me from running away. I was severely chastised by my father and finally took another resolution." Conrad left his father's home and lived the greater part of the time, during fifteen years, among the Indians. In this manner, he became familiar with the Indians' habits, customs, and language. Such was his education; like Lincoln's, it was daily contact with men and things. In 1720, while his father was absent in Europe, "I married my Anna Eve," said Weiser, "and was given in marriage by Rev. John L. Haeger, Reformed clergyman, on 22d of November, in my father's home, in Schoharie."

Nine years later, Conrad followed his father's people to Pennsylvania and settled in the Tulpehocken Valley, and in 1731 his public life commenced.

Previous to this time, nearly all the negotiations between Pennsylvania and the Six Nations were held at Albany and, as a natural consequence, were under the direct influence of the Mohawk nation. The Schoharie exodus and the Tulpehocken land purchase opened the eyes of the Iroquois to the value of their Pennsylvania land claims. Here was a country, they thought, well worthy of closer attention. And since the Mohawks had never aided in the Indian conquests on Pennsylvania soil, why should they have any part in the income from land sales there? And they never did receive any portion of this money until a division arose among the Iroquois, and the Mohawks sold to the Susquehanna Land Company of Connecticut, the Wyoming region. For these reasons, doubtless, the great Onondaga Council sent Shikellamy, an Oneida chief, to the forks of the Susquehanna, in 1728 to guard the interests of the Six Nations in Pennsylvania. He had general oversight over the Shawanese and Delaware Indians. These tribes were soon given to understand that in their future dealings with the proprietary government, it would be necessary to consult him; that all their business would be done in the future in the same manner as the affairs of the Six Nations were accomplished, which was through their appointed deputy.

About 1745, Shikellamy was appointed to the full vice-regency over these tributary tribes, with Shamokin for his seat. He was shrewd and clear in his efforts to promote the interests of his people and was well aware that up to this time, there had been little or no intercourse between the government of Pennsylvania and the Six Nations. With true Indian shrewdness, he knew where to begin his negotiations.

The weak spot in Indian affairs was the effort to control the liquor traffic. Almost with the colony's beginnings, the Society of Friends had thrown their influence against the iniquity of selling rum among the Indians. At one time, all such traffic was forbidden by statute. The Indians petitioned again and again against the trade and how it was conducted. Yet whenever they experienced the effects of prohibitory law, they immediately begged that rum might be sold to them again. It is more than probable that these latter requests were inspired by the traders, whose business was very much impaired by the loss of the rum trade. Various laws and proclamations were issued with little effect. The Delaware and Shawanese Indians complained bitterly of traders who carried rum back into the woods and met their young men returning from hunting and trapping and, in this manner, robbed the old men, the women, and the children of the tribe of the very necessities of life. Accordingly, in 1731, Shikellamy gave the authorities of Pennsylvania the understanding that friendly relations with the Six Nations could not exist unless the liquor trade with their subjects, the Delawares and the Shawanese, was regulated. This led the Assembly to urge Governor Gordon to embrace every opportunity "to renew and maintain the same goodwill and friendship for the Five Nations which the honorable William Penn always expressed to them in his lifetime, and this House will readily defray the necessary charges which shall attend a treaty with these people."[3]

This report met with Governor Gordon's hearty approval. In his reply to the Assembly, he declared that immediate negotiations with the Six Nation Indians were necessary for the security of the province, and since the expense would be greater than at any previous treaty, he appreciated the Assembly's promptness in having the money ready for any emergency. The governor further explained that the Six Nations "had from time to time complained of the abuses put upon them" by the great quantities of rum brought among them by the traders, making it almost impossible for them to control their tributary tribes. "And yet," said the governor, "it is found altogether impracticable to carry on a trade with them and to furnish them with necessaries for their hunting and clothing, which is the only bond and tie of their friendship with us, without some

---

3. *Colonial Records of Pennsylvania*, vol. III. p. 610.

moderate quantities of that liquor; nothing will more sensibly affect them nor more strongly engage them to us, than if I can assure them that now, at this present meeting of the Representatives of all our people we have taken such measures as will furnish them with as much liquor as they shall judge really necessary for them, and yet that it shall be so restrained as that the ill consequences arising from large quantities . . . shall be effectually prevented."

The governor then asked the Assembly to pass a bill that would permit the selling of rum among the Indians and, at the same time, prevent any evils from arising through drunkenness. The Assembly attempted to pass such a bill, but a large majority defeated it. The Friends in the Assembly thought that if the governor would be more careful in the selection of the men licensed as traders and if he would personally examine them and use more stringent means to enforce the existing laws, it would be much better than any additional legislation. It would thus appear that the governor based the Indian complaints upon a lack of legislation, while the Assembly insisted that the cause of the trouble arose from inefficiency in the executive department. It was finally agreed that the governor should issue a proclamation warning all offenders of the penalties of the law and that a messenger be sent to the Six Nations, inviting them to come to Philadelphia and offering them a present of ten pounds.

"Shikellamy," the governor said, "is willing to undertake such a journey; he is a trusty, good man and a great lover of the English." His affection for the English resulted from his intimacy with Conrad Weiser. The embassy's purpose, which he was chosen to accomplish, was to secure the friendship and alliance of the Six Nations. James Logan forcibly set forth the immediate necessity of this in 1731 when at the request of the governor, he explained to the Assembly that the unrestrained traffic in rum had driven a large number of Shawanese Indians to the Ohio River region in 1730, that a Frenchman had been among them all the previous winter, with an interpreter and a gunsmith who did all the repairing gratuitously. Logan further explained that the Shawanese chiefs had been on a visit to the governor of Canada and were highly pleased with their reception. A map of Louisiana, published in London in 1721, was then produced, and Logan showed the Assembly "the exorbitant claims of the French" wherein they laid down the water parting between the Susquehanna and the Allegheny Rivers as the western boundary of Pennsylvania. This claim Logan declared was fraught with much danger to the province, and measures should be taken immediately to stop it. He suggested that a treaty be held with the Six Nations since they have absolute authority over the Shawanese Indians and are the only power that can hold them in the English interest or have any influence in persuading them to return east of the mountains. To accomplish this, Logan insisted that it would be necessary to have such legislation as would assure the Indians that the liquor traffic was being regulated. He further urged that the sincere friendship of the Six Nations was the first requisite.

From this report, the instructions for Shikellamy were drawn. Logan's knowledge of the importance and power of the Iroquois Indians over the surrounding tribes was drawn from Conrad Weiser. Not until after the coming of the Schoharie Germans did the Pennsylvania authorities have any definite knowledge of the importance of the Six Nations. Shikellamy was to make the journey to Onondaga during the summer of 1731. He appeared in Philadelphia in December, bringing with him a Cayuga chief and Conrad Weiser; the latter he introduced as the official interpreter of the United Nations. This action of Shikellamy's indicated the Iroquois mistrust of all provincial interpreters, whose interests, the Indians felt, were too closely allied with the Delaware tribes. In Weiser, the Iroquois had a man who shared their contempt for the Delaware Indians and who they declared was an adopted son of the Mohawk nation.

Shikellamy reported that the Iroquois councils were very glad to hear from the governor of Pennsylvania. It was, of course, too late in the season now for them to think of coming to Philadelphia, but in the spring, when the days were longer, they would most surely come. In confirmation of their goodwill and friendship, they sent the governor a present of a bundle of dressed deer skins. Shikellamy was given ten pounds for his journey, and Conrad Weiser was paid forty shillings for interpreting his report. The Six Nations did not send deputies to Philadelphia during the spring of 1732, as they had promised. The traders on the Allegheny reported that the French were gaining the friendship of the Shawanese and that these Indians still complained about the Pennsylvania laws not being strong enough to prevent such great quantities of rum from being sold among them; Peter Chartiers had only prevented war. Indeed, these Indians declared that it had not been five years since the Six Nations had tried to persuade the Ohio Indians to go to war against the English. They said this was one reason they removed to the Allegheny country. Another reason, they alleged, was because some escaped negro slaves found refuge among them, and they feared that the English would not like it. Conrad Weiser well knew that these were not *bona fide* causes. And unless the Six Nations could be held in the interests of the English, the Shawanese and the Delaware Indians on the Ohio would join the French. Every effort was therefore used to persuade the Six Nations to send deputies to Philadelphia.

At last, in late August 1732, a deputation of Oneida, Cayuga, and Onondaga chiefs arrived, authorized to speak for the nations not represented. Early in this conference, complaints were made, probably by the Assembly's party, against the private nature of the council. Conrad Weiser was selected to interview the leading Indians and learn their pleasure in the matter. The wary chiefs expressed a willingness to deal in a more public manner if desired yet, at the same time, were entirely content to continue the secret sessions. Thus, they played into the hands of both the governor's faction and the Assembly's party. Weiser was invariably successful in preventing any serious friction, and the conference continued, a vigorous test of diplomatic skill on each side. Thomas Penn spoke for the province the words which Conrad Weiser and Richard Peters put into his mouth. After dwelling at some length upon his father's policy, he asked them how they stood toward the French, their former enemies. What do your allies think of the French? How do these people treat you?

After a day spent reflecting, the Six Nations replied that they had no great faith in the governor of Canada or his people, who had deceived them. "Yet the Six Nations were not afraid of the French. They were always willing to go and hear what they had to propose. Peace had been made with the French. A tree had been planted big enough to shelter them both. Under this tree, a hole had been dug, and the hatchets had been buried therein.

Nevertheless, the chiefs of the Six Nations thought that the French charged too much for their goods, so they recommended their people to trade with the English, who would sell cheaper than the French." The Indians knew what would be pleasing to the ears of the governor. They expressed their pleasure in having a son of the great Onas in their midst. Then growing more familiar, they told Penn that when they were at Montreal in 1727, the French Governor told them that he was going to make war upon Corlear[4] and desired that the Six Nations might remain neutral.

One of their chiefs answered, saving, "Onontejo,[5] you are very proud. You are not wise to make war with Corlear and to propose neutrality to us. Corlear is our brother; he came to us when he was very little and a child. We suckled him at our breasts; we have nursed him and taken care of him till he is grown up to be a man. He is our brother and of the same blood. He and we have but one ear to hear with, one eye to see with, and one mouth to speak with; we will not forsake him nor see any man make war upon him without assisting. We shall

---

4. Corlear, the Indian name for the governor of New York.
5. Onontio, the Indian name for the governor of Canada.

join him, and if we fight with you, we may have our own father[6] Onontejo to bury in the ground."

But back of all this pleasing talk, which was more or less meaningless to the Iroquois diplomat, was the promise that if Pennsylvania removed all her traders from the Ohio, the Six Nations would see that the French traders were removed, and then if the governor desired it, the Shawanese would be ordered to go East again and live near the settlements. At the close of this conference, the council declared that Conrad Weiser had been very serviceable and exhibited unusual tact in managing the Indians; therefore, he should be paid twelve pounds.

The Iroquois were true to their promise and tried every means short of war to induce the Shawanese to come back and live east of the Allegheny Mountains. The governor of Pennsylvania sent them a large belt of wampum as an inducement. The Shawanese replied that they were very well fixed where they were and that the wampum had never been received. This independent spirit of these Shawanese Indians so offended the Iroquois that one of their deputies to these Indians spoke with such force and reproved them with such vigor that the Shawanese themselves became angry, and after the council, some of their warriors treacherously murdered the Iroquois deputy. This stirred the Six Nations to revenge the outrage with a war upon the Shawanese. But most probably, through the intercession of Conrad Weiser, the Iroquois leaders were induced to ask for advice from the governor of Pennsylvania. Thomas Penn condoled with them for the loss of a great man and sent them "six handkerchiefs to wipe and dry away (the) tears,"[7] encouraging them to maintain peace at all hazards. Since the offending Shawanese tribe had fled south to Carolina, would it not be better to overlook the matter? Pennsylvania would withdraw her request to remove the remaining Shawanese tribes from the Ohio country. To confirm the governor's good feelings, a present of two strouds was sent with the letter, and the messengers were given a liberal present of powder, lead, and blankets. The expense of the entertainment of the Indians who came to Philadelphia on this mission was paid, and Conrad Weiser was given money "with which to guard their comfort" on the road home. The Six Nations concluded to refrain from war with the Shawanese Indians, but these difficulties led them to remain, as much as possible, away from the influence of Pennsylvania.

---

6. The French taught the Indians to call the governor of Canada their father.
7. *Colonial Records of Pennsylvania*, vol. III. p. 610.

II

The Treaty of 1736

RELUCTANCE OF THE IROQUOIS INDIANS TO HOLD A CONFERENCE WITH THE GOVERNOR OF PENNSYLVANIA—THE SIX NATIONS' ESTIMATE OF CONRAD WEISER'S ABILITY—THE DONGAN DEED, THE FIRST IROQUOIS PURCHASE—THE BLUE MOUNTAIN PURCHASE OF 1736—THE SIX NATIONS ESTABLISH A CLAIM TO THE DELAWARE RIVER LANDS—RESULTS OF THIS INNOVATION—PHILADELPHIA ALARMED AT THE DRUNKENNESS AMONG THE INDIANS—THE IROQUOIS DISCOVER LAND CLAIMS AGAINST MARYLAND AND VIRGINIA—THE SHAWANESE ENTER COMPLAINT; ITS CAUSE—SHAWANESE DIPLOMACY—THE BEGINNING OF THE SHAWANESE ALIENATION.

THE authorities of Pennsylvania did not feel that the treaty of 1732 was as strong as it might be until it was confirmed by deputies representing the remaining tribes of the Six Nations. Accordingly, Conrad Weiser was directed to employ his influence with Shikellamy and bring about a conference that would represent the entire Six Nation Confederacy. Year after year went by, and still, the promised visit of the crafty Iroquois was deferred. Finally, at a conference of Delaware and Conestoga chiefs, an appeal was made to them to explain why the Iroquois did not come to Philadelphia as they had promised. Their old men replied that they had been expecting the Iroquois for three years past, but had been informed that they were detained (1) because of many nations coming to treat with them, (2) "because tribes of strange Indians from the north were among them, Indians who had never seen bread, corn or white people, therefore the Iroquois were determined to keep near home as long as these strangers remained in their midst."

The governor gave the Delaware chiefs a large present, urging them to influence the Six Nations to send deputies to Philadelphia and to keep Conrad Weiser thoroughly informed of any Indian news.

This present to the Delawares seems to have had a salutary influence. In less than six weeks, Conrad Weiser reported that over one hundred Iroquois chiefs were on their way to Philadelphia. The long-expected and much-solicited visit came upon the provincial authorities with an embarrassing suddenness. Smallpox was raging in the city. What should be done with the one hundred Iroquois chiefs and their numerous retinues? Conrad Weiser solved the problem by taking the Indians to the governor's mansion at Stenton and inviting the provincial officers and the proprietors to meet them.

The Indians expressed great satisfaction with Conrad Weiser's care for their health. They told the proprietors that at the treaty of 1732, it was agreed that Conrad Weiser and Shikellamy were the proper persons "to go between the Six Nations and this government" and that they were to be employed in all treaties and conferences. Their bodies, said the Indians, are to be equally divided between the sons of Onas and the Red Men, half to the Indian and half to the white man. Conrad Weiser, they said, was faithful and honest, a good, true man who had spoken their words and not his own. Indeed at this time, there was scarcely an honest interpreter in the colonies. Colonel Johnson of New York relates an instance of an interpreter who, in his presence, translated the text of a missionary sermon which read, "God is no respecter of persons," into "God has no respect for such as you." The Indians expressed their gratitude towards Weiser by presenting him with "a dressed skin to make him shoes, and two deer skins to keep him warm." The provincial council, accordingly, directed that a present worth two hundred pounds be given to the Iroquois Indians and Conrad Weiser, "the interpreter, who is extremely useful on all such occasions, and on the present one has been very serviceable, there be given twenty pounds."

Weiser at once suggested to the council that a part of the two hundred pounds be withheld from the Indians until it was ascertained what amount the proprietors were going to pay for the land. Previous to this time, all the proprietary land purchases had been from the Delaware Indians, except the Dongan deed that Penn had secured in England from the former Governor of New York. This deed the Six Nation Indians declared had been given many years before (1696) to the governor of New York to hold their Susquehanna lands in trust and in no way resigned any control or rights.

Weiser had impressed the Pennsylvania officers and proprietors with the power and influence of the Iroquois. Accordingly, no one disputed with them when they claimed indemnity for all Susquehanna lands south and east of the Blue Mountains, then known as the Endless Mountains. With great deference and amid many compliments, the proprietors paid the Six Nation Indians for

STENTON, HOME OF JAMES LOGAN

this land which had all been previously purchased from the Conestoga and Delaware Indians. The Iroquois now received 500 pounds of powder, 600 pounds of lead, 45 guns, 160 coats, 100 blankets, 200 yards of cloth, 100 shirts, 40 hats, 40 pairs of shoes and buckles, 40 pairs of stockings, 100 hatchets, 500 knives, 100 hoes, 60 kettles, 100 tobacco tongs, 100 scissors, 500 awls, 120 combs, 2000 needles, 1000 flints, 24 looking glasses, 2 pounds of vermilion, 100 tin pots, 25 gallons of rum, 200 pounds of tobacco, 2000 pipes, 24 dozen of gartering.

Two weeks after this deed was signed, when most of the influential Indians had gone from Philadelphia, and after the remainder had been drinking excessively for several days, another deed was drawn covering all the Six Nations' claim to the land drained by the Delaware River, and south of the Blue Mountains. Since the Six Nations had never, until this date, laid any claim to the lands on the lower Delaware, this second deed becomes significant. It established a precedent for an Iroquois claim to the lands owned by the Delaware Indians. William Penn had never recognized any Six Nation claims on the Delaware. The Iroquois themselves had never made any such pretensions. It is highly probable that no one at that time realized what might be the outcome of such a deed, which was an indirect way of denying the Delaware Indians all their land claims. It is quite probable that the chief purpose in securing the deed was to place In writing the promise of the Six Nations that they would never in the future sell land within the limits of Pennsylvania to anyone except Penn's heirs.

The deed was carefully read and interpreted for them by Conrad Weiser. The Iroquois were evidently aware that they had gained a most important point. Henceforth Pennsylvania would be their sponsor for claims on the Delaware River, and all ancient disputes with the Delaware Indians on this matter were settled. Pennsylvania had taken sides in the quarrel and, hereafter, must recognize the power of the Iroquois and lay the hand of oppression upon the Delawares. The wise statesmanship of William Penn, who refused to take sides in any Indian differences, was unfortunately no more. His sons were more bent on personal profit than public justice and security. Shikellamy was undoubtedly the Indian agent who accomplished this, and he used Conrad Weiser to bring it to pass. This action clearly marked a change in the Indian policy of Pennsylvania. It was no longer possible to treat the Delaware Indians as formerly. The Six Nations become the favored people, and the Delawares become underlings. Weiser helped Shikellamy sow the seed, which drenched Pennsylvania in blood from 1755 to 1764. In permitting this second deed, Pennsylvania started that series of events with the Delawares, which cost her one of the most remarkable Indian invasions in colonial history. And at the same time, by securing this and thus conciliating the Iroquois, and holding the key to their future attitude, Weiser and the proprietary made a future nation possible. Pennsylvania suffered that a nation might live. She brought upon herself after many years a Delaware war but escaped a Six Nation war, a French alliance with the Iroquois, and the threatening possibility of destroying all the English colonies on the coast.

The provincial Executive was well pleased with Weiser's suggestion to cut the amount of the governor's present from two hundred pounds to something less than seventy pounds. Doubtless, the council considered this a sufficient sum to pay for "brightening the chain of friendship," relighting the "council fire," and opening more thoroughly a "path to Onondaga."

With some force, the council realized that the expenses of Iroquois conferences far exceeded those held with the Delawares and Conestogas.

The authorities were as anxious to have the Indians leave Philadelphia as they had been to have them come. After three or four weeks, the Indians' fear of smallpox had evaporated, and the city's streets were turbulent with drunken chiefs; the governor and council applied to Conrad Weiser to dispatch the dusky deputies as soon as possible. Accordingly, a proclamation was issued and put into the mouth of the street crier, threatening to fine any person ten pounds who should be found selling any strong liquor to the Indians. Horses and wagons were furnished to carry the Indians' presents part way on the home journey. After the deputies had departed, the city authorities breathed more freely, and the provincial Executive realized that a new force had entered into the Indian relations of the colony.

As the old chiefs slowly wound their way deeper and deeper into the forests of the Alleghenies, they no doubt wondered why their request to have the Indian traders removed from the Ohio country was so politely refused and why their petition to have no more strong drink sold to their young men was evaded. Doubtless, the older chiefs questioned the truth of the governor's rebuke when he told them that the Indians should control themselves as the white men did. "All of us here," said the governor, "and all you see of any credit in this place, can every day have as much rum of their own to drink as they please, and yet scarce one of us will take a dram, at least not one man will on any account be drunk, no, not if he were hired to it with great sums of money."

After a year or more of meditation, the Onondaga chiefs concluded that the traders and the white men on the frontiers were not like the people of Philadelphia.

Since Pennsylvania had paid the Six Nations for their Susquehanna claims south of the Blue Mountains, the shrewd Iroquois became aware that neither Maryland nor Virginia had ever paid them for lands southward, which lay within the western borders of those States. They stated that their claims to this region were based upon the conquests of their fathers. They now insisted that Pennsylvania should assist them in securing this land from Virginia and Maryland. The governor, who was evidently following the advice of Conrad Weiser, put the Indians off until he could secure better information about these claims.

The growing discontent among the Shawanese seized upon the recent Iroquois land sale as another source of their dissatisfaction. When these Shawanese heard of the treaty of 1736, one hundred and thirty of their leaders sent a belt to the French, saying, our land has been sold from under our feet; may we come and live with you? The French not only readily consented but offered to come and meet them with provisions. This information came from the Mohawks, who received no share from the recent Iroquois land sale. In the treaty of 1736, the Six Nations had promised to send all the Shawanese back from the Ohio and compel them to live on the Susquehanna lands, where they had asked permission to live forty-five years before. The Iroquois found this a difficult thing to do, especially since the Mohawks received nothing from the late treaty.

Moreover, the Shawanese learned valuable diplomacy lessons from the Iroquois and the French. In August 1737, a message and a belt came to Philadelphia from the Shawanese on the Ohio, saying that the French had always been their friends, that each year they gave them powder, lead, and tobacco, and that these presents enabled them to hold their own against their Indian enemies in the south. Now, if they should return to their Susquehanna lands, as the leading men in Pennsylvania and the Iroquois chiefs desired, they must starve and lay themselves open to their enemies. With genuine shrewdness, the Shawanese declared they had no desire to join the French, and if the Pennsylvania authorities would send them a present as compensation for the land they had lost, they could keep back their enemies and avoid falling into the hands of the French.

The Pennsylvania council, after 1736, always consulted Conrad Weiser on all Indian affairs. Weiser had little or no respect for a Shawanese Indian. The council, while it realized that the Shawanese had no legal claims on the Susquehanna land from a white man's standpoint about land tenure, was inclined to take Weiser's advice and believed that it would be establishing a dangerous precedent to recognize Shawanese claims when they were but sojourners in the country. The Indians had a quite different conception of land tenure, and the Shawanese held that occupancy did, in time, become possession. Therefore, when they received a present of ten pounds from the province and an invitation to a treaty, they swallowed their chagrin and found solace in the sympathy of the French. This paltry present began a series of misunderstandings with these tribes, finally leading to their total alienation from the English cause.

III

The Onondaga Journey

FEUDS BETWEEN THE NORTHERN AND SOUTHERN INDIANS—VIRGINIA BECOMES A PEACEMAKER—GOVERNOR GOOCH SECURES THE CONSENT OF THE SOUTHERN TRIBES—VIRGINIA APPLIES TO PENNSYLVANIA FOR AID—WEISER SENT ON A MISSION OF PEACE—INDIANS STARVING AT SHAMOKIN—WEISER VISITS MADAME MONTOUR—LIFE IN THE WOODS—THE OTKON, THE EVIL SPIRIT OF THE VALLEY—WEISER QUARRELS WITH THE GUIDE—A FAMINE AMONG THE INDIANS—AN INDIAN SEER'S STRANGE VISION—WEISER'S SKILL IN PROCURING PROVISIONS—THE INDIAN GUIDE SAVES WEISER'S LIFE—WEISER AT ONANDAGO—SOME LAWLESS IROQUOIS FRUSTRATE THE PURPOSES OF WEISER'S MISSION—CAUSES OF SUSPENSION OF FURTHER PEACE NEGOTIATIONS.

THE Iroquois confederacy had been at war for years with the Southern Indians. The great mountain valleys of Virginia contained their war trails. Silently along these paths of blood, small bands of ambitious young Iroquois warriors pushed southward every season in search of Muskokee scalps. The white people experienced no serious trouble as long as the Virginia planters remained east of the mountains. But when a century of colonization produced the enterprising frontiersman, the land speculator, and the fur trader, men began to look into the Shenandoah Valley, then friction with the Iroquois Indians commenced. In Pennsylvania, when difficulty of this nature occurred, its settlement was referred to in the next treaty, where, after some discussion, orders were usually given by the old men that their warriors should, for the future, go south by some path further west, and more removed from the haunts of the settler. In Virginia, for a number of years, there had been an enactment authorizing the county authorities to arrest and bring before the magistrates any bands of strange roving Indians, and if said Indians should in any manner try to elude the officers, they would then be justified in shooting the Indians on the spot.

Immediately after the Pennsylvania purchase of 1736, the difficulties so increased that the governor of Virginia concluded that the only solution to the vexatious problem was to bring about peace between the two great confederacies of Indians. Late in the autumn of 1736, Governor Gooch secured the consent of one of the Southern tribes to make peace. Finally, late in the winter, the entire Southern confederacy of Indians agreed to send deputies during the following spring to meet a similar party of peace commissioners from the Iroquois, at some place like Williamsburg, in Virginia. This was more easily accomplished with the Southern Indians, owing to their distance from the influence of the French and the looseness of their confederacy.

When Governor Gooch fully realized what he had accomplished, it became highly desirable to secure (1) an armistice between the two hostile confederacies and (2) to persuade the Iroquois to send peace commissioners to Williamsburg. Therefore, Virginia immediately applied to Pennsylvania for aid in this affair. At that time, Conrad Weiser was the only man able to stay the bloody tomahawk of the Iroquois. It was now midwinter, and the difficulties of sending a messenger to Onondaga seemed insurmountable. Yet if the young men among the Iroquois, who were accustomed to going on the war trail in the early spring, should get started before a messenger arrived, they could not be recalled, and all the peace negotiations would fail for another year if not ultimately.

Accordingly, Conrad Weiser was selected to perform this mission; he started his journey on the 27th of February. The snow on the mountains made horseback riding exceedingly difficult. At Shamokin, on the forks of the Susquehanna River, it was found impossible to get the horses across. After more than a day's delay, a daring Indian crossed and took Conrad and his German companion, Stoffel Stump, safely over in a canoe. Weiser had expected to secure provisions and a guide at Shamokin; he only found a guide.

The Indians there were on the verge of starvation. "I saw a blanket," wrote Weiser in his journal, "given for about one-third of a bushel of corn." Here they first learned what hunger pangs were, and only after great difficulty did Weiser get a small quantity of cornmeal and a few beans. With this scanty store, he determined to plunge into a trackless wilderness toward Onondaga. The Indians reported the streams impassable and the snow waist-deep. Weiser was a man who rarely turned back.

The little party of two white men and two Indians followed the north bank of the west branch of the Susquehanna River. The Indians called this the "Zinachsa" (Ot-zin-ach-son). With and without snowshoes, they traveled, crossing the streams as best they could. At the mouth of Lovalsock Creek, they found the hut of Madame Montour, that remarkable French woman who lived in great favor among the Indians. At first, Madame Montour told Weiser that she had no food, but later, when all the Indians had withdrawn from the cabin, she deftly raised a plank from the floor and, out of her hidden store, fed Weiser bountifully.

They left Madame Montour's with empty provision sacks and snow over four feet deep in the mountains. Their campfire built under the spruce trees would often sink over three feet into the snow before morning. A bed of spruce boughs and a meager breakfast of cornmeal and beans boiled in water was above the average of their comforts. More than once did they stand all night around a sputtering fire while torrents of rain moved the masses of snow on the mountains. After leaving the west branch of the Susquehanna, they followed what the Indians called the lost or bewildered stream. "The woods was so thick," wrote Weiser, "that for a mile at a time, we could not find a place the size of a hand where the sunshine could penetrate even in the clearest day." The swiftness of the stream made it necessary for them all to grasp one long pole while wading across. They often found it impossible to keep warm by walking, owing to the frequent crossings.

In one valley, which might have been the Loyalsock, the storms of March were so frequent and severe that the Indians believed that an evil spirit, "Otkon," lived and ruled there. "It was such a desolate region," said Weiser, "that I often thought I must perish in this frightful wilderness." The Indians told Weiser that if they only had a magician along, he could appease the wrath of "Otkon" by appropriate sacrifices. Weiser sincerely expressed his desire that one of the Indians present might try his skill in this dark art. Near the head of the same valley, they found two skulls securely fastened upon poles. The Indians said these were the remains of two unfortunate Iroquois warriors who, while returning* from a war excursion to the South, encamped here one stormy night with two Carolina Indians as captives. These "prisoners," said Weiser, "who were two resolute men, found themselves at night untied, which, without doubt, had been done by the 'Otkon' and, having killed their captors and taken possession of their arms, had returned home."[1]

On the 28th of March, they ate their last handful of meal, fully expecting to reach the north branch of the Susquehanna River that night, where they supposed they would find an abundant supply of provisions. About the middle

---

1. *Memoirs of the Pennsylvania Historical Society*, vol. I., p. 11.

of the forenoon, they came to Sugar Creek, which was much-swollen by melting snow. They found it too high and rapid to ford. Accordingly, by dint of much patience, having only one small hatchet, they felled a long pine tree, but unfortunately, it did not reach the opposite bank. The stream having already risen a foot since they arrived, its raging currents caught the pine tree and swept it down the stream. The Indian guide now suggested wading the stream and all holding to a long pole. Weiser was decided, in his opinion, that the current was too swift and would sweep them away. The entire party was irritated over the loss of food, and the two Indians "fell to abusing Stoffel." They told him it was his fault that Conrad would not follow the guide's words. When Weiser defended Stoffel, they called him a coward who loved his life so much that he would force them all to die of hunger on the spot. The guide declared that he knew more about this wild country than Weiser, that he was responsible for the party, and they must do as he said. They must build a raft and cross on that if they could not wade. Conrad, with great determination, told them that no raft could be kept right side up in that current, and it would be far better for them to follow Sugar Creek until they reached the Susquehanna and then ascend the river. The guide, with increasing warmth, told him that he did not know what he was talking about. The other Indian, an Onondaga warrior, who had joined the party as a convenient way to return from a Southern raid, insisted that no white man could give him any advice in the woods. Weiser promptly ended all further controversy by slinging his pack over his back and starting down the stream. Stoffel obediently followed. The Indian guide hesitated for some time but finally shouldered his burden and sullenly followed the resolute German. The proud Onondaga remained alone. About a mile down the stream, Conrad found a narrow place where a tree would safely bridge the flood. Here they silently crossed, fired a signal for the stubborn Onondaga, and plunged into the dark forest without a word. Late that night, Ta-wa-gar-et, the Onondaga, came humbly into camp, wet to the skin and nearly exhausted. He told them that after they left, he made himself a raft and attempted to cross. His craft was overturned in the stream, and he was thrown upon an island from which he barely escaped with his life. After some minutes' silence in the camp, the Onondaga asked for Conrad Weiser's pardon for his stillborn conduct. This incident was of no small importance in the negotiations which followed some weeks later at the Onondaga council fire, where Conrad Weiser's words had great weight.

When this starved and tottering embassy reached the Susquehanna several miles above the present site of Towanda, it found the Indians there on the verge of starvation. All the able-bodied men were away vainly searching for game. The old men, squaws, and children had lived on maple juice and sugar for weeks. With all his trinkets Weiser could buy no meal. The women made him a weak soup of cornmeal and ashes boiled separately and then mixed. The two Indians ate so greedily of this that they became quite sick. Conrad gave his portion to the bony little children who crowded around with tears on their stolid faces. Stoffel ate heartily of the soup, and there is no evidence that he experienced the least inconvenience. Later in the evening, in another hut, Weiser succeeded in buying, with twenty-four needles and six shoe strings, five small loaves of cornbread "of about a pound in weight." With Stoffel's assistance, this was quickly consumed. Nothing more could be purchased. Stoffel urged that they abandon the mission, procure a canoe, and float down the river. The high water and the numerous rapids would have made it possible to have reached Shamokin "in six or eight days" if they had been able to procure provisions. Weiser refused to entertain such a suggestion.

He called a conference of the old and wise men and asked them why the game was so scarce. "Twelve years ago," said Weiser, "when I was here, you had a greater supply than all the other Indians. Why is game so scarce now?"

They replied that hunting had strangely failed since last winter. Some of them had found nothing at all. The Lord and Creator of the world, they said, was resolved to destroy all the Indians. One of their seers, an old gray-headed Indian, told Weiser that he had had a vision of God. When he inquired of the Great Spirit why the game was so scarce, he received the following reply: "You inquire after the cause why game has become so scarce. I will tell you. You kill it for the sake of the skins, which you give for strong liquor and drown your senses, and kill one another and carry on dreadful debauchery. Therefore, I have driven the wild animals out of the country, for they are mine. If you will do good and cease from your sins, I will bring them back; if not, I will destroy you from off the earth."

Conrad Weiser then asked them if they believed what the seer had seen and heard. They replied that some of their number believed that it would happen so; others believed it but gave themselves no concern about it. Time will show, they said, what will happen to us. "Rum will kill us and leave the land clear for the Europeans without strife or purchase."

While Conrad Weiser took careful note of these things, they were not to his purpose. He must devise some means of reaching the Onondaga Council before the war parties were organized. How to do this without food and with failing strength was a serious problem. Again, he called the old men together. He told them that he was on a mission for the good of the Six Nations, that he came on behalf of the governor of Virginia and Brother Onas, and something must be done to further his enterprise. After some consideration and delay, the Indians concluded that a hut, whose owners were away on a hunt, should be broken open and as much of the contents as necessary be used for the expedition. A share was given to two Indians, who were directed to go ahead as runners and herald the coming of the embassy. With great thankfulness, Weiser and his little party received their share, about one-third of a bushel of corn. Weiser had this pounded before they started. It was not done without considerable loss. "Hunger," wrote Weiser, "is a great tyrant; he does not spare the best of friends, much less strangers." With less than ten quarts of pounded corn, Weiser pushed on toward Onondaga, following the North Branch of the Susquehanna and doling out the little stock of meal each day with a parsimonious hand.

Several days before they reached the "Great Water Shed," which divides the waters of the Susquehanna from those of the Hudson on the east, the Mississippi on the west, and the St. Lawrence on the north, they waded through soft snow in what seemed an endless forest. On the "8th of April," he wrote, "we were still on the journey, and I was utterly worn out by cold and hunger, and so long a journey, not to mention other hardships; a fresh snow had fallen about twenty inches deep; I found myself still nearly three days' journey from Onondaga, in a terrible forest. My strength was so exhausted that my whole body trembled and shook to such a degree that I thought I should fall down and die; I went to one side and sat down under a tree, intending to give up the ghost there, to attain which end I hoped the cold of the night then approaching would assist me. My companions soon missed me, and the Indians came back and found me sitting there. I would not go any further, but said to them in one word: 'Here I will die;' they were silent awhile; at last, the old man (Shikellamy) began, 'My dear companion, take courage, thou hast until now encouraged us, wilt thou now give up entirely? Just think that the bad days are better than the good ones, for when we suffer much, we do not sin, and sin is driven out of us by suffering. But the good days cause men to sin, and God cannot be merciful; but on the other hand, when it goes badly with us, God takes pity on us.' I was therefore ashamed, and stood up and journeyed on as well as I could."[2]

They crossed the watershed the following day and traveled forty miles to reach the Onondaga Council the next day. Unfortunately, Weiser gives us no report of his negotiations there besides the results. To stay the tide of war, which was strong in the hearts of the Iroquois toward the Southern Indians, was no easy task. At last, the proud Maqua consented to the armistice but refused to

---

2. *Pennsylvania Magazine*, vol. I, p. 165.

send deputies to Williamsburg* They claimed that it was too far to travel. If the Southern Indians wished to treat with the Iroquois, let them come to Albany. Although Weiser failed to accomplish all that was desired, he secured the armistice and saved Virginia from an invasion of Iroquois warriors. He reported to Pennsylvania, and the governor immediately advised Virginia of the mission's results. The governor of Virginia, at once, sent deputies to the Cherokee and Catawba tribes.

When these deputies were in session, a roving band from the Six Nations, either with or without orders or in ignorance of the decisions of the Onondaga Council, fell upon a hunting party of the Cherokees and killed three of them and destroyed five of their horses. This piece of wanton mischief so incited the Southern Indians that they declared that all further peace negotiations with such treacherous people were at an end. In despair, Carolina and Virginia appealed to Pennsylvania. James Logan, the governor* turned the entire affair over to Conrad Weiser, urging him to go to the Six Nations and secure a firm peace if possible.

Several years elapsed before this question came up again, during which time we do not know whether Conrad Weiser did anything or not. The probabilities are that he did nothing. The Indian policy of the province was becoming increasingly the result of pressure, and it naturally inclined to follow the lines of least resistance. And since there was no pressure on the part of the Six Nations upon this point, little was done during the following five or six years.

Another reason might be assigned for the cessation of all efforts to secure peace between the Northern and the Southern Indians, and that is the fact that Conrad Weiser was the only agency through which anything could be done in this line, and during this period, he was more interested in affairs of the church than in those of the state.

IV

Religious Revivals at Ephrata Temporarily Win Weiser Away from Indian Affairs

Religious awakening at Tulpehocken—Beissel's Visit to Weiser—Weiser withdraws from the Lutheran Church—Weiser becomes a Seventh-day Baptist—Weiser burns the Lutheran Catechism—Governor Thomas seeks to draw Weiser away from the Ephrata Influence—Weiser appointed Justice of the Peace—Weiser quarrels with Beissel—A "Spiritual Virgin" makes Trouble at Ephrata—Weiser, the Magistrate, outgrows Weiser, the Church Elder—Weiser leaves the Seventh-day Baptists—His spiritual Return—Weiser becomes interested in the Moravian Missionaries—Weiser travels with Zinzendorf—Weiser saves Zinzendorf's Life—The Moravians turn away from Weiser—Weiser secures the Release of two Moravians from the Jail in New York.

AT the time of Conrad Weiser's arrival in Pennsylvania, there was an unusual awakening in the eastern part of the province upon religious subjects. In a few years, the people of Tulpehocken, who were largely Lutherans, agreed that none but Protestants and people of like persuasion should be permitted to live among them. Peter Miller, a highly educated man from Germany, was called among these Tulpehocken people to be their teacher. He served them for four years. Conrad Beissel,[1] the leader and organizer of the Seventh Day Baptists at Ephrata, had for some years made the conversion of the Tulpehocken people the subject of regular prayer.

---

1. See Dr. M. G. Brumbaugh's *History of the Brethren* for a full account of these Men.

THE CLOISTERS AT EPHRATA

Beissel and several of his disciples finally visited Tulpehocken and were received by Conrad Weiser, the elder of the church, and Peter Miller, the teacher, "with the consideration due to him as an ambassador of God."[2] When Beissel was about to return from this remarkable journey, Peter Miller and Conrad Weiser accompanied him for six miles over the mountains. The subject of conversation between these men is not known. The sermons and prayers of Beissel are not recorded. We only know the results, and they are of themselves remarkable enough. A division was caused in the Lutheran congregation at Tulpehocken. Conrad Weiser, Peter Miller, and some elders withdrew from the Church.

A new question now faced these seceders from the faith of their fathers. What should they do? They could not endorse "Separatism," even if the country was full of "Laodiceans, Naturalists, Ishmaelites, and Atheists." Weiser and his little band of the dissatisfied felt the supreme need for some church government, some system with an organization. Weiser's was eminently an orderly mind. He was a leader and an organizer. The authors of the *Chronicon Ephratense* speak of him as a "man who had received from God remarkable natural gifts and sound judgment, and therefore carried weight with him into whatever sphere he might turn, whether of nature or of the church. He was the teacher's (Peter Miller) main-stay, for they were on intimate terms together, which death itself did not destroy."

Weiser's unrest soon led him to visit Ephrata, where he sought a long interview with Beissel. This strange man had a remarkable and powerful influence upon Weiser, so much so that the latter was instrumental in securing the complete surrender and final conversion of Peter Miller himself. Both of these men were baptized by Beissel in May 1735. For some time after this, Peter Miller lived in a hermitage near Tulpehocken. This place of abode was erected for him by the Ephrata Brethren.

For a time, all went well in the church; Weiser became exceedingly zealous in the new faith. On one occasion, we are informed that in company with Peter Miller and others of the new converts, he went to the house of Godfried Fidler, where he burned the Lutheran catechism, the Psalter, the Heidelberg catechism, and several other time-honored books of devotion.[3]

Weiser gave liberally of his possessions for the "upbuilding of the new enterprise" at Ephrata. According to the custom of these people, he allowed his beard to grow until it reached such dimensions that even his former acquaintances

---

2. *Chronicon Ephratense.*
3. See C. Z. Weiser's *Life of Conrad Weiser.*

failed to recognize him. Beissel led a proselyting party, composed of the twelve fathers in the church, into New Jersey. Weiser was one of these honored fathers, and he added very materially to the church's standing through his influence in public affairs. Indeed he was very enthusiastic in his support of the Seventh Day Fraternity and especially of Beissel. Most of Weiser's friends were exceedingly sorry to see him join such a religious body. The chronicler of the Ephrata history, who despised the ways of the world, declares that "the country could neither wage war nor make peace with the Indians without him." So important, indeed, was Weiser to the provincial authorities that Governor Thomas used all his public and private influence to win him away from these strange people. The governor fully realized that Indian affairs would suffer unless his rising power in the province was drawn away from the allurements of this peculiar form of worship. In the language of the Chronicler, Governor Thomas "well understood the art of dissimulation" and "took measures to bring him over to his (Governor Thomas's) side again, to cope with which the good brother was by no means competent. The former took hold of the matter very shrewdly, spoke in praise of the organization at Ephrata, and that he was not disinclined to come into closer relations with such a people. This he could well say, for he went to the trouble to visit the settlement with a following of twenty horses and accompanied by many people of quality from Virginia and Maryland. He was worthily received by the Brethren, though the Superintendent and the Mother Superior of the sisters held themselves aloof, tie (Governor Thomas) declared himself well pleased with the institution. But when he saw that the families also had their own household in the settlement, he wanted to know what the object of this was; on being told that they, too, had entered the celibate state, he regarded it as something curious. Having made a favorable impression on the Brother,[4] he[5] now tendered him the office of a justice of the peace, which the Brother would then no doubt have gladly accepted if it were not against the principles of his people; he did so, however, only on condition that the congregation would permit it. At his request, a council was held to decide whether a Brother of this confession might be allowed to hold a government office. The fathers thought that this could not be done. But the Superintendent thought differently and asked them whether they had a right to respect a Brother's conscience. And when he" [Conrad Weiser] "was asked about it, he declared that his conscience did not forbid him to accept, upon which full liberty was granted him. The

---

4. Conrad Weiser.
5. The Governor.

governor also allowed him to withdraw from court whenever such matters come up as it were against his conscience."[6]

After this time, if we are to believe the Ephrata chronicle, Conrad Weiser became increasingly occupied with the business of the magistracy and less and less interested in the affairs of the Brethren. Other more potent reasons operated to turn Weiser away from the Seventh Day Fraternity. A difference soon sprang up between Weiser and the Superintendent. The difficulty began when the Tulpehocken branch of the Ephrata Church asked for a preacher in addition to Peter Miller, their teacher. Several preachers were tried, even the celebrated "Elimelech," but none remained. "After the priestly chair was now empty again," said the Chronicler, "Conrad Weiser incautiously seated himself in it and thereby opened the door for the tempter to try him." It must be borne in mind that the forms of the "Seventh Day Baptists" permitted householders to live in membership with the single brothers and the virgins. While Beissel placed a high value upon those who took celibacy vows, he had room in his heart for the householder or married people. Yet one is led to suppose that the order rituals placed a somewhat modified definition upon the bonds of marriage. In the mysterious style of the chronicler, it is hinted that since baptism had considerably weakened the ties of matrimony, "there were spiritual courting! through which the void," in Conrad Weiser's "side might easily have been filled again." It appears that Beissel warned Weiser of this danger, real or imaginary. Whatever this mystery was, it remained locked in the bosom of Beissel.

"In this severe trial," said the chronicler, "Conrad Weiser in his God-enamored condition found himself, and because he did not take sufficient heed to himself, the tempter assailed him anew, and would probably have overcome him, had not God put it into the heart of the sister to seek out the convent and have herself re-baptized by the Superintendent (Conrad Beissel), then the cords of the tempter were torn, and they again became as strangers to each other."[7]

It appears that one time at a foot washing, Beissel warned Weiser of the danger he was in from temptations of the "female sex." Sometime after this, Weiser found occasion to rebuke Beissel for assuming that he was the Christ because Beissel had remarked that "when he stood in the breach for a deceased brother, the blood was forced from his fingernails." Out of these things, a coldness grew between the two brothers. Finally, for reasons he saw best to keep to himself, Weiser forbade Beissel, the Superintendent, from frequenting the Sisters' Convent. The extent of Weiser's authority among the Brethren is unknown, yet we

---

6. *Chronicon Ephratense*, pp. 82, 83.
7. *Chronicon Ephratense*, p. 75.

are told that he placed the penalty of severe punishment upon Beissel if he did not obey. For some time, Weiser believed things were not as they should be at the Cloisters. One spiritual virgin consulted him, who, as justice of the peace, had become the leading man on the bench at the county court, complaining of Beissel. Whether the Superintendent was guilty or the virgin was jealous is shrouded in doubt.

It is recorded that the virgin offered herself in marriage to Beissel and was refused, and when he placed others, in the Sisters' Convent, in positions above that occupied by herself, she brought these charges against Beissel. Conrad Weiser immediately reported the entire affair to the governor. Two solitary brothers, believing that Beissel was innocent, went to Conrad Weiser and implored him not to stain his hands in innocent blood. He promised them that if it were possible to withdraw the case, he would do so. But meanwhile, the governor had written him to give the parties a hearing and send the case to Lancaster Court for trial. Then Weiser had another interview in the presence of "a housefather"; the "virgin" again confessed that she assisted Beissel in making way with an illegitimate child.

The Brethren insisted that Beissel was innocent and that the virgin was imbittered because her sister had been appointed Mother Superior instead of her. Be this as it may, the "virgin" recanted all her charges when Weiser told her that by the laws of the province, her own life was endangered by the admission of such a crime. The Brethren were afterward more than convinced that her testimony was false because, soon after she left the order, she became engaged to be married to another man and died just before the wedding. The Brethren declared this was the justice of heaven, slaying the wicked in their sins.

Weiser, after this, is said to have turned away from the Brethren and been received into his former church with much rejoicing. Just why he left the Ephrata Fraternity is not clear, but we find the following letter, which he wrote to the Brethren, that in a measure explains itself:

Conrad Weiser, your former Brother, has the following to say to you in this writing, on behalf of the poor sighing souls, of whom there are not a few among you, who are groaning day and night unto God because of the Pharaohic and Egyptian bond service with which the Congregation is so heavily laden and burdened that it scarcely can endure any.

Besides which this bond service is much worse than the Egyptian, for the latter was for the payment of debts, but with that under which the Congregation

BETHANIA, BROTHERS' HOUSE, EPHRATA

is in bondage, no debts can be paid. Yea, what am I saying? Pay? The more one lets oneself come under this service, the more one sinks into debt.

But they who withdrew from it because they see that no debts can be paid with this bond service and that one cannot fulfill it so long as one lives are refused fellowship as though they were evil-doers, and are expelled from the congregation, etc.

Weiser went further and recommended a reformation in the church and offered to go and assist in it. This gratuity being refused, we find Weiser for a long time estranged from the Brethren.

The warm intimacy and love between Weiser and Peter Miller became, after a time, the means of drawing Weiser back to the community once more. When he again visited Ephrata after his prolonged absence, no one censured him, and no one turned from him. Weiser inquired for Beissel, who came forward and received him with open arms into "the sisters* home, where his old acquaintances rejoiced with him that he had found again his piece of silver which had been lost."

Soon after, at a love feast, the Brethren reincorporated Weiser into the "spiritual communion; although," said their historian, "we willingly yield to his mother church the honor of garnering in his body."[8]

These experiences tended to alienate Weiser from the public affairs of the State. Indeed, no sooner was he away from the community at Ephrata than a group of earnest Moravian missionaries interested him deeply in their plans for the conversion and improvement of the Indians.

Spangenberg, Zeisberger, and Zinzendorf applied to Weiser for aid and guidance. As early as November 8, 1737, Bishop Spangenberg wrote: "I have made the acquaintance of a certain man, Conrad Weiser, who was nurtured in the faith of the Reformed Church, but who has for some time been identified with the Seventh Day Baptists." Weiser instructed several men in the Mohawk tongue and advised them about the best methods to convert the Indians. He urged the adoption of the French plans in a measure. Before sermons were preached, smith shops should be opened, and the guns and hatchets of the Indians gratuitously mended. Weiser's plan was that a concrete favor should be given before an abstract truth was elucidated. He was especially desirous that a smithy should be established at Shamokin.

After Weiser had gone on several mission journeys with the Moravians, Governor Thomas, who was well aware of Weiser's importance in the Indian

---

8. *Chronicon Ephratense*, p. 86.

policy of the province, used every possible means to draw him away from these people.

When Count Zinzendorf, in 1742, applied to Conrad Weiser to accompany him to Onondaga and introduce him to the Six Nation Indians, Governor Thomas urged him not to go. Weiser hesitated but finally concluded to guide Zinzendorf as far as Shamokin. He had already been entertaining the Count for some time; indeed, Zinzendorf was at Weiser's house when that notable party of Iroquois sachems stopped there on their return from a treaty at Philadelphia. With Weiser's assistance, these Indians were won over to the Moravian project of establishing a mission among them. They replied to Zinzendorf's offer: "Brother, you have journeyed a long way from beyond the sea to preach to the white people and the Indians. You did not know that we were here; we had no knowledge of your coming. The Great Spirit has brought us together. Come to our people; you shall be welcome; take this fathom of wampum; it is a token that our words are true."

On the journey to Shamokin, Weiser named the mountains they crossed "Thurnstein" in honor of Zinzendorf. At Ostonwacken, they waited upon Madame Montour, who burst into tears when she saw Zinzendorf and heard that he had come to preach the gospel, the truths she had almost forgotten. Zinzendorf remarks in his journal that Madame Montour was a French woman captured in Canada when she was ten years old. She had forgotten most of her early teachings and believed that Bethlehem, the Saviour's birthplace, was in France and that his crucifiers were Englishmen." Some of the French missionaries extensively taught this perversion.

After his return from the west branch of the Susquehanna River, Zinzendorf desired to go up into the Wyoming Valley, where the Shawanese Indians lived. Weiser did all in his power to prevent the Count from undertaking this journey but to no avail. Zinzendorf found a cold reception among the Shawanese. These Indians were suspicious and could not comprehend why he came among them. They scorned his missionary projects and, in their hearts, believed that he came to take possession of their land, and if he did not do it at first, he would eventually accomplish it.

One day, when the Count had his tent removed from the vicinity of those occupied by his daughter and servants so that he might examine some packages of letters recently forwarded from Germany without the possibility of interruption, a stealthy Indian scout peered upon him from a leafy thicket. When he reported to the wise men, they declared that the white man was arranging and reading his deeds to their land. Accordingly, a plot was laid to murder the Count. The hour was fixed, and the Indian selected to strike the blow.

COUNT ZINZENDORF

In the meantime, Conrad Weiser had been much troubled about Zinzendorf. "His prolonged absence bodes ill," thought Weiser. The interpreter's mind was filled with a presentment that some hidden danger was threatening the Count. He at once started for Wyoming, where he arrived just in time to discover the plot and save the life of this remarkable missionary.

"His presence," wrote Zinzendorf of Weiser, "and the bold authority with which he dealt with the Shawanese put an end to their evil purposes."[9]

In the winter of 1745, Zeisberger and Frederick Christian Post were among the Mohawk Indians learning their language. For some time, the colonial Governors looked suspiciously at the Moravians, believing them to be in league with the French. The governor of Pennsylvania shared strongly in this prejudice. And since Conrad Weiser belonged to the governor's party, he also received the Moravians' suspicion and distrust. They turned away from him and said many bitter things against him. To what extent Weiser merited the Moravians' ill will is unclear. The probability is that he differed from the Moravians in the method designed for the conversion of the Indians; from this difference, a coldness arose between them. That Weiser always felt kindly towards the Moravians is certain. When the governor of New York, under the impression that Zeisberger and Post were spies in the interest of the French, had them arrested while they were in the Mohawk country and thrown into jail because they refused to take the oath, then it was that Conrad Weiser interceded with Governor Thomas and secured their pardon from Governor Clinton.[10]

After Weiser had found disappointment with the Brethren at Ephrata and lost interest in the Moravians, he turned with renewed zeal to public affairs and the interests of the Indians.

---

9. See *Life of Zeisberger*, pp. 117, 119.
10. See Letter from Weiser to Spangenberg.

V

The Alienation of the Delawares

Weiser's Indian Policy—The Delaware Indians lose their Power—The Shawanese Treaty of 1701—The Shawanese Conference of 1739—The Delawares from Ohio come to Philadelphia—Trouble grows out of the "Walking Purchase"—Weiser's Attitude toward the Delaware Indians—Weiser opposed to the Quakers—Weiser grasps the Ohio Problem—The Iroquois hold the Balance of Power—Weiser's Policy in the Interest of the Six Nations—The Conference of 1742—The Indians dissatisfied with their Presents—The Six Nations complain of the Squatters in the Juniata Valley—The Iroquois drive the Delawares from their Hunting Grounds—Canassatego chastises the Delawares—They are dismissed from the Conference—The Six Nations claim Western Maryland and Virginia—Difficulties over Indian Expenses—The Indians and Governor eulogize Conrad Weiser—Conrad Weiser entertains the Iroquois Deputies—Maryland in trouble with the Six Nations—The friendly Delawares driven from Home.

DURING the period from 1735 to 1742, as has been seen, Conrad Weiser was largely engaged in church affairs. The Indian relations were not pressing, though silent influences were at work, which in a few years led to important results. Had Conrad Weiser shown the same zeal for the Delaware and Shawanese tribes that he did for the Iroquois, many difficulties might have been avoided. It was the nature of the Indians to tolerate no compromise, which made it difficult for the province of Pennsylvania to avoid being dragged into the quarrel brewing between the Six Nation Indians and their allies, the Delawares. Weiser's policy was invariably in favor of the Iroquois and, therefore, necessarily against the Delawares and Shawanese.

After William Penn's time, the old men of the Delawares continued to come to Philadelphia each autumn and receive a few trivial gifts. In October 1738, Allummappees came and had the chain of friendship brightened to the extent of thirty pounds worth of presents, he and the other old men of his tribe having brought skins to the value of eight pounds and presented them to the governor. This was almost the last of the old *regime* in Indian affairs. A set of younger men were coming into power among the Delawares, and they were susceptible to the influence of the Shawanese. These tribes came into the province from the south about 1699 and were permitted by William Penn to live among the Delaware Indians. The Conestoga Indians pledged themselves to the good behavior of these new arrivals.

In 1701 the Shawanese tribes made a firm treaty of peace and friendship with William Penn. They promised to submit to the laws of Pennsylvania and to refrain from alliances with other Indians or white men. They further promised to trade with no one except Pennsylvania traders, provided the governor would permit none but licensed traders to come among them. After the death of William Penn, an increasing number of complaints came from these Indians about the unrestrained traffic in rum, which unlicensed traders brought among them. This, together with the various land sales made by the Delawares and the Iroquois, led the majority of the Shawanese to move to the Allegheny and Ohio Rivers.

The provincial authorities of Pennsylvania fully realized the importance of having these Shawanese tribes east of the mountains again, evident that the French were rapidly winning them over as allies.

Consequently, in 1739 several Shawanese chiefs were induced to come to Philadelphia. At this conference, when the governor put the plain question of loyalty to past agreements, the Indians desired that their reply might be postponed until morning, saying that it was their custom to do public business only during the sun's rising and not during the setting. In the morning, they showed that all past agreements had been kept by them quite as faithfully as by the white men. And since Pennsylvania had, about a year previous, promised to issue an order forbidding the sale of any more rum among them, they had sent one of their young men to the French as an agent to induce them "for all time, to put a stop to the sale of rum, brandy, and wine." With the full understanding that the rum traffic was to be stopped, the Shawanese confirmed the old treaty of 1701 and promised not to join any other nation. A wagon was furnished to carry their old men, baggage, and liquors some distance from Philadelphia.

The following year, Conrad Weiser was called to Philadelphia to serve as an interpreter for a party of eastern and western Delawares and a group of Iroquois.

The Friends Meeting House, where the conference was held, was crowded with curious people. The Allegheny Indians, fresh from French overtures, were full of complaints.

"We are great hunters," they said, "but your young men have driven the game off. We want you to keep your young men away. We want our guns and axes mended free."

The governor readily promised them all they asked and gave them a present worth 150 pounds. This was a more valuable gift than those usually bestowed upon the Delawares, and it is more probable that giving it aroused jealousy among the eastern Delawares.

The Allegheny Indians were then told not to believe false stories and were urged to look upon Philadelphia as their home. At this point in the conference, the governor turned to the Six Nation chiefs and charged them with a violation of good faith. It appears that an Iroquois Indian had nearly killed a white man on the Minisink lands,[1] and when the governor of Pennsylvania demanded the person of the offending Indian, his tribe refused to give him up. This, the Pennsylvania authorities insisted, was a breach of former treaties. The Iroquois deputies at Philadelphia acknowledged this, and Shikellamy, who had control of the Six Nation affairs in the province, pledged himself that the offender should be delivered if possible. Since the Indian code recognized that one favor deserved another, the Iroquois asked that Pennsylvania use her influence to secure the liberty of two of their children, who were prisoners among the Catawba Indians in Carolina. Governor Thomas promised to write to the governor of Virginia about it.

The following spring, a complaint was received from the eastern Delawares, saying that the white people had taken possession of certain lands in Bucks County which had never been purchased. The governor at once produced the deed of the celebrated Walking Purchase, together with a map showing them conclusively that their claims upon these desirable lands were all covered by the writings. A letter was also shown to them from the Iroquois chief declaring that their cousins, the Delawares, owned no lands and, therefore, had no right to sell land. This letter went further and begged the proprietors not to accept any land grant from any Delaware Indians. All these documents were sent to the Delawares' sachems, with the provincial Council's request that the Delawares should live peacefully and friendly with their neighbors, the English.

---

1. The Minisink Lands were a part of the territory covered by the Walking Purchase, over which there was so much dispute among the Indians.

A notice was also sent to these once-favored people that the deputies of the Six Nations were expected to be in Philadelphia in May (1742), and if the Delawares chose to come down at their own expense and be present, no objections would be offered.[2]

The Delawares slowly realized that Indian affairs were not conducted as they were. To what extent Conrad Weiser was instrumental in divorcing the Pennsylvania policy from the Delaware interests is not clear; that he was a potent and tireless factor in arousing interest for the Iroquois is evident. Since Weiser was an ardent advocate of the governor's party and threw his influence against the Friends who were in public office, he was probably instrumental in developing that policy which rudely pushed the Delaware Indians into the background.

In the State election of 1741, Weiser took an active part and used all his influence to persuade his German brethren from supporting Quakers for representatives. In an open letter to his "worthy countrymen," Weiser said,

> You have been told, it seems, that if you took not care to choose Quakers, you would be caught in the same slavery you came hither to avoid. It grieves me to think that any should give themselves the liberty to invent and propagate such falsehood. The Quakers are a sober, industrious people, and so far as they have been concerned in government, we have shared in their protection, but we see there are amongst them who shew they have the same pashions and give way to them as much, full as much as other men, and we want such (for assemblymen) as will make up our breaches and not widen them, but as to the slavery that has been mentioned, you may be assured that whomsoever you shall chuse, by much the greater part will be English, and there is no nation in the world more jealous and careful of their laws than the English nation, and therefore you may fully trust them, and that you may be directed by wisdom in your choice, and that peace, love, truth, and good-will amongst men may prevail is the hearty prayer of your friend,
>
> Conrad Weiser.
> Tulpehockin, in Lancaster County,
> the 20th of Sept., 1741[3]

---

2. *Colonial Records*, vol. IV., p. 481.
3. From MSS. found among the Smith Papers at the Falls of the Schuylkill.

In this same letter, however, Conrad Weiser reveals the fact that he is thoroughly aware of the situation relative to French encroachments, and since he uses his knowledge on this subject for campaign purposes, it is more than evident that the people, and especially the German people, were also awakening to the danger. "The French Nation," said Weiser in this letter, "is many thousands strong in America and possessed of Canada, a large and well-fortified country to the north of us, and to the west of us they are possessed of the great river Meshasigg, which extends in its several parts far and wide, one part of it generally going where traders go (Logstown, on the Ohio, below the present site of Pittsburgh), to deal with our Indians, is within the bounds of pensilvana, insomuch that between that and the west branch of the Susquehanna, is but a short land carriage, and all the Indians near the aforesaid great Rivere (Ohio), are in league with the enemy, and it is an easy matter for the french with the help of these Indians, to come this road and lay this province waste in a few days."

The prophetic vision of Conrad Weiser would indicate that no man in the province knew its geography better or realized the coming danger more clearly. Few Englishmen as early as 1741 had any knowledge of the country beyond the Allegheny Mountains or knew the nature and extent of the French claims. Conrad Weiser seems to have been the one man keenly alive to the situation. Colonel Johnson of New York was indeed exerting all his influence against the French and endeavoring to hold the Iroquois aloof from any alliance, yet Colonel Johnson's influence availed but little, at that time, beyond the Mohawk tribes.

All persons well-informed about Indian affairs were thoroughly aware that the Iroquois held the balance of power. Should a struggle between the French and English ever come, the Six Nations could decide the matter through their alliances. Accordingly, they were courted on all sides. The French missionaries obtained a foothold in the west and soon caused a division among* the Senecas, thus securing the tributary tribes on the Allegheny to the arms of France. Colonel Johnson held the Mohawks finally to the English interests, while Conrad Weiser, who was given the most honored seat at the Onondaga Council hires, held the three central nations, the Cayugas, Onondagas, and Oneidas, in sympathy with Pennsylvania and the English, thus neutralizing the French influence until the Albany purchase of 1754 drove the western Pennsylvania Indians into the arms of the French.

It was under a sense of this impending danger that Conrad Weiser was led to bend the Indian policy of the province away from the Delaware and Shawanese tribes and unite it with the interests of the Six Nations. Because of these facts, it is not difficult to comprehend why the Delawares were now given to understand that if they attended the approaching conference with the Iroquois at Philadelphia in 1742, they were at liberty to come, provided they would bear their expenses. At all previous conferences, the Delawares had been entertained at the province's expense. They felt this policy change keenly, but for many years they remained silent, ruminating over their wrongs.

The conference of 1742 was called to pay the Six Nations for that portion of the land purchased from them in 1736, which lay west of the Susquehanna River. At the time of the purchase, the Indians were unwilling to receive pay for this portion. It included all the lands in Pennsylvania west of the Susquehanna River and south and east of the Blue Mountains.

The Senecas were not present at this meeting because of a famine reported to be among them. The Mohawks were absent because they were not considered to have any claims upon Susquehanna lands. The three remaining nations of the Iroquois received for this section of land, which now comprises the counties of York, Cumberland, Adams, and most of Franklin, "500 pounds of powder, 600 pounds of lead, 45 guns, 60 stroud match coats, 100 blankets, 60 kettles, 100 tobacco tongs, 100 scissors, 500 awl blades, 120 combs, 100 duffil coats, 200 yards of half-thick, 100 shirts, 40 hats, 40 pair stockings, 100 hatchets, 500 knives, 100 hoes, 2000 needles, 1000 flints, 24 looking glasses, 2 pounds of vermilion, 10 tinpots, 1000 tobacco pipes, 24 dozen of gartering, 200 pounds tobacco, 25 gallons of rum."[4]

The Indians promptly expressed dissatisfaction with the amount when these goods were divided. They admitted that it was all agreed upon, but they felt sure that if the proprietors were present, they would pity their wretched condition and give them more. Then with genuine Iroquois skill, their leader begged the governor, since he had the keys to the proprietors' chest, to open it and take out a little more for them. The governor replied that the proprietors had gone to England and taken the chest's keys with them. The Indians replied, saying, we know that our lands are growing more valuable. "Land is everlasting, and the few things we receive for it are soon worn out and gone; for the future, we will sell no lands, but when Brother Onas[5] is in the country, and we will know beforehand the quantity of goods we are to receive."

The Indians went a step further and declared that the governor did not keep his word regarding lands that had not been sold. "Your people daily settle on these lands (Juniata Valley)," said the Indians, "they spoil our hunting. The

---
4. *Pennsylvania Colonial Records*, vol. IV., pp. 566, 567.
5. Meaning the sons of William Penn.

white man's horses and cows eat the grass which formerly our deer fed upon. You must remove the settlers from the Juniata." The governor replied that he had ordered the magistrates of Lancaster County to go there and drive off the squatters; he was unaware that any had stayed after that. Here the Indians interrupted the speaker and said that the persons sent for this purpose did not do their duty; instead of removing the settlers from the Juniata, they made surveys for themselves; these men were in league with the squatters. In strong language, the Indians insisted that more effectual means must be employed and honest men selected for the work.

The governor promised them that all this would be done, but since they demanded the removal of the Juniata squatters with such promptness, the governor would call their attention to the fact that many Delaware Indians above the mouth of the Lehigh River, on the Minisink lands, had refused to give peaceful possession of the territory secured by the Walking Purchase. Accordingly, in the presence of the Delaware Indians who were attending the treaty at their own expense, Canassatego, the Iroquois speaker, said,

> You informed us of the misbehavior of our cousins, the Delawares, with respect to their continuing to claim and refusing to remove from some land on the River Delaware, notwithstanding their ancestors had sold it by deed under their hands and seals to the proprietors for a valuable consideration, upwards of fifty years ago, and notwithstanding that they themselves had about (five) years ago, after a long and full examination, ratified that deed of their ancestors, and given a fresh one under their hands and seals, and then you requested us to remove them, enforcing your request with a string of wampum. Afterward, you laid on the table by Conrad Weiser our own letters, some of our cousins' letters, and the several writings to prove the charge against our cousins, with a draught of the land in dispute. We now tell you that we have perused all these several papers. We see with our own eyes that they (the Delawares) have been a very unruly people and are all together in the wrong in their dealings with you. We have concluded to remove them and oblige them to go over the River Delaware, and to quit all claim to any lands on this side for the future, since they have received pay for them, and it has gone through their guts long ago. To confirm to you that we will see your request executed, we lay down this string of wampum in return for yours.[6]

---

6. *Penna. Colonial Records*, vol. IV., pp. 578, 579.

The above statements, which sound as if the governor's Council had inspired them, seem to have wholly overlooked the fact that when John and Thomas Penn were persuading the chiefs of the Delaware Indians to confirm the deeds which covered the Walking Purchase, they promised that said papers would not cause the removal of any Indians then living on the Minisink Lands.[7]

Whoever furnished the material for Canassatego's speech was careful that he should not be aware of this promise. The Delawares were given no opportunity to defend themselves. Indeed, as soon as Canassatego had finished the above address to the governor, he turned to the Delawares and, taking a belt of wampum in his hand, spoke as follows:

> COUSINS:—Let this belt of wampum serve to chastise you; you ought to be taken by the hair of the head and shaken severely till you recover your senses and become sober; you don't know what ground you are standing on or what you are doing. Our Brother Onas' case is very just and plain, and his intentions are to preserve friendship; on the other hand, your cause is bad, your head far from being upright, you are maliciously bent to break the chain of friendship with our Brother Onas. We have seen with our eyes a deed signed by nine of your ancestors above fifty years ago for this very land and a release signed not many years since by some of yourselves and chiefs now living to the number of fifteen or upwards. But how came you to take upon you to sell land at all? We conquered you; we made women of you; you know you are women and can no more sell land than women. Nor is it fit that you should have the power of selling land since you would abuse it. This land that you claim is gone through your guts. You have been furnished with clothes and meat and drink by the goods paid you for it, and now you want it again like children as you are. But what makes you sell land in the dark? Did you ever tell us that you had sold this land? Did we ever receive any part, even the value of a pipe shank for it? You have told us a blind story that you sent a messenger to inform us of the sale, but he never came amongst us, nor we never heard anything about it. This is acting in the dark and very different from the conduct

---

7. The Indians (Delawares) request that they he permitted to remain on the present settlements and plantations, though within that purchase, without being molested. In answer to which the assurances that were given on this head at Pennsbury, were repeated anti confirmed to them. *Penna. Archives*, 1st series, vol. I., p. 541.

our Six Nations observe in their sales of land. On such occasions, they give public notice and invite all the Indians of their united nations and give them a share of the present they receive for their lands. This is the behavior of the wise United Nations, but we find that you are none of our blood. You act a dishonest part, not only in this but in other matters. Your ears are ever open to slanderous reports about our brethren. . . . And for all these reasons, we charge you to remove instantly; we don't give you liberty to think about it. You are women, take the advice of a wise man and remove immediately. You may return to the other side of the Delaware, where you came from, but we don't know whether, considering how you have demeaned yourselves, you will be permitted to live there or whether you have not swallowed that land down your throats, as well as the land on this side. We, therefore, assign you two places to go—either to Wyoming or Shamokin. You may go to either of these places, and then we shall have you more under our eye and shall see how you behave. Don't deliberate but remove away and take this belt of wampum.

Conrad Weiser interpreted this into English, and Cornelius Spring turned English into the Delaware tongue. While this rebuke was still smarting on the ears of the Delawares, Canassatego, taking up another belt of wampum, said to them, "This serves to forbid you, your children, and grandchildren, to the latest posterity, forever meddling in land affairs, neither you nor any who shall descend from you are ever after to presume to sell any land, for which purpose you are to preserve this string in your memory of what your uncles have this day given you in charge. We have some other business to transact with our brethren and therefore depart the Council and consider what has been said to you."

The Delawares sullenly withdrew to brood over their insult. They were well aware that nobody had ever disputed their right to sell land during the days of William Penn. And for many years after this, they found a sympathetic ear among the Friends around Philadelphia, who were very much dissatisfied with the governor's Indian policy.

A careful examination of Canassatego's address on this matter suggests that he drew most of his facts from the governor's representatives. Whether Conrad Weiser assisted in inspiring this rebuke or not is unknown, yet he, with the others, permitted it and thus scattered seed which in time caused more bloodshed in peaceful Pennsylvania than the Walking Purchase ever did.

The Delawares, having been ordered out of the house, the shrewd Iroquois turned their attention to more important business. They claimed that Maryland and Virginia were settling on land owned by the Six Nations, which had never been sold to the white man. The Iroquois then asked for the governor of Pennsylvania to intercede and demand damages payment. "That country (Western Maryland and Virginia)," said the Indians, "belongs to us by right of conquest. We have bought it with our blood and taken it from our enemies in fair war, and we expect as owners of that land to receive such a consideration for it as the land is worth. We desire you (the governor of Pennsylvania) will press him to send us a positive answer; let him (the governors of Virginia and Maryland) say yes or no; if he said yes, we will treat with him; if no, we are able to do ourselves justice, and we will do it by going to take payment on ourselves."

The Six Nations were well aware of their vantage ground, knowing that the English colonies dare not refuse their request.[8] This was virtually a declaration of war unless terms of their own making were complied with at once by Virginia and Maryland. The governor of Pennsylvania promptly promised to intercede and, if possible, secure payments. He told the Indians that after the last treaty (1736), James Logan did write to the governor of Maryland about the land but did not receive one word from him on the subject. "I will write him again," said the governor, "and I have no doubt, but he will do you justice. We caution you meanwhile not to allow any acts of violence to be committed."

In a secret session, however, the governor and Council concluded to write to Maryland at once, demanding a satisfactory reply and that the letter should be sent by a special messenger at public expense. It was also decided to give the Indians a present in addition to what had been received for land. The governor and Council were desirous of making this present quite liberal but feared to name a large amount lest the Assembly might not approve it. For some time, the Assembly had been expressing dissatisfaction with the recent management of Indian affairs and hinted that the Legislature should have some voice in the Indian policy of the province if it was expected to defray the expenses. In this case, the governor consulted with the Assembly speaker, agreeing that the presents should be up to 300 pounds. The amount of this gift had no small influence in preventing an Indian outbreak because, at that very time, the governor of Maryland became alarmed over a rumor that the Shawanese and Delaware Indians had joined the French in a conspiracy to destroy the frontier settlers in Maryland and Pennsylvania. Shortly after the Six Nation chiefs left Philadelphia, this rumor became quiet. The Indians were greatly pleased with

---

8. *Penna. Colonial Records*, vol. IV., p. 571.

the magnitude of their present and asked for wagons to haul their goods home, and they also requested that the nun bottle, which had been so tightly corked while they were in Philadelphia, be now uncorked on the way home. The board decided to furnish them with twenty gallons of rum, and Conrad Weiser was asked to estimate the cost of transporting them to Onondaga. Weiser's estimate was £100, which sum the treasurer declared he could not advance without an order from the Assembly. James Logan then offered on behalf of the proprietors to advance £40 of the hundred, and the speaker and a few members of the Assembly, who were in town, were consulted to know if they were willing to have the remainder of the money advanced on the credit of the Assembly.

Just before the Indians departed, they told the governor and his Council that the business they had transacted was very important. It "requires a skillful and honest person to go between us, one in whom both you and we can place confidence. We esteem our present interpreter to be such a person, equally faithful in the interpretation of whatever is said to him by either of us, equally allied to both. He is of our nation and a member of our Council, as well as yours. When we adopted him, we divided him into equal parts, one we left for ourselves and one we left for you. He has had a great deal of trouble with us, wore out his shoes in our messages, and dirty'd his clothes by being amongst us so that he is as nasty as an Indian. In return for these services, we recommend him to your generosity. And on our own account, we give him five skins to buy him clothes and shoes with."[9]

To this, the governor replied: "We entertain the same sentiments of the ability and probity of the interpreter as you have expressed; we were induced at first to make use of him in this important trust, from his being known to be agreeable to you, and one who had lived amongst you for some years in good credit and esteem with all your nations and have ever found him equally faithful to both. We are pleased with the notice you have taken of him and think he richly deserves it at your hands. We shall not be wanting to make him a suitable gratification for the many good and faithful services he has done this government."[10]

A few days previous, Conrad Weiser presented his bill for £36 18s. 3p. to the Council, which, having been examined, was pronounced a just and very moderate one. The Council then, "taking into consideration the many signal services performed by the said Conrad Weiser to this government, his diligence and labor in the service thereof, and his skill in the Indian language and methods

---

9. *Penna. Colonial Records*, vol. IV., p. 581.
10. *Penna. Colonial Records*, vol. IV., p. 582.

of business, are of the opinion that the said Conrad Weiser should be allowed, as a reward from the province at this time, the sum of £30 at least, besides the payment of his account."[11]

Conrad Weiser conducted this delegation of over two hundred Indians, ninety of whom were sachems and chiefs, with their presents and baggage into the forests toward Shamokin. At his house, in Tulpehocken, the entire party tarried some time. Here, in an open meeting, Weiser induced them to reveal the strength of the tribes in alliance with the Six Nations. They told him that outside of their own tribes, they could control 5000 warriors and that on "the great River Missysippy," above the mouth of the Ohio, were tribes of unknown number in alliance with the Six Nations, and on the north side of Lake Huron were several flesh-eating tribes, "who do not plant corn or anything else, but live altogether upon flesh, fish, roots, and herbs, an infinite number of people of late becomes allies to the Six Nations."[12] Conrad Weiser secured and forwarded this information so that the province might realize the importance of keeping the friendship of the Iroquois Indians.

In the meantime, Governor Thomas had addressed a letter to Conrad Weiser asking his opinion upon the Iroquois attitude toward Maryland. When Weiser's reply reached the Council, it was decided that a letter should be sent to the governor of Maryland with Weiser's suggestions enclosed. While these letters were being transmitted by a special messenger at public expense, word came that some Nanticoke Indians were imprisoned in Maryland, and unless they were released, their allies would make trouble. This report was scarcely read before a letter came from Governor Ogle himself. On behalf of the Maryland Council, he asked for the advice and assistance of Pennsylvania in this trouble with the Six Nations. Governor Thomas at once engaged Conrad Weiser to accompany the Maryland messenger to the country of the Six Nations and to act as interpreter. The purpose of this Maryland mission was to invite the Iroquois to a treaty to be held the next spring (1743) at Harris' Ferry (Harrisburg). While the Iroquois were deliberating upon this matter, a little affair occurred with the Delaware Indians, which materially increased the misunderstanding and hard feeling between these tribes and the governor and further illustrated that Conrad Weiser exerted none of his influence towards keeping the Delawares in a peaceful frame of mind. Indeed, it would seem in our colonial history that when any province took sides in an Indian quarrel or feud, it was sure to bring on war with the other faction.

---

11. *Penna. Colonial Records*, vol. IV., pp. 576, 577.
12. *Penna. Colonial Records*, vol. IV., p. 586.

In November 1742, Captain John and Titami, two worthy old Delaware chiefs, who had once been leaders of their people, and had always been warm friends of the white man, sent a petition to the governor on behalf of themselves and several others who had for many years been living near the Friends.

In this petition, the Indians claimed to have embraced the Christian religion "and grown into considerable knowledge thereof," and given these facts, they begged permission to remain where they were near the English and under the same laws. They further petitioned that a portion of land might be set apart for their use.

The governor called Titami and Captain John into the Council's presence and asked them questions regarding their knowledge of Christianity. From which interview, it appears, said the governor "that they had very little if any at all." He then asked them if they knew the nature of last summer's treaty with the Six Nations. Not satisfied with this, the governor ordered that Canassatego's speech be read to them and asked them if they understood. They replied that they did but had not been fully informed of its purposes by the Delawares.

The governor told them that the bad behavior of the Delawares had brought all this upon them. The two old gray chiefs acknowledged it and expressed concern for their countrymen's conduct. Titami then said that he had three hundred acres of land granted to him by the proprietors, and he merely asked permission to live there in peace and friendship with the English.

Captain John said that he did not currently own any land, but he intended to buy some if he might be allowed to live among the English. The Indians were then told to withdraw from the room while the matter was considered. The Council concluded that it would be highly improper to grant the petition because the Six Nations might resent it, and it might be the means of reviving the late troubles with the Delawares.

The Indians were called in, and the governor told them that he had "some knowledge of them and their good behavior towards the English, he would agree, provided they could obtain the consent of the chiefs of the Six Nations, that they two should be suffered to remain in the neighborhood of the English, but that Captain John must remove from the land where he now dwells, that being the property of persons who bought it from the proprietors, and they were to understand that the other petitioners were by no means to be included in this permission, nor any other of the Delaware Indians, whom they call their cousins, nor any besides themselves and their proper families dwelling in the same house with them; and this the governor frequently repeated to them that they might not pretend misapprehension, and with this answer, they were dismissed."[13]

To compel these old men to ask permission from the Iroquois was asking more than the pride of a Delaware could endure. The two old chiefs were never heard of again in public places; they quietly drew back into the forests, and their friends among the white men never knew why they left their former haunts. Slowly the young warriors among the Delawares learned the old men's cause of sorrow, and a store of revenge was laid up toward a day of retribution.

While the Delawares were brooding over these things, and the Six Nations were playing a fast and loose game with the deputies from Maryland, a condition of things sprung up in Virginia, threatening an Indian outbreak.

---

13. *Penna. Colonial Records*, vol. IV., p. 625.

VI

The Virginia Trouble of 1743

VIRGINIA DENIES THE IROQUOIS LAND CLAIM—IROQUOIS WARRIORS TAKE VIRGINIA SCALPS—THOMAS MCKEE'S ACCOUNT—MCKEE PLEADS WITH THE SHAWANESE INDIANS—MCKEE RUNS FOR HIS LIFE—VIRGINIA'S ACCOUNT—WEISER GOES TO SHAMOKIN TO LEARN THE TRUTH—GOVERNOR THOMAS' OPINION—THE PENNSYLVANIA ASSEMBLY FURNISH MONEY—WEISER ATTEMPTS TO MAKE PEACE—A SECOND TRIP TO SHAMOKIN—WEISER SPEAKS TO THE INDIANS—VIRGINIA ACCEPTS WEISER'S MEDIATION—THE IROQUOIS ANGRY ABOUT THE JUNIATA SQUATTERS—VIRGINIA FORCED TO ACCEPT THE IROQUOIS' TERMS—WEISER GOES TO ONANDAGO TO ARRANGE A TREATY—AN INDIAN BANQUET—WEISER AT THE ONANDAGO CONFERENCE—WEISER MAKES PEACE—THE LANCASTER TREATY OF 1744 ARRANGED.

SINCE the treaty of 1736, Virginia had given little or no attention to the Iroquois land claims. After the treaty of 1742, Maryland, we have seen, opened negotiations at the great Onondaga Council Fire, but Virginia did nothing; in fact, she denied that the Six Nations had the right to any land in Western Virginia. To what extent these things irritated the Iroquois is not known. These Indians were accustomed to being fawned upon by the French on one side and the New York and Pennsylvania authorities on the other. It is highly probable that at their council fires after the deputies had returned from the Philadelphia conference of 1742, some hard things were said about Virginia.

Be this as it may, the facts remain that a party of Iroquois warriors started south immediately after the return of the Philadelphia deputies. This party claimed to have gone out against their old enemies, the Catawba Indians. They came down the Susquehanna River in canoes until they reached John Harris' Ferry, the first important white settlement on their route. Here they secured a pass from a magistrate of Lancaster County for their safe passage through the inhabited parts of Pennsylvania. With this, they started across the country in a southwestward direction toward the Shenandoah Valley. They traveled civilly and without molesting anyone until they readied Virginia, where they fell in with a party of settlers, and a severe engagement ensued in which several lives were lost on each side. The Indians made a hasty retreat towards New York.

Sometime in January 1743, Thomas McKee, a Lancaster county trader living on the Susquehanna, went up to the "Bigg Island"[1] to trade with the Shawanese Indians. One morning some of these Indians came running into McKee's store greatly excited, saying that they had heard the "Dead Halloo" several times and that it seemed to come from the "Bigg Island." The Indians shouted over to know what was wrong and received the reply that the white people had killed some of their men. McKee went over in a canoe and spoke to these Iroquois warriors in his usual friendly manner. The Indians shook their heads and turned away from him. The Shawanese Indians immediately held a council, and McKee was allowed to attend. One of the Iroquois warriors made a speech to the Shawanese. He told them that when his party was in Virginia, they camped one night near a white man's house, and the next morning when three of their party went there, a quarrel broke out. Four white men tried to tie the Indians: knives were drawn, and lives would have been lost had the white men refused to let the Indians go. They ran to the camp, and the entire Iroquois party packed their bundles and hurried off. A large party of white men followed them; after traveling a long distance, the Indians found they were pursued. They then stopped at a house where several men invited the Indians into the building, asking them to leave their arms outside. Several Indians did this, but the more cautious remained outside, suspecting some ill designs of the Virginians. These Indians were uneasy until they got those in the house out again, when they all started off at a good pace and kept it up for the remainder of the day. The following morning a large party of white men came upon them, firing continually. A boy in the rear was killed. Then the Indian captain ordered his men to turn and fight. Several white men were shot, including the color bearer. A sharp engagement followed in which the tomahawks were freely used. Ten Virginians and four Indians were killed, and many were injured on each side. The Indians carried their wounded away and cared for them. Ten able-bodied Indians were sent home to Onondaga to report and receive orders. These runners were told by their captain "that as there were different sorts of white people; if they should

---

1. "Big Island" was on the west branch of the Susquehanna River, at the present site of Lock Haven.

meet any on the road, they should not meddle with them, lest they should by mistake kill any of those who were in friendship with them."[2]

The Shawanese at the "Bigg Island" were greatly disturbed by this report. Although Thomas McKee tried to convince them that the bonds of friendship between the Iroquois and the Pennsylvanians were as strong as formerly and that the sons of Onas were in no way responsible for what had happened in Virginia; therefore he hoped that the Shawanese would protect him while he was among them. One of the Indians replied that all white people were of one color, and as one body, they would aid one another in case of war. When McKee inquired if any of the Shawanese had seen his servant who had been sent to Chiniotta for skins, he was told that they had not seen his man, and if they had, they most certainly would have killed him. This alarmed McKee very much. He got up and took an old Shawanese Indian with him into his storehouse; after presenting him with two or* three twists of tobacco, he tried to convince him of what would happen to the Shawanese Indians if they broke their Pennsylvania treaty by killing a white man.

The old Indian promised to do what he could in council. After some time, he called McKee out of his store and told him that the Shawanese were very angry in the council.

A short time after this, a white woman, who the Iroquois had taken prisoner in Carolina, came to McKee in the dark and told him secretly that the Iroquois Indians had given the Shawanese permission to do with him as they thought fit. And that the Shawanese had gone out some distance into the woods to hold a council in privacy upon the matter. The woman told McKee that if he did not make his escape, he would surely be killed. The trader needed no further hints. He told his man, and they decided to leave the store and all the goods behind and escape. They traveled for three days and nights through the uninhabited parts of the country until they believed they were out of danger.

McKee's account was the Indians' side of the story. The white people in Virginia, where this occurred, reported that as soon as the Indians reached Virginia, they commenced killing the settlers' hogs and cattle, and in one instance, a man's horse was killed. They said that the Indians brought all this difficulty upon themselves by these outrages. The settlers tried to approach the Indians with a flag of truce but were fired upon, and several were killed.

Conrad Weiser was immediately dispatched to Shamokin to learn the truth. A grandson of Shikellamy, in the presence of Weiser and the Indian sachems, told the entire story. He said,

---

2. *Penna. Colonial Records*, vol. IV., p. 632.

there were twenty-nine in the party which crossed the Potomac. They wanted to go to some justice of the peace to get their passes renewed, but they could find none. There were no deer to be killed. They would have starved if they had not killed a hog now and then, which they did at Jonontere. On the other side of said hills, they laid down their bundles and sent three of them (their men) to look for the road they must go. These three men were met by two white men, who asked them many questions till a third person of the white came up, then they all at once took hold of the Indians' guns, but the Indians would not let them go out of their hands. One of the Indians took out his knife and threatened to stab the white man, upon which they let go the guns and went their way, and the Indians returned to their company and told what had happened to them.[3]

The captain told them not to pay any attention to this. The next day the Indians were followed again by the white men with guns and pitchforks. The remainder of this report was substantially similar to McKee, the trader. The serious question growing out of Weiser's negotiations was which story to believe.

Governor William Gooch, of Virginia, in writing to Governor Thomas of Pennsylvania, said: "If what the Six Nations insist upon be true, that we are the aggressors, the matter has been greatly misrepresented to me."[4]

Governor Thomas, in his reply, said:

> From the interpreter's private conversation with Shikellimo (Shikellamy), you will observe that the Six Nations insist upon the Virginians' having been the aggressors; and to be plain, from all the circumstances I have been able to collect, I am of that opinion. . . . If the inhabitants of the back parts of Virginia have no more truth and honor than some of ours, I should make no scruple to prefer an Iroquois' testimony to theirs. The Indians own that they killed some hoggs to assuage their hunger, which joined to their threats last year, in case they were not paid for their lands, seems to me to have been the fatal cause of the skirmish.[5]

These opinions of Governor Thomas were probably reflections of Conrad Weiser's judgment. So strong was the influence of this sturdy German that

---

3. *Penna. Colonial Records*, vol. IV., pp. 644, 645.
4. *Penna. Colonial Records*, vol. IV., p. 654.
5. *Penna Colonial Records*, vol. IV., p. 653.

Virginia did not insist upon carrying her point but, after some little "flurry and bluster,"[6] concluded to do as Weiser thought best.

The first thing that Governor Thomas did when he heard of the difficulty in Virginia was to send Conrad Weiser, in all possible haste, to Shamokin to use his influence in assuring the Six Nations and all the Indians in alliance with them that Pennsylvania and the sons of Onas stood faithfully by the former treaties of friendship. The governor's second thing was to report this action to his Assembly with the statement: "I doubt not of your giving the proper orders to the treasurer for defraying what expenses shall be incurred on this occasion."[7] The Assembly promptly replied, "whatever sums of money shall become necessary to expend to these good purposes, we shall cheerfully pay and give the proper orders to the treasurer to this end."[8]

In the meantime, the governor had written Conrad. Weiser, saying: "I will do all I can to procure you a handsome reward for the trouble and fatigue you must necessarily undergo in the persecution of this matter at this bad season of the year." Conrad Weiser had a difficult affair to manage. No definite instructions were given to him.

"I leave it to your own judgment," wrote the governor, "how far it may be proper for you as our agent to proceed in it. . . . I need not say anything more to you, who know so much."

Thus, this honest-hearted and strong-willed German was left to get Virginia out of her difficulty as best he could. And Virginia was at that time loudly insisting that she was not in the wrong, that the Six Nations commenced it, and that their land claims were hollow subterfuge. Furthermore, Pennsylvania herself was in a very precarious position. Should the Six Nations go to war with Virginia, Pennsylvania could not remain neutral and be expected to provision the bands of Iroquois warriors who passed through her borders; and this the Indians would demand as a right: and if it was refused, there would be war in Pennsylvania. Then to add to the difficulties of Weiser's mission, the settlers west of the Susquehanna had no love for the Indians, and under the excitement of the Virginia rumors, there was great danger of their doing some rash thing for which all Pennsylvania would be held responsible. Weiser knew how easy it would be for these things to bring on a general Indian outbreak. He alone, at

---

6. R. Peters, Secretary of the Pennsylvania Provincial Council, writing to Conrad Weiser, February 1743. says: "The Virginia Governor seems to swear and talk big. but it being grounded on a mistake of his own. I suppose he will take shame for it." (From the manuscript collection of C. Weiser's letters in the Library of the Penna. Historical Society.)

7. *Penna. Colonial Records*, vol. IV., p. 634.

8. *Penna. Colonial Records*, vol. IV., p. 637.

that time, measured the influence of the French. To foment this quarrel would be exactly to their liking. Should the Iroquois turn against the English, the Shawanese would remember their unanswered petitions about rum, the Delawares would recall the Walking Purchase, and what a harvest this would be for the French. Weiser did not know, however, that Europe was just on the eve of the war of the Austrian Succession. But he did know that should such an outbreak arise and the Iroquois be lost to the English, victory must crown the French in their struggle for empire in America.

The fate of a future nation was at stake when Weiser started through the snow for Shamokin in January 1743. He received his orders on the evening of January 30, and the next morning, with Thomas McKee, he was pushing through the forests. They crossed the trails of Indian scouts who had been watching the actions of the white men. A few days later, they reached a Shawanese village where twenty-five warriors ran into a trader's house when they saw Weiser coming. They sat down in the corner of the house where their arms were. Each Indian had a cutlass in addition to their gun. When he dismounted from his horse, the Indian trader's wife told Weiser that these Indians were unfriendly and had been plotting mischief.

Weiser went into the house and shook hands with them. "Their hands trembled," wrote Weiser, "and none of them hardly looked to my face till I sat down and began to talk with them."[9] Weiser soon won the friendship of these Indians, and they accompanied him to Shamokin.

At that place, the representative Indians of many tribes and nations were waiting for the news. Twenty-five wise men met at Shikellamy's house. In addition to the regular Five Nation embassies, there were present Sachsidowa, chief of the Tuscaroras, Allummappees and Lapapeton of the Delawares, and the "Great Hominy," chief of the Shawanese, and also Andrew, son of Madame Montour, who served as interpreter for the Delawares. Since Shikellamy was in mourning for his cousin who was killed in the recent skirmish in Virginia, Weiser first directed his speech to the old chief, saying, "Brother, Shikellimo, you have just cause to mourn for the loss of your cousin killed in Virginia lately; I am also sensible of the grievous accident, but as the public welfare calls for your aid at this time, I have been sent to comfort you, and to wipe away the tears from your eyes, and, in short, to put your heart at ease, for which purpose I present you with these two shrouds."[10]

---

9. *Penna. Colonial Records*, vol. IV., p. 641.
10. *Penna. Colonial Records*, vol. IV., p. 641.

Weiser called the company's attention to former friendship treaties, William Penn's many favors shown to the Indians, and the protecting care of the great King of England over his red children in America. He then insisted: (1) That a delegation with Shikellamy at its head be sent at once to Onondaga to inform the Six Nations at their great Council Fire that we are all of one body, one heart, and one mind; (2) That the goods which the Shawanese Indians had stolen, from the trading houses be returned. This will be a direct violation of former treaties if this is not done. If the traders are not desired among you, send them home unmolested; (3) That measures be taken to meet the governor of Virginia and have this unfortunate accident settled. The Indians, after many councils and lengthy deliberations, agreed to all these things, Weiser having been quite generous in making presents of match coats to the most influential of the chiefs. When Thomas McKee lied from his trading house, the Shawanese Indians filled it. Weiser, at this meeting, so influenced Shikellamy that the old chief forced the Shawanese to return the stolen goods to McKee.

After Weiser's return from Shamokin, a letter was received from Governor Gooch consenting to the mediation offered on the part of Pennsylvania and expressing a hearty desire to have the affair made up amicably. Therefore, Weiser was sent a second time to Shamokin and instructed to arrange for reconciliation between Virginia and the Six Nations and to arrange for a conference with Maryland, who was still waiting for an opportunity to meet the Iroquois. When Weiser reached Shamokin the second time, he found the Indians who had been sent to Onondaga as deputies on behalf of the Virginia affair had returned. They thanked him for his concern for the misfortunes that befell their warriors in Virginia. "We take it," they said, "as a particular mark of friendship. We assure you that notwithstanding the unjust treatment our warriors met with in Virginia, we did not allow our heads to be giddy nor to resent it as it deserved, which might have occasioned a violation of treaties and the destruction of many."[11]

The speaker then turned his speech from Conrad Weiser, the individual, to Conrad Weiser, the governor's representative. "Brother Onas," he said, "the Dutchman on Scokooniady (Juniata) claims a right to the land merely because he gave a little victual to our warriors who stand very often in need of it. This string of wampum serves to (the speaker then took two strings of wampum in his hands) take the Dutchman by the arm and to throw him over the big mountain within your borders. We have given the River Scokooniady for a hunting place to our cousins, the Delawares, and our brethren, the Shawanese, and we

---

11. *Penna. Colonial Records*, vol. IV., p. 647.

ourselves hunt there sometimes. We, therefore, desire you will immediately by force remove all those that live on the said River Scokooniady."

Here he laid down two strings of wampum. Then directing his speech to the governor of Maryland, he said: "You have invited us to come to your town, and you offered to treat with us concerning the messages we sent by our brother, the governor of Pennsylvania, and to establish good friendship with us. We are very glad you did so, and we thank you for your kind invitation.

"Brother, we have a great deal of business and things of moment under our deliberation, and it will take the best of the day (this summer) before we can finish them. We, therefore, desire you will set your heart at ease and think on nothing but what is good; we will come and treat with you at Canataquany (a place near Harris' Ferry) tomorrow morning (next spring) since you live so near the sea and so far from us. We accept kindly of your invitation. Our brother, the governor of Pennsylvania, recommended your messages to us, which he would not have done if he had not been satisfied your intentions were good; we, therefore, promise you by these strings of wampum to come and treat with you at the aforesaid place."

The speaker laid down four strings of wampum and, turning to the Shawanese, said: "Brethren, . . . you believe too many lies and are too forward in action. You shall not pretend to revenge our people that have been killed in Virginia. We are the chief of all the Indians. Let your ears and your eyes be open toward us, and order your warriors to stay at home, as we did ours."

Then turning to Pennsylvania again, he said: "Brother Onas, your back inhabitants are people given to lies and raising false stories. Stop up their mouths; you can do it with one word. Let no false stories be told; it is dangerous to the chain of friendship."[12]

During all these negotiations, not a word was said about Virginia. After the public conference, Weiser asked Shikellamy why the Iroquois were not willing to come down and treat with Virginia.

Shikellamy asked him if "he could not guess."

Weiser said, "no."

"How could they come down," said Shikellamy, "with a hatchet stuck in their heads; the governor of Virginia must wash off the blood first, and take the hatchet out of their head and dress the wound (according to custom he that struck first must do it) and the Council of the Six Nations will speak to him and be reconciled to him and bury that affair in the ground that it never may be seen

---

12. *Penna. Colonial Records*, vol. IV., p. 649.

nor heard of any more so long as the world stands. But if the Virginians would not come to do that, he (Shikellimo) believed that there would be a war."[13]

Shikellamy also told Weiser that the Six Nation warriors would not disturb the people of Pennsylvania. They would go directly to Virginia from the Big Island in the west branch of the Susquehanna River. Weiser, the Tuscarora chief, Shikellamy, and two Delaware chiefs brought this information to Philadelphia. The governor told the Delaware chief that he was sorry that their uncles, the Iroquois, had occasion to find fault with the behavior of the Delaware Indians and the back inhabitants. You both spread false stories among the Indians. "I hope you will take good notice of what they (the Iroquois) said to you about it in my presence."[14]

To Shikellamy, the governor gave ten pounds and compliments. He gave six pounds each to Shikellamy's two sons; to Sachsidowa, the Tuscarora chief, he gave five pounds. These same Indians also received free entertainment while in Philadelphia. Conrad Weiser knew where Pennsylvania money would bring the best returns in Indian affairs. When Virginia received his report, she came to terms promptly. A present of one hundred pounds' value was placed in the hands of Governor Thomas by Virginia. Governor Gooch wrote: "We request that you will be pleased to send your honest Interpreter once more to the Indian chiefs, and if possible prevail with them to accept through your hands a present from us of one hundred pounds sterling value, in such goods as you may think proper, as a token of our sincere disposition to preserve peace and friendship with them, and as an earnest that we will not fail to send commissioners next spring, at the time and place that shall be agreed upon, to treat with them concerning the lands in dispute."[15]

The provincial Council of Pennsylvania agreed that Conrad Weiser should be sent at once to Onondaga to arrange the meeting time and place and to deliver the generous present sent by Virginia. When Weiser arrived at Onondaga and had exchanged the usual greetings with the Indians, Tocanontie, known as the "Black Prince" of the Onondagas, expressed great satisfaction at Weiser's arrival, saying, you never come without good news from our brethren in Philadelphia.

Weiser smiled "and told him it was enough to kill a man to come such a long and bad road over hills, rocks, old trees, and rivers and to fight through a

---

13. *Penna. Colonial Records*, vol. IV., p. 650.
14. *Penna. Colonial Records*, vol. IV., p. 651.
15. *Penna. Colonial Records*, vol. IV., p. 654.

cloud of vermin and all kinds of poison'd worms and creeping things, besides being loaded with a disagreeable message, upon which they laughed."

Weiser went about this mission with a marked degree of care. He had Shikellamy with him, and they held several secret preliminary interviews with the leading men before the great Council Fire took place. At these interviews, Weiser was told that the Six Nations had put the settlement of this Virginia affair into the hands of the Onondaga Nation, that all the Iroquois had great "regard for Onas and his people, that they would do anything for them in their power, and they looked upon the persons who kept house for Onas (meaning the governor) as if Onas was there himself." Then Weiser listened to Jounhaty, the captain of the Indians in the Virginia skirmish, relate the circumstance with all its details.

After this, the captain gave a feast to which Assaryquoa[16] and Onas[17] were invited together with eighteen chiefs. "The feast consisted of a cask of rum of about two gallons; several songs were sung before the feast began, in which they thanked Assaryquoa for visiting them; they also thanked Onas for conducting Assaryquoa and showing him the way to Onondaga; the sun was praised for having given light, and for dispelling the clouds; then the cask was opened, and a cup of about three-fourths of a gill was filled for Canassatego, who drank to the health of Assaryquoa; next him drank Caheshcarowano to the health of the governor of Pennsylvania, and after this manner, we drank round," wrote Weiser. "The next time the cup was first reached to me by Jounhaty, who attended the feast, I wished long life to the councellors of the Six Nations, and drank my cup, so did Shikeliimo and the rest; after that, the kettle was handed around with a wooden spoon in it, every one took so much as he pleased, whilst we were drinking and smoking, news came that a deputation of Nanticoke Indians arrived at Cachiadachse from Maryland; the house of Canassatego was ordained for them since the town house was taken up by Onas and Assaryquoa; after all the rum was drunk* the usual thanks was given from every nation or deputy with the usual sound of Jo-haa, and we parted."[18]

Several days after this, there was a grand collecting of the head men from the surrounding tribes and nations. Many ceremonies were observed in receiving them. Finally, when the great Conference took place, Weiser spoke to them with all the profuseness of Indian metaphor. Pelt after belt of wampum was used, and the magnitude of Virginia's present was made to dazzle in the Indian*

---

16. Governor of Virginia, represented by Weiser.
17. Governor of Pennsylvania, represented by Shikellamy.
18. *Penna. Colonial Records*, vol. IV., pp. 661, 662.

eyes. Weiser offered to make peace with them on behalf of Virginia and then demanded their reply.

"All the wampum," wrote Weiser in his journal,[19] "were hung over a stick laid across the house about six foot from the ground, several kettles of hominy, boiled Indian corn and bread was brought in by the women, the biggest of which was set before Assaryquoa (Conrad Weiser) by the divider; all dined together; there were about sixty people. After dinner, they walked out, every nation's deputies by themselves, and soon came in again and sat together for about two hours; then Zilla Woolie proclaimed that Assaryquoa was to have an answer now immediately; upon which all the men in town gathered again, and the house was full, and many stood out of door (so it was in the forenoon when the message was delivered to them).

"Zilla Woolie desired Assaryquoa to give ear, Tocanuntie being appointed for their speaker, spoke to the following purpose: 'Brother Assaryquoa, the unhappy skirmish which happened last winter betwixt your people and some of our warriors was not less surprising to us than to you; we were very sorry to hear it, all amongst us were surprised; a smoke arose from the bottomless Pitt, and a dark cloud overshadowed us; the chain of friendship was endangered and disappeared, and all was in confusion. We, the chiefs of the United Nations, took hold of the chain with all our strength, we were resolved not to let it slip before we received a deadly blow. But to our great satisfaction, in the darkest time, our Brother Onas enter'd our Door and offer'd his Mediation- He judged very right to become mediator betwixt us. We were drunk on both sides, and the overflow of our galls and the blood that was shed had corrupted our hearts, both yours and ours. You did very well to come to our fire and comfort the mourning families. We thank you; this belt shall serve for the same purpose to comfort the families in mourning amongst you.'"

The speaker laid a belt of wampum on the table, and Conrad Weiser, on behalf of Virginia, thanked them. The Indian speaker laid down a belt of wampum for every proposition upon which he spoke. Under the eighth belt, he thanked the governor of Virginia for the present the old and wise men of that country had sent them by the governor of Pennsylvania. "Let this string of wampum serve to assure you . . . that we will come down within the borders of Pennsylvania to a place called Canadequeany next spring and will be very glad of seeing your commissioners there; we will treat them as becomes brethren with good cheer and pleasure. We will set out from our several towns after

---

19. *Penna. Colonial Records*, vol. IV., p. 665.

eight moons are passed by, when the ninth is just to be seen, this present moon, which is almost expired, not to be reckoned, upon which you may depend."[20]

Thus Conrad Weiser prevented war between Virginia and the Six Nations. Such a war must eventually have involved the other colonies. Weiser also arranged for a treaty to take place at Lancaster the following year (1744) where Maryland and Virginia could meet to buy out the Iroquois land claims, which these astute diplomats had so skillfully established within their borders, and where Pennsylvania could suppress all disputes and renew her old chains of friendship.

---

20. *Penna. Colonial Records*, vol. IV., pp. 665, 667.

VII

The Lancaster Treaty

VIRGINIA TREATS WITH THE INDIANS—VIRGINIA ALSO DENIES LAND CLAIMS BUT OFFERS PRESENTS—THE IROQUOIS ESTABLISH THEIR CLAIM TO WESTERN VIRGINIA—THE CAUSE OF THE INDIAN COMPLAINT AGAINST VIRGINIA—VIRGINIA ATTEMPTS TO TEACH THE INDIANS HISTORY—THE IROQUOIS REPLY—THE IROQUOIS' OPINION OF THE CATAWBA INDIANS—THE INDIANS WANT TO SEE THE PROMISED PRESENTS—TWO VIEWS OF THE DEED—PENNSYLVANIA THE MEDIATOR—THE JUNIATA SQUATTERS—THE MURDER OF JOHN ARMSTRONG—PENNSYLVANIA MAKES A PRESENT TO THE INDIANS—FRENCH *VERSUS* ENGLISH DRINKING GLASSES—IMPORTANCE OF THE TREATY—WEISER'S SUGGESTION—MARYLAND HESITATES——WEISER DISTRUSTED—LANCASTER IN 1744—THE ARRIVAL OF THE INDIANS—THEY PITCH THEIR CAMP—THE INDIANS' PUBLIC WELCOME—AN INDIAN DANCE—INDIAN BEHAVIOR—MARYLAND'S ATTITUDE AT THE OPENING OF THE TREATY—MARYLAND DENIES THE INDIAN LAND CLAIM—THE IROQUOIS REPLY—THE INDIANS' VERSION OF THE DONGAN DEED—MARYLAND'S REPLY—MARYLAND GIVES THE INDIANS A PRESENT—PUBLIC OPPOSITION TO A SECRET TREATY—BANQUET GIVEN TO THE INDIANS IN THE COURT HOUSE—THE INDIANS CHRISTEN THE GOVERNOR OF MARYLAND—SIGNING THE DEED—SHIKELLAMY REFUSES TO SIGN—THE INDIAN DEED TO MARYLAND—THE DEED FINALLY SIGNED.

THE different colonies anticipated the approaching treaty at Lancaster with no small degree of anxiety. A French war was expected at any time. Unless the Six Nations and their allies were held in the colonial interest, it was conceded by all that the French would secure their friendship. Then the entire frontier of Virginia, Maryland, Pennsylvania, and New York would be open to their marauding expeditions. The fear of such results naturally aided in bringing

Virginia and Maryland into a conciliatory attitude towards the Indians. Conrad Weiser was the leading spirit in securing this condition of affairs. The governor of Pennsylvania used Weiser to keep him informed of the actions of the Indians and asked him to write out his suggestions in full about the approaching treaty.

In acknowledging Weiser's letter, the governor's secretary said: "I handed your communication to the governor, who is very well pleased with every part of it, and most where you say that Maryland may treat first before the Virginia people arrive, but there the governor has ordered me to tell you that they will not consent to treat separately, but both at the same time, and of this, you may certainly depend, and accordingly arrange with the Indians."

Governor Thomas experienced many difficulties in working out Conrad Weiser's plans. The Maryland government had been bitterly divided upon the subject since 1742 when the governor recommended this subject to the Maryland Assembly. The Legislature concurred, but a dispute at once arose about the method of appointing commissioners to the treaty. The Assembly insisted upon the right to appoint half of the commissioners and to draw up their instructions. Governor Bladen looked upon this as a usurpation of his powers and declined to confirm their proceedings. The House would not yield, and negotiations were suspended. The governor finally appointed the commissioners on his own account.

Before this dispute was settled at Annapolis, the Virginia commissioners arrived and were informed by the Maryland delegates that Conrad Weiser was a suspicious character and not to be trusted. The Maryland distrust of Weiser was so great that it caused the Virginia commissioners to write home for new instructions relative to an interpreter. In this letter, dated at Annapolis, May 20, 1744, they say that the Maryland commissioners "have great suspicion of Mr. Weiser, and we believe that they will not solely rely upon him; we submit it to your Honor whether it will not be proper for us to have your command to have another if we find it necessary, this we think we are not at liberty to do by our instructions, which are positive as to Weiser; but if your Honor thinks proper to write us by the Post to Philadelphia, a liberty to take another, we shall either do it or not as we see occasion."

Before the Virginia delegation left Annapolis for Philadelphia, Weiser's letter to the Maryland commissioners containing his plans was received. In reporting this letter to Governor Gooch, the Virginia commissioners say, "Before we left Annapolis, there was an express from Conrad Weiser, with an artful letter relating to the Indian affairs, which they say is Logan, tho' Weiser signs it; a good deal of expense is proposed in favor of the Indians, and they are persuaded that there will arise some difficulty, by our having no other interpreter but Weiser."[1]

In this letter to Maryland, Conrad Weiser insisted that much more could be accomplished in this treaty if the governor himself would come to Lancaster instead of sending commissioners and that the Indians, on such occasions, would only talk with the governor. After a long wrangle, Maryland sent commissioners. When the Virginia delegation reached Philadelphia and came under the influence of Governor Thomas, we hear nothing more derogatory to Conrad Weiser. Indeed, the subtle influence of the Indian diplomat appears in the letters of these commissioners to Virginia.

The little town of Lancaster was sixteen years old at the time of the treaty. Only a few brick and stone buildings overlooked the home-like cluster of wooden houses. The treaty was held in the Court House, a two-story brick building erected in 1739. There were two courtrooms, one on the first floor capable of holding eight hundred persons. The one upstairs was supplied with a huge fireplace. To this room, the February session of court was accustomed to adjourn.

With their numerous followers, the commissioners and the governor of Pennsylvania had been assembled in Lancaster several days before the Indians arrived. On Friday, June 22, while the commissioners were all dining together in the Court House, the long-expected delegation of Indians appeared. The procession headed by Canassatego numbered two hundred and fifty-two. A number of the women and children were mounted on horseback. A great crowd of people followed them. When they came in front of the Court House, their leaders saluted the commissioners with a song which was an invitation to the white people to renew all former treaties and to make good the one now proposed.

Conrad Weiser conducted this motley procession of sachems, chiefs, warriors, squaws, and Indian children to some vacant lots on the outskirts of the town. Here the authorities had placed some poles and boards to assist the Indians in building their wigwams, which were largely constructed from the boughs of the trees in the adjacent woods. It was said of these Indians that they would not permit themselves to be entertained in houses made by white men. On these lots, their cabins were placed according to their rank, the Onondagas being first.

When the commissioners and the curious people in Lancaster came out to view the Indian camp, Conrad Weiser requested them not to talk much

---

1. See Journal of William Black, Secretary of the Virginia Commissioners, in *Pennsylvania Magazine of History and Biography*, vol. I., pp. 129, 238.

about the Indians nor to laugh at their dress or behavior since many of them understood English and might take offense at such remarks, which would make it more difficult to conduct the treaty.

That afternoon the commissioners assembled in the Court House to welcome the Indians. After shaking hands with all, Governor Thomas seated himself in the center on the judges' bench. The Virginia commissioners, Col. Thomas Lee and Col. William Beverely, took position on the right. The Maryland commissioners, Hon. Edmund Jennings and Hon. Philip Thomas, were on the left. Around the large half-oval table, which stood down and in front of the judges' bench sat the secretaries, William Peters, of Pennsylvania, in the center, William Black, of Virginia, on the right, and Witham Marshe, of Maryland, on the left. According to their rank, the Indians also took a position on the ascending steps that flanked the judges' bench. The body of the house was filled with attendants of the treaty and spectators.

After a hearty speech of welcome by Governor Thomas, interpreted by Conrad Weiser, "a good quantity of punch, wine, and pipes were given to the sachems, and the governor and all the commissioners drank to them, whom they pledged. When they had smoked some small time, and each drank a glass or two of wine and punch, they retired to their cabins,"[2] where they had been bidden to rest a few days before commencing the business of the treaty.

The following day the Indians all remained in their wigwams while the commissioners, with Governor Thomas and Conrad Weiser, went to visit the Seventh Day Baptists at Ephrata, their Sabbath day. That evening Witham Marshe and James Logan went to the Indian camp to witness one of their dances, which Marshe describes in the following manner:

> Thirty or forty of the younger men formed themselves into a ring, a fire being lighted (notwithstanding the excessive heat) and burning clear in the midst of them. Near this sat three elderly Indians who beat a drum to the time of the others dancing, when the dancers hopped round the ring after a frantic fashion, not unlike the priests of Bacchus in old times, and repeated sundry times, these sounds: 'Yo-hoh! Bugh!' Soon after this, the major part of the dancers (or rather hoppers) set up a horrid shriek or halloo! They continued dancing and hopping after this manner for several hours and rested very seldom. Once, while I stood with them, they did seat themselves; immediately thereupon, the three old men began to sing an

2. *Marshe's Journal*, p. 14.

Indian song, the tune of which was not disagreeable to the white bystanders. Upon this, the young warriors renewed their terrible shriek and halloo, and formed themselves into a ring environing the three old ones, and danced as before . . .

These young men are surprisingly agile, strong, and straight-limbed. They shoot both with the gun and bow and arrow most dexterously. They likewise throw their tomahawk (a little hatchet) with great certainty and at an indifferent large object for twenty or thirty yards distance. This weapon they use against their enemies when they have spent their powder and ball, and destroy many of them with it. The chiefs who were deputed to treat with the English by their different nations were very sober men, which is rare for an Indian to be so if he can get liquor. They behaved very well during our stay with them, and sundry times refused drinking in a moderate way. Whenever they renew old treaties of friendship or make any bargains about lands they sell to the English, they take great care to abstain from intoxicating drink for fear of being overreached, but when they have finished this business, then some of them will drink without measure.[3]

The Maryland commissioners had no intention of recognizing any Indian claims to land within the borders of their province. Their position was based upon the following facts: (1) In 1652, Maryland bought from the Minquas or Susquehanna Indians all their claims on both sides of the Chesapeake Bay up to the mouth of the Susquehanna River. (2) In 1663, eight hundred Seneca and Cayuga Indians from the Five Nation Confederacy were defeated by the Minqua Indians aided by the Marylanders. The Iroquois never relinquished this war until a famine had so reduced the Minquas that in 1675 when the Marylanders had withdrawn their alliance, the Minquas were completely subdued by the Five Nations, who now claimed a right to the Susquehanna lands to the head of the Chesapeake Bay. From these facts, Maryland claimed that the Iroquois right was merely from conquest, and this was surrendered when Governor Dongan of New York obtained his deed from the Six Nations for their land on the Susquehanna River because (1) Penn had bought that deed in 1696; (2) the Conestoga Indians had confirmed it in 1699; (3) the Conestoga Indians (the remnant of the ancient Minquas) were put on a reservation In Pennsylvania in 1718, and when they for a second time confirmed Dongan's deed it was done in

---

3. *Marshe's Journal*, pp. 14, 15.

the presence of the Onondaga deputies; (4) Pennsylvania had purchased these conquest lands from the Iroquois in 1736, as far north and west as the Blue Mountains. Therefore, the Six Nations had no land claims within the borders of Maryland.

When the Maryland commissioners came before the Indians at Lancaster, they said that when they were first notified of this demand in 1737, they felt that, upon second thought, the Indians would withdraw it since there could be no possible reason for such a claim.

Speaking directly to the Indians, they said: "It was very inconsiderately said by you that you would do yourselves justice by going to take payment yourselves; such an attempt would have entirely dissolved the chain of friendship subsisting not only between us but perhaps the other English and you. We assure you our people, who are numerous, courageous, and have arms ready in their hands, will not suffer themselves to be hurt in their lives and estates."[4]

The Indians were then told that the old and wise people of Maryland had reflected upon these rash threats of the Iroquois deputies and concluded to hold a treaty whereby they could learn by what right the Six Nations claimed this land. "We are desirous of brightening the chain of friendship, and for this purpose, we have brought a quantity of goods with us. We are not satisfied with the justice of your claim for land, but we have brought the goods along to show our brotherly kindness and affection for the Red Man."

The next day Canassatego arose to reply to the Maryland commissioners. This remarkable Iroquois orator "was a tall well-made man." He "had a very full chest and brawny limbs. He had a manly countenance mixed with a good-natured smile. He was about sixty years of age, very active, strong, and had a surprising liveliness in his speech." . . .[5] Canassatego referred in very complimentary language to the selection of Lancaster as a place of meeting and the generous reception which had been tendered them.

Then turning to the Maryland commissioners, he said:

> You tell us that when about seven years ago you heard by our brother Onas of our claim to some lands in your province, you took no notice of it, believing, as you say, that when we should come to reconsider that matter, we should find that we had no right to make any complaint of the governor of Maryland and would withdraw our demand. And when about two years ago we mentioned it again to

---

4. *Penna. Colonial Records*, vol. IV., p. 703.
5. From *Marshe's Journal*, p. 12.

our brother Onas, you say we did it in such terms as looked like a design to terrify you; and you tell us further that we must be beside ourselves in using such rash expressions as to tell you we know how to do ourselves justice if you should still refuse. It is true we did say so, but without any ill design, for we must inform you" that when we first asked brother Onas to intercede for us, we desired him to also write to "the Great King beyond the seas, who would own us for his children as well as you, to compel you to do us justice. And two years ago, when we found that you paid no regard to our just demands, nor that brother Onas had conveyed our complaint to the Great King over the seas, we were resolved to use such expressions as would make the greatest impressions on your minds, and we find that it had its effect, for you tell us that your wise men held a council together and agreed to invite us, and to inquire of our right to any of your lands; and if it should be found that we had a right we were to have a compensation for them; . . . this shows that your wise men understood our expressions in their true sense. We had no designs to terrify you but to put you to doing us the justice you had so long delayed. . . . We are well pleased to hear that you are provided with goods and do assure of our willingness to treat with you for these unpurchased lands. . . . You tell us that you have been in possession of this land "above one hundred years, but what is one hundred years in comparison to the length of time since our claim began—since we came out of this ground? For we must tell you that long before one hundred years, our ancestors came out of this very ground, and their children have remained here ever since. You came out of the ground in a country that lies beyond the seas, there, you may have a just claim, but here you must allow us to be your elder brethren and the lands long before you knew anything of them. We were so well pleased with the Dutch when they came here over one hundred years ago "that we tied their ship to the bushes on the shore and afterward liking them still better the longer they stayed with us and thinking the bushes too slender, we removed the rope and tied it to the trees, and as the trees were liable to be blown down by high winds, or to decay of themselves, we, from the affection we bore them, again removed the rope, and tied it to a strong big rock (here Conrad Weiser said that they meant the Oneida country), and not content with this, for its further security we removed the rope to the

Big Mountain (Onondaga country), and there we tied it very fast and rolled wampum about it. After this, when the English came and became one people with us as the Dutch were, they (the English) found that the rope which tied the ship to the great mountain was only fastened with wampum, which was liable to break and rot and to perish in a course of years, he, therefore, told us that he would give us a silver chain which would be much stronger and last forever.

We have been good friends ever since, yet we are sensible that with all the advantages of the white man's guns and knives and hatchets, we are each year growing poorer, deer are growing scarcer. We are losing much since the white man came among us, and particularly from that pen and ink work going on at the table (pointing to the secretaries), and we will give you an instance of this.

Our brother Onas, a great while ago, came to Albany to buy the Susquehanna lands of us, but our brother, the governor of New York, who, as we suppose, had not a good understanding with our brother Onas, advised us not to sell him any lands, for he would make an ill use of it, and pretending to be our good friend he advised us, in order to prevent Onas or any other person from imposing upon us, and that we might always have our land when we should want it, to put it into his hands, and told us he would keep it for our use, and never open his hands, but keep them close shut, and not part with any of it but at our request. Accordingly, we trusted him, and put our lands into his hands and charged him to keep it safe for our use; but sometime after, he went away to England and carried our land with him, and there sold it to our brother Onas for a large sum of money; and when at the instance of our brother Onas we were minded to sell him some lands, he told us that we had sold the Susquehanna lands already to the governor of New York and that he had bought them from him in England, tho' when he came to understand how the governor of New York had deceived us, he very generously paid us for our lands over again. . . . We have had" the Maryland deeds "interpreted for us, and we acknowledge them to be good and valid, and that the Conestoga or Susquehanna Indians had a right to sell those lands unto you, for they were then theirs, but since that time we have conquered them, and their country now belongs to us, and the lands we demand satisfaction for are no part of the land comprised in those deeds—they are the Cohongorontas (Potomac) lands.

These we are sure you have not possessed one hundred years, no nor above ten years.

The Maryland commissioners replied as follows:

We have considered what you said concerning your title to some lands now in our province and also of the place where they lie. Altho' we cannot admit your right, yet we are so resolved to live in brotherly love and affection with the Six Nations that upon giving us a release in writing for all your claim to any lands in Maryland, we shall make you a compensation to the value of three hundred pounds currency.

A parcel of goods with the prices attached were spread out upon the table in the Court House for the part payment of this three hundred pounds. After the Indians had examined these, they expressed dissatisfaction with the attached prices. Accordingly, a council was held, and Conrad Weiser was called to advise them. He sat down among them, and after some discussion, the Indians agreed to take the goods at the valuation of £220 15s. In addition, the Maryland commissioners presented the Indians with $100 in gold, which was received with the Red Man's shout of "Jo-hah." These Maryland presents were probably the result of Conrad Weiser's persistent influence, urging the necessity of the colonists' outdoing the French if they would hold the friendship of the Iroquois.

Early in these negotiations, Virginia and Maryland closed the Court House doors to all visitors from these two States. When this was enforced, it produced great indignation among many. No measures were taken to exclude Pennsylvania visitors until the Maryland deed was ready for the Indians' signatures, then out of fear of undue influence on the part of those present from Pennsylvania, who were supposed to be in the interests of the proprietors, a strictly secret session was held. In this meeting, which is not referred to in the treaty proceedings, the Indians refused to sign the release. Considerable delay was occasioned until Conrad Weiser explained the demands of the Maryland commissioners "in so clear a manner that there came such an amicable determination as proved agreeable to each party."[6] The "amicable determination" spoken of by Marshe was the verbal promise of the Indians to sign the deed when it was engrossed.

To celebrate what seemed to the commissioners as a diplomatic victory, it was decided to give the Indians a great dinner. The tables were spread in the Court House. Twenty-four chiefs of the Six Nations were invited, together with

---

6. *Marshe's Journal*, p. 19.

a large number of the citizens of Lancaster. Five tables were covered with a great variety of palatable dishes. The Indians were seated at two separate tables, with Canassatego at the head of one, the other Indians taking place according to rank. The three secretaries, assisted by Thomas Cookson, prothonotary of Lancaster County, William Logan, and Col. Rigbie, carved the meat and served the Indians. Conrad Weiser stood between the governor's table and the Indians, informing them when the governor drank to their health and giving general directions to the order of the ceremonies. The Indians were served in addition to the meats, with cider and wine mixed. The sachems "seemed prodigiously pleased with their feast, for they fed lustily, drank heartily, and were very greasy before they finished their dinner, for, bye the bye, they make no use of forks."[7]

The Indians were now feeling in a jovial state of mind, and they seized upon this opportunity to perform the ceremony of giving to the governor of Maryland an Indian name. Since Penn's days, they had called the governor of Pennsylvania brother Onas, Virginia's governor, was known among them as Assaraquoa, but Maryland had no name by which it was known. Accordingly, after much demonstration and speech-making, the commissioner of Maryland representing the governor, the absent official, was christened by the Indians "Tocary-ho-gon," meaning excellent position between Assaraquoa and Onas. Conrad Weiser was the interpreter for these ceremonies, which ended with all drinking bumpers of wine to the King's health.

Governor Thomas and the commissioners said Marshe, "indeed, all the persons present, except the Indians, gave several huzzas, after the English manner, on drinking the King's health, which a good deal surprised them, they having never before heard the like noise."

At the close of these ceremonies, the governor and commissioners retired for about an hour when Mr. Marshe produced an engrossed copy of the land deed from the Indians. Some difficulty had been anticipated in getting the Indians to sign it.

"Here, by the order of our commissioners," said Marshe, "I produced the engrossed release for the lands with the seals fixed. We were obliged to put about the glasses pretty briskly, and then Mr. Weiser interpreted the contents of it to the sachems, who conferring among themselves about the execution of it, the major part of them seemed very inclinable to sign and deliver it.

"But upon Shikellamy, an Oneida chief's remonstrance, some of the others, with himself, refused for that day executing it, which refusal of Shikellamy's, we imputed, and not without reason, to some sinister and underhanded means

---

7. *Marshe's Journal*, p. 20.

SHIKELLAMY, THE ONEIDA CHIEF

made use of by Pennsylvania to induce the sachems not to give up their right to the lands by deed, without having a larger consideration given them by the province of Maryland than what was specified in the release. Shikellamy, who, before we had esteemed one of our fastest friends, put us under a deep surprise and confusion by his unfair behavior; yet we in some measure extricated ourselves out of them by the honest Canassatego's and the other sachems to the number of sixteen, delivering the deed, after the forms customary to the English, to which there were a great many gentlemen signed their names as witnesses. Mr. Weiser assured the commissioners that he, with Canassatego and some other chiefs, would so effectually represent the unfair dealings of Shikellamy and his partisans in Council that he did not doubt to induce him and them totally to finish this business on Monday next, manage all the insinuations and misrepresentations agitated by the enemies of Maryland, and, indeed, Mr. Interpreter proved successful, as is evident in the transactions of Monday, and may be seen in the printed treaty."[8]

Weiser's diplomatic skill is well illustrated in this affair. The Maryland commissioners, who were loud in expressions of Weiser's duplicity and treachery before the treaty, were now his warm friends. Shikellamy, intimate with Weiser for many years, finds his confidence not shaken.

To what extent the Maryland commissioners were aware that Weiser secured such changes in the deed to satisfy Penn's heirs and Shikellamy is unknown. Marshe himself seems to be entirely oblivious to such a change.[9] The celebrated boundary dispute between Maryland and Pennsylvania was then pending, and the deed Shikellamy refused to sign would have given Maryland an Indian title to a large portion of land claimed by Pennsylvania. Marshe reflects this idea, which was the opinion of the Maryland commissioners when he said, we "thereby gained not only some hundred thousand acres of land for Lord Baltimore, who had no good right to them before this release but an indisputable and quiet enjoyment of them to the several possessors, who in fact had bought of that Lord's agents."[10]

The release, which the Six Nations did eventually sign for Maryland, recognized an undetermined boundary line between Pennsylvania and Maryland and in no way tried to fix that boundary as Marshe and the commissioners from Maryland supposed. The release reads for all "lands lying two miles above the uppermost forks of Patowmack or Cohongoruton River, near which Thomas

---

8. *Marshe's Journal*, pp. 19, 20.
9. See note by Dr. Egle, in *Marshe's Journal*, p. 21.
10. *Marshe's Journal*, p. 21.

Cresap has a hunting or trading cabin, by a north line to the bounds of Pennsylvania. But in case such limits shall not include every settlement or inhabitant of Maryland, then such other lines and courses from the said two miles above the forks to the outermost inhabitants or settlements, as shall include every settlement and inhabitant in Maryland, and from thence by a north line to the bounds of Pennsylvania, shall be the limits. And further, if any people already have or shall settle beyond the lands now described and bounded, they shall enjoy the same free from any disturbance of us in any manner whatsoever, and we do and shall accept those people for our Brethren, and as such shall always treat them. We earnestly desire to live with you as Brethren and hope you will show us all brotherly kindness; in token thereof, we present you with this belt of wampum."[11]

Shikellamy never signed this deed. Since Canassatego was a superior sachem, we have no record of Shikellamy's views. We only know that the old man was always opposed to the immoderate use of strong liquor and stood aloof from men under its effects.

Marshe gives us the following interesting account of how the release was finally secured on the following Monday when the commissioners and the Indians met at George Sanderson's Inn instead of the Court House. "When the several chiefs who had not signed the deed of release and renunciation of their claim in lands in Maryland did now cheerfully and without any hesitation execute the same, in the presence of the commissioners and Mr. Weiser; which latter they caused to sign and deliver in behalf of a nation (Mohawk) not present, both with his Indian name of Tarach-a-wa-gon and that of Weiser. Thus we happily effected the purchase of the lands in Maryland by the dexterous management of the interpreter."[12]

The Indians seemed perfectly satisfied with what they had received for their Maryland claims. Shikellamy's opposition was based on a determination not to recognize that Maryland had any land claims north of the disputed boundary line. We have no record of Shikellamy's views; he probably had his own reflections when he witnessed the bestowing of a broad gold-laced hat upon an Iroquois chief who was actively securing the signatures to the deed.

During the same days that these Maryland negotiations were pending, the Virginia commissioners also had their affairs in progress. The previous difficulties between the Iroquois and Virginia, which Conrad Weiser so fortunately settled, put the commissioners into a genial frame of mind. They met the Indians

---

11. *Penna. Colonial Records*, vol. IV., pp. 719, 720.
12. *Marshe's Journal*, p. 22.

on the following grounds. "You wrote us in 1736, through the governor of Pennsylvania, that you expected some consideration for your lands in Virginia. When we received this letter, we examined all our old treaties and found that the Five Nations had given up all their land claims to the King of England, who had possession here over one hundred years ago; therefore, we hold our title under the Great King.

"Fearing that there might be some mistake about your claim, we asked the governor of New York to look into it. He sent his interpreter to you in 1743, who laid this before you at a council held at Onondaga. You replied that if you had any demand or pretension on the governor of Virginia in any way, you would have made it known to the governor of New York. Now, this corresponds to what you said to the governor of Pennsylvania in 1742 because then you only laid claim to land in Maryland. We are pleased with your good faith and disposition towards friendship. We have with us a chest full of new goods. The key is in our pockets. You are our brethren, the Great King is our common father, and we will live with you as Christians ought to do in peace and love. Therefore, we beg you to tell us upon what foundation you claim land in Virginia, when and what Indians did you ever conquer in Virginia? If it appears that you have any right to these lands, we will make you satisfaction."

The Iroquois made the following reply:

> We own the land. We claim it by right of conquest—a right too dearly purchased and which cost us too much blood to give up 'without any reason at all,' as you say we have done at Albany; but we should be obliged to you if you would let us see that letter, and inform us who was the interpreter, and whose names are put to the letter; for as the whole transaction can't be above a year's standing, it must be fresh in everybody's memory, and some of our council would easily remember it; but we assure you, and we are well able to prove, that neither we, nor any part of us, have ever relinquished our rights, or gave such an answer as you say is mentioned in your letter. Could we, so few years ago, make a formal demand by James Logan and not be sensible of our right? And hath anything happened since that time to make us less sensible? No. . . . All the world knows we conquered the several nations living on the Susquehanna, Potomac, and on the back of the great mountain (Blue Mountains), in Virginia. . . . We know very well that it has often been said by the Virginian that the Great King of England and the people of that colony conquered the

Indians that lived there, but it is not true. We will allow that they have conquered the Sachdagughroonans and drove back the Tuscaroras and that they have on that a right to some part of Virginia, but as to what lies beyond the mountains, we conquered the nations residing there, and that land, if ever the Virginians get a right to it, it must be by us . . .

We are glad to hear that you have brought a big chest of 'new goods' and that you have the key in your pockets; we will open all our hearts to you that you may know everything in them. . . . You may remember that about twenty years ago you had a treaty with us at Albany, you took a belt of wampum and made a fence with it on the top of a mountain. You said that we were to stay west of that fence, and you would remain east of it. That is the mountain we mean, and we desire that treaty may be confirmed. After we left Albany, we brought our road a great deal more to the west that we might comply with your proposal, but though it was of your own making, your people never observed it but came and lived on our side of the hill, which we don't blame you for, as you live at a great distance near the seas, and can't be thought to know what your people do in the back parts, and on their settling contrary to your proposals on our new road, it fell out that our warriors did some hurt to your people's cattle of which a complaint was made and transmitted to us by our brother Onas. And we, at his request, altered the road again and brought it to the foot of the great mountain where it now is, and the nature of the country makes it impossible for us to move it any further west . . .

We had not been long in the use of this new road before your people came like flocks of birds and sat down on both sides of it, and yet we never made a complaint to you, though you must have been sensible those things must have been done by your people in manifest breach of your own proposals made at Albany; and therefore as we are now opening our hearts to you, we cannot help complaining. . . . The affair of the road must be looked upon as a preliminary to be settled before the grant of lands, and that either the Virginia people must be obliged to remove more easterly, or if they are permitted (to remain in Shenandoah Valley), to say that our warriors marching that way to the southward shall go shares with them in what they plant.[13]

---

13. *Penna. Colonial Records*, vol. IV., pp. 709, 713.

THE LANCASTER TREATY

A few days later, the Virginia commissioners endeavored to set the Indians right upon the history of their past treaties.

> If the Six Nations have made any conquests over Indians that may at any time have lived on the west side of the great mountains of Virginia, yet they never possessed any lands there that we ever heard. That part was altogether deserted and free for any people to enter upon, as the people of Virginia have done by order of the Great King, very justly as well as by an ancient right as by its being freed from the possession of any other, and from any claim even of you the Six Nations, our brethren, until within these eight years. Our first treaty was one of friendship made at Albany in 1674. The next one was made at the same place in 1686, when you declared the Five Nations to be subjects of the Great King, our father, and gave up to him all your lands for his protection. You acknowledged this in a treaty with the governor of New York the following year. These are the very words that you used on that occasion; have you forgotten them? 'O brethren, you tell us the King of England is a very great King, and why should you not join with us in a very just cause when the French joins with our enemies in an unjust cause? O brethren, we see the reason for this, for the French would fain kill us all, and when that is done, they would carry all the beaver trade to Canada, and the great King of England would lose the lands likewise; and, therefore, O great Sachem beyond the great lakes, awake, and suffer not those poor Indians that have given themselves and their lands under your protection to be destroyed by the French without a cause.'[14]

This plea on the part of the Iroquois in 1687 was occasioned by the threats of the war of the Palatinate (1689–1697).

> The last treaty you made with us you have not reported correctly. "Your brethren, the white people in Virginia, are in no article of that treaty prohibited to pass and settle to the westward of the great mountains," but the Indians tributary to you are by that treaty forbidden from passing to the eastward of those mountains, or to the southward of the Potomac River. It was further agreed in that treaty that no Indians should pass through the forbidden territory without

---

14. *Penna. Colonial Records*, vol. IV., p. 717.

passes. Therefore, "what right can you have to lands that you have no right to walk upon but upon certain conditions? . . . You have not observed this part of your treaty, and because we have not strictly enforced it, some trouble has arisen. We can show you this treaty and the names of the Indians who signed it. Brethren, this dispute is not between you and Virginia; you are setting up your right against the Great King, who is our common father and means to do justice to all his children. Brethren, there would have been no trouble about the road you speak of if you had taken our advice and made peace with the Catawba Indians. Then you could have stayed out of Virginia, and there would have been no dispute between us."

Then the Virginia commissioners once more expressed their goodwill toward the Iroquois and told them their willingness to settle for those disputed lands.

From this point in the proceedings, the Indians showed no disposition to argue the land question with the Virginia commissioners based on old treaties. They knew their power. They knew that the war between France and England had commenced. They knew that the French were bidding high for the Iroquois alliance. For these reasons, they were probably determined to force recognition of their land claims and give the English, in individual colonies, an opportunity in the aggregate to outbid the French. Therefore, the Iroquois took another tack. They said:

The world was at first made on the other side of the great water different from what it is on this side, as may be known from the different color of our skin and our flesh, and that which you call justice may not be so amongst us. You have your laws and customs, so have we. The Great King might send you over to conquer the Indians, but it looks to us that God did not approve of it; if He had, He would not have placed the sea where it is as the limits between us and you.

Brother Assaraquoa, though great things are well remembered among us, yet we don't remember that we were ever conquered by the Great King or that we have been employed by that Great King to conquer others; if it was so, it was beyond our memory. You tell us we have not kept our peace with the Catawbas; we tell you that the Catawbas have broken faith with us. They have called us women. The war must continue between them and us until one or the other of us is destroyed. For this reason, the road must be kept open between us and the Catawba country. You have some very ill-natured people living along this road; we desire that you who are in power may know who they are and arrange that our warriors may have a reasonable amount of victuals when they are in want. You know very well when the white people came first here, they were very poor; but now they have got our lands and are by them become rich, and we are now poor. What little we had for the land goes soon away, but the land lasts forever.

You told us you had brought with you a chest of goods and that you have the key in your pockets, but we have never seen the chest nor the goods that are said to be in it. It may be small and the goods few. We want to see them and are desirous to come to some conclusion. We have been sleeping here these ten days past and have not done anything to the purpose.[15]

This brought the Virginia commissioners to the point, and the Indians were promised that the goods should be seen on Monday. The Indians were told that enough had been said about the titles to the land. The chests were opened, and the goods were spread before them. "They cost," said the commissioners, "two hundred pounds, Pennsylvania money, and were bought by a person[16] recommended to us by the governor of Pennsylvania, with ready cash. We ordered them to be good in their kinds, and we believe they are so. These goods and two hundred pounds in gold which now lie on the table, we will give you, our brethren of the Six Nations, upon conditions that you immediately make a deed, recognizing the King's right to all the lands that are or shall be by his Majesty's appointment in the colony of Virginia."

The commissioners also guaranteed the Indians an open road to the Catawba country, promising that the people of Virginia should perform their part if the Indians performed theirs. The Iroquois understood this to mean that their war parties should be fed while passing through Virginia and that their warriors should abstain from shooting the farmers' hogs, cattle, or chickens.

The following day the Virginia commissioners gave the Indians one of the promised hundred pounds in gold in order, they said, to make the "chain of union and friendship as bright as the sun, that it may not contract any more rust forever." Another day was consumed in presenting the other one hundred

---

15. *Penna. Colonial Records*, vol. IV., 720, 721.
16. Probably Conrad Weiser.

pounds in gold and promising to recommend the Iroquois to the favor of the King of England. Canassatego was given a camblet coat, and the chiefs were given passes for their warriors who intended to go through Virginia.

When the treaty was over, the Indians believed that they had established land claims in Virginia, that the open road was guaranteed, that their warriors were to be fed while passing through the State, and that they had sold land only to the headwaters of the streams feeding the Ohio River. The Virginians, on the other hand, believed that they had extinguished all Iroquois land claims forever within the charter limits of their State.

Pennsylvania, guided by Conrad Weiser, was the mediator and peacemaker in this treaty. Virginia and Maryland were compelled to make financial provisions for the Indians before coming to the treaty. They were induced to lay aside their opposition to Iroquois land claims and settle in such a manner as would secure the friendship of the Six Nations, thus thwarting the schemes of the French and protecting the frontiers of the English from the Carolinas to New England.

While Pennsylvania was thus leading the astonished Maryland and Virginia commissioners through the hidden paths of Indian diplomacy, she had troubles of her own in settling with those keen-witted natives. Since the purchase of 1736, traders and squatters had been greatly attracted by the lands in Juniata Valley. This region lay beyond the limits of the previous purchases, and whenever settlers took possession of unpurchased land, Indian outrages were sure to occur.

Sometime before this treaty, John Armstrong, a trader, with two of his men, and their horses loaded with merchandise, were following the Allegheny path towards the Ohio for trade. An Indian who claimed to have been wronged by "Jack" Armstrong in a bargain followed the trader until he was about to cross the Juniata at the Narrows when they murdered Armstrong and his men and plundered their goods. This matter was placed in the hands of Shikellamy at Shamokin, who caused the murderers to be apprehended, and after giving them a hearing, ordered two of them to be sent to jail at Lancaster to await trial at the hands of the white man.

While Shikellamy's sons were conveying the prisoners to Lancaster, the friends of John Mussemeelin, one of the prisoners related to some important Delaware sachems, induced Shikellamy's sons to allow Mussemeelin to escape. The other Indian was locked safely in prison. At the Lancaster Treaty, the governor of Pennsylvania demanded of the Iroquois that they command their subjects, the Delawares, to surrender Mussemeelin to the province's authorities. The governor invited the Indians to Lancaster to witness the trial. The Iroquois were also given to understand that they must cause a search to be made for the stolen goods and have them or their value restored to the heirs of Jack Armstrong. Before they replied to this demand, the Six Nations knew that a present was awaiting them from Pennsylvania, equal to, if not greater, than those given by Virginia or Maryland.

The Iroquois' reply is characteristic of the Indians' idea of justice.

> We join with you in your concern for such a vile proceeding, and to testify that we have the same inclinations with you to keep the road clear, free, and open, we give you this string of wampum. Brother Onas, these things happen frequently, and we desire that you will consider them well and not be too much concerned. Three Indians have been killed at different times at Ohio, and we never mentioned anything of them to you, imagining it might have been occasioned by some unfortunate quarrels. . . . We desire you to consider these things well and to take the grief from your hearts we give you this string of wampum.
>
> We have reproved the Delawares severely for their conduct and will see that the stolen goods are restored. On our return home, we will order the Delawares to send Mussemeelin to you for trial, but not as a prisoner. You have the guilty Indian now in jail. We will expect you to do Mussemeelin justice and return him to his people in safety.

After mutual congratulations between Pennsylvania and the Six Nations, a present of goods to the value of three hundred pounds was given them on condition that they stand aloof from the French and keep Pennsylvania thoroughly informed of all the movements of the enemy and also of the secret designs of the French allies. The Indians were then told of the war's progress and the glorious victories of the English over the French.

When the Indians replied to this little expression of loyal pride in the prowess of English arms, they said, "You tell us you beat the French; if so, you must have taken a great deal of rum from them, and can the better spare us some of that liquor to make us rejoice with you in the victory. The governor and commissioners ordered a dram of rum to be given to each in a small glass, calling it a 'French glass.'"

The next day Canassatego, turning to the governor of Pennsylvania, said: "We mentioned to you yesterday the booty you had taken from the French and asked you for some of the rum which we supposed to be part of it, and you gave us some, but it turned out unfortunately that you gave us it in French glasses, we desire now you will give us some in English glasses."

The governor replied, "We are glad to hear that you have such a dislike for what is French. They cheat you in your glasses as well as in everything else. You must consider that we are at a distance from Williamsburg, Annapolis, and Philadelphia, where our rum stores are, and that although we brought up a good quantity with us, you have almost drank it out; but notwithstanding this, we have enough left to fill our English glasses, and will show you the difference between the narrowness of the French and the generosity of the English towards you."

To this, the Indians gave five "Yo-hahs." The governor and commissioners called for some rum and some middle-sized wine glasses. They all drank to the health of the King of England and the Six Nations and so ended the treaty "by three loud huzza's in which all the company joined."

VIII

The Iroquois Struggle for Neutrality

CAUSES FOR SIX NATIONS' NEUTRALITY—ATTITUDE OF COL. JOHNSON AND CONRAD WEISER—FRENCH OVERTURES—POSITION OF SIX NATIONS—DIFFICULTIES BESETTING NEUTRALITY—PETER CHARTIERS DIVIDES THE SHAWANESE—THE SHAWANESE APOLOGIZE—THE SHAWANESE REPRIMANDED BY PENNSYLVANIA—RENEWED EFFORTS TOWARD A CATAWBA PEACE—WEISER AGAIN ATTEMPTS TO MAKE PEACE BETWEEN THE NORTHERN AND SOUTHERN INDIANS—WEISER'S LETTER—WEISER BEFRIENDS SHIKELLAMY—WEISER GOES TO ONANDAGO—WEISER REPORTED HIS INTERVIEW WITH THE INDIANS—INSTRUCTIONS FOR THE ALBANY CONFERENCE, 1745—PENNSYLVANIA OBJECTS TO A UNION OF THE COLONIES—PENNSYLVANIA COMPELLED TO TREATS WITH THE INDIANS AFTER THE CONFERENCE ADJOURNS—THE INDIANS FOIL THE INSTRUCTIONS OF THE COMMISSIONERS—DIFFERENCES BETWEEN THE GOVERNOR AND THE ASSEMBLY—GOVERNOR THOMAS RESIGNS—THE MOHAWKS JOIN THE ENGLISH—THE FRIENDS OPPOSE THE USE OF INDIAN ALLIES IN WAR—WEISER BEGINS TO OPPOSE NEUTRALITY—WEISER CRITICISES THE WHITE MAN'S INDIAN POLICY—JOHN KINSEY AND THE PENNSYLVANIA ASSEMBLY CHAMPION IROQUOIS NEUTRALITY—REASONS GIVEN BY THE IROQUOIS AND THE FRIENDS FOR NEUTRALITY—NEUTRALITY INCREASES THE INDIAN TRADE IN PENNSYLVANIA.

AFTER the Lancaster treaty, the Iroquois journeyed leisurely home entertaining a very good opinion of themselves. They felt that their position, geographically, was one of good fortune. The English had paid well for their friendship; now, what would the French do? Father Onontio, the governor of Canada, had invited them to come and see him. They would go. French presents could be received as readily as those of the English. The Iroquois knew their strength. Had they not been courted by both nations? Let it continue. The

Indian had better rest securely in his neutrality and enjoy the bounty of two rival nations. Thus reasoned the wise men of the Six Nations, and such were the conclusions reached at the great "Council Fires" held for the Confederation at Onondaga.

At the same time, the subtle influence of the French was rapidly gaining headway among the Senecas. The persuasive Col. Johnson of New York was also steadily gaining the Mohawks for allies. Alone stood Conrad Weiser holding the Indian policy of Virginia and Pennsylvania in his hand and urging neutrality. For four years, this struggle went on, often threatening to split the ancient confederacy of the Six Nations into fragments.

At Lancaster, the Iroquois deputies had promised to inform the governor of Pennsylvania of the movements of the French. This they did faithfully. Scarcely two months after the treaty, word came through Shikellamy and Conrad Weiser that the governor of Canada had sent an embassy to the Onondagas to condole with them on the recent death of one of their chiefs. This embassy advised the Indians to remain neutral during the war, and the French would soon destroy the English. Onontio would see that the Indians had all the powder and lead they needed, and since the cowardly English traders at Oswego had run away, he would take the trading station at that place under his care and furnish the Indians with all the goods they needed at very low prices.

Shikellamy then informed Weiser that the Council of the Six Nations had decided to send word to the governor of Canada that the Iroquois did not approve of Onontio's "intention to take the House at Oswego to himself, which could not be done without bloodshed." They declared that the undertaking was fraught with danger and insinuated that the French were mean and cowardly to attack the English "in their backs." They advised, and the Indian councils loved to give advice, that Onontio act "more honorably as becometh a warrior and go around by sea and face the English." With much pertinence, the Indians asked why this war should be carried on across their territory. Why could not the French and English face each other across the water? Why should the Indians be asked to take sides? The Six Nations desired to remain neutral, and why could they not be allowed to do so? In this effort, the Indians were aided by Conrad Weiser and the province of Pennsylvania. New York and the New England colonists used every effort to induce the Iroquois to take up the hatchet against the French. Virginia and the South clamored for peace between the Catawbas and the* Six Nations. The French then exerted every possible influence to induce the Indians to turn against the English, and neutrality was urged wherever this was not popular among the Indians.

This struggle of the Iroquois for neutrality was beset with difficulties. Division was already shaking the Confederacy to its foundations. There was a strong French party predominating among the Senecas and western nations. There was also a strong English party predominating among the Mohawks and their eastern allies, who, under the influence of Col. Johnson and the New England agents, were anxious to fight the French. Then the great central nation, the Onondagas, flanked by the Cayu- gas and the Oneidas, listened to the voice of Conrad Weiser and tried to follow a neutral course. Their path was, however, beset with difficulties.

The neutral nations were held responsible for the acts of the allies of the entire Confederacy. Peter Chartiers, a half-breed and a trader among the Shawanese came under French influence. He persuaded his people to remove from the Allegheny River and come nearer to the French forts on the Mississippi. The Iroquois forbade this. As a result, Chartiers caused a division among the Shawanese, and a portion of them joined the French. Then rumors of Indian raids upon the frontiers of Pennsylvania, Maryland, and Virginia were in everybody's mouth. Governor Thomas directed Conrad Weiser "to employ some of the Delaware Indians at Shamokin as scouts to watch the enemies' motions, and to engage the whole body of Indians there, and to harass them in their march, in case they should attempt anything against us, and afterwards to join our remote inhabitants for their mutual defence."[1]

Beyond injuring a few traders, Chartiers did no mischief in Pennsylvania. Scaroyady, an Oneida chief, was put in control of the Shawanese affairs by the Onondaga Council. Before the war was over, Chartiers found his party uncomfortably in the minority. Under the subtle influence of Scaroyady, many of the disaffected Shawanese deserted Chartiers and came back under the Iroquois dominion.

In less than three years, they apologized to Pennsylvania for their actions, saying:

> We have been misled, and have carried on a private correspondence with the French without letting you or our brethren, the English, know of it. We traveled secretly through the bushes to Canada, and the French promised us great things, but we find ourselves deceived. We are sorry that we had anything to do with them. We now find that we could not see, altho' the sun did shine, we earnestly desire that you would intercede with our brethren, the English, for us, who

---

1. *Penna. Colonial Records*, vol. V., p. 6.

are left in Ohio, that we may be permitted to be restored to the chain of friendship and be looked upon as heretofore the same flesh with them.[2]

Conrad Weiser was consulted about the sincerity of the Shawanese and their statements. Weiser had always been outspoken in his contempt for these Indians. He had often asserted that they were renowned for their treachery. Governor Thomas, who reflected Weiser's opinions of the Shawanese, expressed himself in his message to the Assembly in no mild terms. Just what Weiser said on this occasion does not appear, but doubtless, his views shaped the policy of the commissioners at Lancaster (1748), who severely reprimanded the Shawanese for their conduct. Then Taming Buck, a Shawanese chief, in reply to the reprimand, said,

> we . . . are sensible of our ungrateful returns for the many favors we have been all along receiving from our brethren, the English. . . . We came along the road with our eyes looking down to the earth and have not taken them from thence until this morning when you were pleased to chastise us and then pardon us. We have been a foolish people and acted wrong, altho' the sun shone bright and showed us very clearly what was our duty. We are sorry for what we have done and promise better behavior in the future. We produce to you a certificate of the renewal of our friendship in the year 1739 by the Proprietor and Governor. Be pleased to sign it afresh that it may appear to the world we are now admitted into your friendship, and all former crimes are buried and entirely forgot.[3]

This request of the Shawanese was rejected. The commissioners refused to sign the certificate. The Shawanese were told that it was sufficient for them to know that they were forgiven on condition of future good behavior, and when that condition was performed, it would be time enough to sign treaties of friendship. Whether Conrad Weiser advised this course or not is uncertain. He could at least have prevented it, and induced Pennsylvania to make a valuable peace with the Shawanese, now when they were so humble. The French would have eagerly seized such an opportunity and made the most of it. With colonial short-sightedness, Pennsylvania considered the treaty of Aix-la-Chapelle as

---

2. *Penna. Colonial Records*, vol. V., p. 311.
3. *Penna. Colonial Records*, vol. V., pp. 315. 316.

something permanent. Indian concessions were, therefore, no longer a necessity. While other tribes received presents at Lancaster in 1748, the Shawanese merely had their guns and hatchets mended. The Iroquois had kept their pledges made in 1744, and the haughty Shawanese were brought to their knees before the English. They went away from the treaty in disgrace. And after the manner of Indians brooded long over such treatment. In this affair, Conrad Weiser again permitted seed to be sown, which in a few short years led the Shawanese into a French alliance and steeped western Pennsylvania in blood.

When the news reached Pennsylvania and Virginia in the autumn of 1744 that Peter Chartiers had led a party of the Shawanese to join the French, it was believed that the Catawba Indians were at the bottom of it. Indeed, it was feared that unless the long-projected peace between the Iroquois and the Catawbas could be consummated, the entire Muskokee confederation would join the French, thus exposing the whole southern frontier to Indian outrages. As a result, renewed efforts were made by Virginia and Carolina to bring about the much-desired Iroquois peace. Although the Six Nations at the Lancaster treaty of 1744 declared that such a treaty was impossible, and although the mountains were alive with their war parties during the autumn of 1744, so great was Governor Gooch's faith in the influence of Conrad Weiser that he wrote to Governor Thomas in November 1744, enclosing the result of his efforts with the Catawba Indians during the summer.

The Catawbas declared that such a peace would be highly desirable. They had faithfully followed the advice of Governor Gooch and had not permitted one of their men to go to war with the Iroquois, they said,

> For these four years last past, though notwithstanding, they, the Six Nations, are constantly upon us and have killed forty-odd lately. We would be willing to send deputies to treat with the Six Nations if we knew that they would be kindly received, but we remember that we treacherously killed a party of the Six Nations' deputies a few years ago; how then would it be possible for us now to send deputies to the Iroquois in safety? We have already sent our belt and other tokens to the Six Nations by way of the governor of South Carolina and have never yet received any answer or token from them other than constant war. We desire that a letter may be written to Conrad Weiser, instructing him to get a letter from the Six Nations signed by their own hands, with tokens also, as we have already done before, and to recall their warriors that no more hostilities may be committed.

We earnestly desire that a peace may be concluded and that Conrad Weiser may assure the Six Nations that if they will send their deputies to us with a messenger, we will receive them with brotherly love in our arms; and we also desire that the governor of Pennsylvania will take all proper measures for the concluding of a peace, which we do assure you will be greatly to our satisfaction. We expect to know by the spring of the year the result of this matter, and till then, shall rest satisfied.

His X mark.
Signed by the King of the Catawbas
October 1744

Governor Gooch placed this affair entirely in the hands of Governor Thomas of Pennsylvania, saying,

If you had not the management of this affair, I should apprehend great difficulty in prevailing with the Six Nations to accept their offer, but when I consider the address of the person[4] it is submitted to, all suspicions (apprehension) vanish. Whatever expense you are at on this occasion shall be thankfully repaid by,

Sir,
your most obed't &
humb. Serv't,
Will. Gooch.[5]

Governor Thomas recommended to the Assembly that Conrad Weiser be sent to Onondaga to see if it were possible to bring about peace. The Assembly favored the suggestion and offered to defray such necessary expenses as Virginia did not meet. The governor's letter to Weiser asking him to go to Onondaga arrived while Court was in session at Lancaster. Going into the heart of the Iroquois country during the war, when French intrigue was working among the Indians, was dangerous. The proposal to bring about peace at this time was a proposition that none but Conrad Weiser would for a moment have

---

4. Conrad Weiser.
5. *Penna. Archives*, vol. I., pp. 663, 664.

entertained. He postponed his reply to the governor's letter until the Court adjourned and he could go home and consider it in the quiet.

On the 10th of February, 1745, he sent his reply to Secretary Peters, saying:

> I shall never be wanting in your Honour's service whatever- may be required of me that tends to the Honour of your government and the good of the Public, and am very willing to undertake a journey to Onondaga in the spring to put the finishing hand in behalf of Onas, to so good a work, and I do not doubt of success, if what is said by the Catawba King be no deceit, which I fear it is. My reasons are thus. The Catawbas are known to be a very proud people and have, at several treaties they had with the Cherokees, used high expressions and thought themselves stout warriors for having deceived the leader of the Iroquois deputies. I should have been better pleased to see the said King's name with some of his countrymen's signed to the letter they sent to Governor Gooch; some of that nation's names are known to the Six Nations, the Interpreter should also have signed. Most Indian interpreters are traders and people not to be depended on. However, I ought to leave this to Gov. Gooch. The Catawbas are also known to be an irregular people; they have no counsel; the richest or greatest among [them] calls himself a King with the consent of his brothers, cousins and proves often the greatest full (fool); acts all what he does as an arbitrator, the rest don't mind him, and after all, sends him to the grave with a broken head. This is what those who were prisoners among them all agree. If that one article is true with them, that they will own that they treacherously murdered Garontowano and some of his men, a peace no doubt will be made between those poor wretches. I shall soon go up to Shamokin to see Shickellimy and shall then have an opportunity to talk a great deal with Shickelimy, and if he seems inclined for peace, I will let him know of Governor Gooch's request to your Honor; otherwise not, and will on my return from Shamokin wait upon your Honor to receive the necessary instructions. I should be well pleased if the Six Nations would make Williamsburg the place of Congress, but question very much whether they will not think of given up too much or submit so much to the Catawbas, they the Six Nations will refuse at once, and therefore that point must be given up, your Honour said enough about that in the letter; as for a third place, I shall be more able

to give my sentiments about that when I return from Shamokin.⁶

Then Weiser soliloquizes about the probable dangers of a trip to Onondaga at that time.

> I shall hardly meet any Frenchman who can hurt me, and if there are more, I think they will have more to fear from me than I from them. The Counsel of the Six Nations have always looked upon me as their friend and one of their own nations. It will be dangerous for a few Frenchmen to meddle with me amongst the Indians; they will soon find their mistakes.

Weiser then said that he has much more to fear from a family of white people living in his own valley. He declares that the Heans "are worse than any French and Indians, and I do not know yet whether my wife and children will be so far out of fear that I can leave them; the Heans has still their friends, as they had this twenty years, other ways not one soul of the family would in this day be in the province, or if they had had their due, they would have been out of the world. I do not know how to do, the whole neighborhood is afraid of them, and the many felonies they have committed and hitherto escaped punishment will be sufficient cause for several good families to move to some other place. I did expect at least that they would all be bound to stay in their own houses in time of night and behave well in all respects, but I find their time is not yet come."

The governor evidently took this matter of the Heans in charge, for Weiser wrote, thanking the governor for interesting himself in the misfortunes "that threatened me and my family." The introduction of these things indicates Weiser's reluctance to go to Onondaga while the war was in progress. "As for the time to set out," he said, "I think it almost impracticable before the middle of May because for the creeks, and for food in the woods for horses, and the southern Indians cannot expect an answer in their own towns before the latter end of August next if everything goes well; I should have liked it much better, if they had sent two or three old men as deputies, I would have traveled with them to the Mohawk's Country by way of Albany, and having got the opinions of the counsels of the Mohawks, I would have acted accordingly without any danger to the Catabaws; I intend to go round by Albany now if I do go." Since the Mohawks were avowedly in the English interests, it was quite clear in

---

6. *Penna. Archives*, vol. I., pp. 671, 672.

Conrad Weiser's mind that Albany would offer the safest route into the Onondaga country.

Weiser fully realized that Shikellamy was the door into the secrets of the Onondaga Council, and if communications were to be kept open during the winter, something must be done for the faithful old Indian. Early in the winter, Weiser sent his son Sammie to Virginia after one of his honest debtors. On the way, he met several Iroquois Indians returning from raids against the Catawbas, who told him that "Unhappy Jake," one of Shikellamy's sons, had been killed in an engagement with the Catawbas. For this reason, Weiser was doubtful about the prospect of peace between the Northern and Southern Indians. He also felt that it was the province's duty to send some tribute or offer to wipe away old Shikellamy's tears. Such a present, Weiser suggested, "would not only be satisfactory to Shikellamy, but very agreeable and pleasing to the council of said nation; and, consequently, some little service done to ourselves." In a postscript, Weiser adds: "It is customary with the Indians that let what will happen, the chiefs or people in trust with them, don't stir to do any service or business to the public, when they are in mourning, till they have in a manner, a new commission as before said, in being fetched out of mourning and invested with new courage and dispositions."[7]

The governor evidently sent Weiser instructions to procure a present for Shikellamy, since under the date of February 11, 1745, Weiser wrote to Richard Peters: "I could get no goods in Lancaster fit for anything, . . . have therefore sent my son to Philadelphia to purchase from Mr. Shippen, if you wish you may change the order." It would appear that the governor had changed the order to three pieces of strouds instead of three match coats. Weiser wrote, "I think it would be extravagant to give it all to Shikellamy; I intend to set out for Shamokin the 25th of this instant and shall take but three match coats and one-half duzend of silk handkercher, and leave the rest until I receive orders from you what to do with. I think there must be a mistake, hope it is not in my order."[8]

Weiser saw to it that every possible attention was paid to Shikellamy. Three years before, he recommended the Moravian missionaries establish a free smith shop at Shamokin and continually urged building a house for Shikellamy.

Shortly after the Lancaster treaty of 1744, Shikellamy, doubtless following the suggestion of Conrad Weiser, took from his recently acquired means and employed eight men, Germans, under the direction of Weiser to build a house

---

7. *Penna. Archives*, vol. I., p. 666.
8. *Penna. Archives*, vol. I., p. 673.

for him. Conrad said they were seventeen days building "a locke house," which was "49½ foot long and 17½ wide and covered with shingles."⁹

In the latter part of May 1745, Conrad Weiser, Andrew Montour, Shikellamy, and his son set out for Onondaga. At Tioga, a messenger was sent ahead to apprise the natives of their coming. Indians from all the nations except the Mohawks assembled in great numbers to hear what Conrad Weiser had to say. There appears to be a general stir among the natives since they arranged to meet at Oswego and go to Canada to hold a treaty with the French Governor. They would have started the day before Weiser arrived if his messenger had not appeared. Weiser asked the Indians how such proceedings comported with their previous promises at Lancaster. They told him that they knew perfectly well what they were doing. We know, they said, that "the French Governor of Canada will try to gain upon us . . . the French are known to be a crafty people . . . but it will be in vain for him, as we have already agreed what to say to him and will not go from it."¹⁰

Weiser delivered the Catawhas' message, substituting Williamsburg as the place of meeting instead of a town among the Southern Indians, knowing full well that they would resent any such suggestion. He apologized for the past conduct of the Catawbas as best he could and urged the Indians to send deputies for the sake of Assaryquoa and Onas, if for no other reason.

The Indians, through the Black Prince, their speaker, replied that no council fire had ever been kindled at Williamsburg, but they would be willing to send deputies to Philadelphia. And then, with characteristic Iroquois caution, declined to send them this summer, offering many excuses and promising to send them next summer (1746). The Indians were very much incensed at the reported conduct of Peter Chartiers and asked why Onas did not declare war against him at once.

"After the council was over," said Weiser, "the Black Prince invited all the deputies and the chiefs of Onondaga, myself and company, to a dinner; we all went directly to his house; he entertained us plentifully with hominy, dried venison and fish, and after dinner, we were served with a dram round."¹¹

While at dinner, Weiser learned from their conversation that many favored war with the Shawanese and peace with the Catawbas. He also learned from an old sachem in confidential conversation that the Six Nations deemed it in their best interests to maintain—strict neutrality between the French and the English, "and therefore would not join with either nation in the war unless

---

9. *Penna. Archives*, vol. I., p. 661.
10. *Penna. Colonial Records*, vol. IV., p. 778.
11. *Penna. Colonial Records*, vol. IV., pp. 781, 782.

compelled to it for their own preservation. That hitherto, from their situation and alliances, they had been courted by both but should either prevail so far as to drive the other out of the country they (the Indians) should be no longer considered. Presents would be no longer made to them, and in the end, they should be obliged to submit to such laws as the conquerors should think fit to impose on them."wwwwwwww

When Weiser reported this to Governor Thomas, a message was promptly sent to the Pennsylvania Assembly, quoting this part of Weiser's report and calling attention to the fact that the Iroquois had received a belt of wampum from the French Governor, upon which was wrought the figure of a hatchet. Since the Indians received this, Governor Thomas looked upon the act with suspicion, "and by no means a good omen to us. There is but one probable means of securing them," continued the governor, "and that is to persuade them by outbidding the enemy to an open declaration for us: money, notwithstanding their reasoning, having always been the prevailing argument with them. Should the present opportunity be lost, it is much to be feared that the intrigue of the French in the ensuing winter will seduce and entirely alienate them from us. But supposing the best of them, that their inclinations are with us, and that they are resolved to preserve a neutrality if their allies break it and take up the hatchet against us, they (the Iroquois) must either join them (the allies) or fly to us for protection, which can in no way be so effectually secured to them as by a union of all the British northern colonies for that purpose. This is a matter which very nearly concerns the quiet and safety of the people of Pennsylvania, and as such, I recommend it to your most serious consideration,"[12]

The difficulties which beset the Iroquois in their remarkable struggle for neutrality and the dangers threatening the colonies should the Six Nations join the French led to Governor Thomas' suggestion, the execution of which was not attempted until the great Albany conference of 1734. The Assembly approved the governor's suggestions and expressed regrets that his health was such as to prevent him from attending the treaty at Albany. It also approved the choice of commissioners, especially since two out of the three were members of the Assembly. This treaty was to be held in October 1745 at Albany. The Pennsylvania commissioners were instructed to treat either jointly with New York or separately,

> as you shall judge most for the honor and interest of the government you represent, taking especial care that you do not suffer the least diminution of either in the course of the treaty. You are, by the

---

12. *Penna. Colonial Records*, vol. IV., pp. 772, 773.

province interpreter, Mr. Weiser, who is ordered to attend you, to inquire by all private ways and means:—

1. Into the truth of the Iroquois conference at Montreal.
2. You are to demand satisfaction from the Six Nations for all goods plundered from our traders by the Shawanese under Peter Chartiers.
3. You are to make the Iroquois aware that such robbery is a clear breach of former treaties,—but you are at the same time to be very careful not to do or say anything that may impeach the title of the Honorable proprietors of this province to the lands upon Ohio by virtue of the Royal Grant to them made.
4. You are to expostulate very freely with the Six Nations over their breach of faith made to Conrad Weiser last spring when they promised a cessation of hostilities with the Catawbas until the deputies should meet in Philadelphia next spring, now they have allowed their warriors to go against the Catawbas. This is treachery, and you are to tell them so.
5. You are to show a disinclination to believe any Iroquois stories about Catawba treachery, and unless the Six Nations are willing to give security for future good behavior, you are to threaten a withdrawal of mediation offered by the King's government in America.
6. If this security is offered as effectually as the circumstances of these people will admit. You are to renew the offer of mediation on my behalf at Philadelphia next spring.
7. You are to show them that their receiving a belt of wampum from the French is looked upon by us as an act of hostility.
8. You are to remind them of the long friendship existing between them and the English and recount to them the many favors shown them by the English.
9. You are to persuade them into a continuance of our former friendship, and if you find them cordially disposed to it and can have any dependence upon their sincerity, you are to present them with the two hundred and fifty pounds voted by the Assembly in such goods as you shall think most acceptable to them.
10. You would be further instructed, were I at liberty to act upon my own judgment [and here is the only point in which the governor's Indian policy differed from that of the Assembly], to join with

the government of New York in urging the United Nations to an open declaration against the French, and in promising them, in that case, an aid of men, arms and ammunition for their defense.[13]

John Kinsey, Speaker of the Pennsylvania Assembly and a prominent member of the Society of Friends, was the leading spirit among the commissioners who met at Albany in October 1745. Here were assembled the governor of New York, commissioners from Massachusetts and Connecticut, and four hundred and sixty Indians representing five of the six united nations. There were none of the Senecas present; they had sent word that it was a time of great sickness and mortality among them. To what extent this report was true is unknown, but since the French influence was strongest among the Senecas, the French probably restrained them from attending the Albany treaty.

The Pennsylvania deputies with Conrad Weiser rode on horseback across New Jersey to Elizabethtown and took a boat there for New York, where a sloop carried them to Albany. The governor of New York received them kindly and took a copy of their instructions. The states' commissioners held a conference to decide whether they should treat jointly or separately with the Indians. New York, Massachusetts, and Connecticut favored a joint treaty. It "would show our union, and consequently, have greater weight with the Indians."

Pennsylvania objected to a joint treaty because (1) it would take time to prepare an address that all could endorse; (2) it would necessarily introduce subjects of no concern to Pennsylvania; (3) since the New England colonies insisted that the Six Nations should declare war against the French, Pennsylvania must oppose it until the Legislatures of the colonies could be consulted; (4) an Indian war would be injurious to all the colonies, as it would be the means of drawing open hostilities upon all our borders; (5) the Six Nations wished to remain neutral, the Indians were not disposed to fight each other, and should we enlist the Six Nations on the English side, we might expect what occurred during the last war, "when the Indians of the opposite parties passed each other without fighting and only scalped the white people"; (6) if we induce the Six Nations to declare war with the French we must provide for them. This cannot be done without the consent of our colonial assemblies, and not doing this would betray the Indians. How do we know now what our assemblies may do?

The Pennsylvania objections had but little influence. The other colonies were determined to push the Six Nations into a war with the French. Massachusetts said it was unreasonable that the entire burden of the war should rest

---

13. *Penna. Colonial Records*, vol. IV, pp. 776, 777.

on one province while the others remained neutral, and if the neutral colonies were determined not to bear their share of the war expenses, they should not use influences to prevent the Iroquois from becoming allies of the New England provinces. The attitude of New England tried the patience of long-suffering New York, who, while incensed, stood along with Pennsylvania in her opposition to the course taken by New England. New York insisted that New England had been too precipitate in her declaration of war, and the other governments were not obliged to follow her example. Proper provisions were not yet made for war. New York had done all she could to prepare for such an event, and New England must remember that provinces with a long-unprotected frontier should not be dragged into a war for which they were unprepared.

It was finally decided that Pennsylvania should treat separately with the Indians after the business of the other provinces was completed. In this joint conference, the Indians were given to understanding that unless they declared war against the French, the English would consider it an unfriendly act. The Indians replied that they had many allies and that it would be necessary to consult them before making a decision. "We will, therefore, before we make use of the hatchet against the French or their Indians, send four of our people, who are now ready, to Canada to demand satisfaction for the wrongs they have done our brethren (the English) and if they refuse to make satisfaction, then we will be ready to use the hatchet against them whenever our brother, the governor of New York, orders us to do it."[14]

The Mohawk influence colored this reply. The Indians gained time and succeeded in putting off the demands of New England without losing their standing among the English, and as a closing stroke to their negotiations, they presented a belt of wampum to New York and the New England provinces with the request that "you, our brethren, should all be united in your councils," and of one mind, "and if anything of importance is to be communicated to us by any of you, this is the place where it should be done."

After the treaty had concluded and the governor of New York had returned to New York City, the Pennsylvania commissioners held their conference with the Indians, pressing the points outlined in their instructions from Governor Thomas. The Indians listened with great deference and answered as follows:

> Our going to Montreal was at the invitation of the governor of Canada; we told him that formerly we had inconsiderately engaged in wars but that we looked upon this war between the English and

---

14. *Penna. Colonial Records*, vol. V., p. 18.

French only and did not intend to engage on either side; for that the French and English made war and made peace at pleasure, but when the Indians engaged in wars they knew not when it would end. We also told the French that they knew, and all the world knew, the countries on which we were settled, and particularly the Lakes were ours; and, therefore, if they would fight our brethren, the English, they ought to fight on the salt water, and that they must not come over our land to disturb them, or to obstruct the trade at Oswego; that they, the French, had two trading houses on those lakes, with which they ought to be contented. The governor of Canada promised that he would do this unless the King of France, his master, ordered otherwise.

News having arrived that the English had taken Cape Breton, the Canadian Governor called all the Indians around him, his allies as well as the Iroquois deputies, and holding in his hand a large belt of wampum in which the figure of a hatchet was worked, said, 'Children, you who are my allies must live and die with me, they cannot deny me assistance; as for my children of the Six Nations, I know you love your brethren, the English, and, therefore, I shall not say much to you; perhaps you would not be pleased with it. But, children,' said he, 'should know their duty to their father.' Then speaking to us all he desired such who loved him to go with him and assist him in defending Quebec; and that those who went with him need not take anything with them save their tobacco pouches; that he would provide guns, pistols, swords, ammunition, provisions, and everything, even paint to paint them; and thereupon delivered the belt to the interpreter, who threw it at the feet of the Indians present, some of whom inconsiderately, and without any consultation first, had took it up and danced the war dance; and afterward divers of the Indians present, chiefly the praying Indians, went with the French Governor to Quebec, where they staid eight or ten days, but no notice was taken of them, nor any arms or necessaries so much as a knife provided for them; nor were they permitted to speak to the governor, which so exasperated the praying Indians that they left Quebec and are since gone against their common enemies to the southward.

This frank report of the Montreal conference weakened the commissioners' determination to press the other provisions in their instructions. The Indians made no satisfactory explanation about the Catawba affair or Peter Chartier's treatment of the Pennsylvania traders other than to say, "Your traders go very far back into the country, which we desire may not be done because it is the road of the French."

Possibly, the Pennsylvania traders traveled as far west as the French route to the Mississippi River *via* Detroit and the Wabash. At any rate, the restitution of the traders' property was not pressed, and the commissioners seemed satisfied with the Iroquois statement relative to the war raids against the Catawbas since they promised to restrain their warriors. "It is not in our power," they said, "to restrain our warriors, as the English can do until peace be finally concluded. This the Catawbas know."

The Indians were told that the governor of Pennsylvania would expect a full answer to these points in the spring. They were then feasted on a pair of oxen and some beer and were told that "since winter was approaching, they would want clothing to preserve them from the cold, and powder and lead to acquire their livelihood by hunting, we, therefore, provide the goods which now be before you, to wit: Four half bars of lead, six pieces of strouds, two pieces of striped blankets, one piece of Shrewsbury cotton, eight dozen knives, four pieces of Indian blankets, four pieces of half thicks."

It is unclear how this present would cost two hundred and fifty pounds which the Pennsylvania Assembly appropriated for that purpose. The Indians, however, knew nothing of this and received their gift with grateful hearts. They held a short conference among themselves and returned, thanking the commissioners for the present, saying, "We are poor and have little to return; however, out of what we have, we present you with six bundles of skins which you see. These we desire may be accepted as a token of our affection."

It would appear that Pennsylvania's influence in this Albany treaty was very slight, yet the fact that Pennsylvania warmly supported the neutrality policy of the Six Nations lent them strength in their hour of greatest need.

During the winter of 1745 and 1746, numerous rumors were afloat that the Iroquois were about to revolt and join the French. Governor Thomas feared that the young men of the Six Nations, being of a warlike disposition, could not be restrained and would join the French in the spring. The old men would wink at this until the entire Confederacy would finally be arrayed against the English. Then the whole frontier would be exposed to savage depredations.

The governor made every effort to persuade the Pennsylvania Assembly to join with New York and the New England colonies in a general treaty with the Iroquois in July 1746. Since most of the Assembly was composed of members of the Society of Friends, that body opposed the movement. Said the Assembly to the governor; it was feared that the purposes of such a congress were:

> to engage the Indians of the Six Nations in the war against the French and to join in the expedition against Canada. If so,", "our uniting with the other governments in the congress proposed will be of little use since it cannot be doubted, but that provision is made to defray the expense which shall arise thereby and that these Indians will pay greater regard to the directions of the Crown than to the joint request of all the colonies. Besides, the governor must be sensible that men of our peaceable principles cannot consistently therewith join in persuading the Indians to engage in war. If it be thought there be any real danger of the Indians deserting the British interest and going over to the French, and that to preserve them steady in their friendship, further presents are necessary to secure them in their fidelity to the Crown of Great Britain, and amity with the inhabitants of this and the neighboring colonies, and the governor can think his health and business will permit his negotiating this affair in person, we shall be willing to pay the expense to arise by it.

John Kinsey, Speaker
4th mon., 24th, 1746[15]

While these things were pending, Governor Thomas, whose health had been rapidly failing since the Lancaster treaty of 1744, resigned, and Anthony Palmer, a member of the Council, agreed to serve as President of the Council until Penn's heirs should select another Governor. In conducting Indian affairs, the Assembly and Conrad Weiser each had unlimited confidence in the ability of Governor Thomas, and after his departure, they each became more assertive and dictatorial when consulted upon these matters.

Early in the spring of 1747, Colonel Johnson, the Indian agent for the province of New York, assisted by Mr. John Henry Lydius, induced the young men among the Mohawks and several straggling tribes in that vicinity "to take up the hatchet" against the French. To what extent these two men and the province of New York equipped these Indians for war is not known, but on their behalf, Colonel John Stoddard wrote to Governor Shirley of Massachusetts, setting forth the necessity of the colonies furnishing six or seven hundred pounds to fit

---

15. *Penna. Colonial Records*, vol. V., p. 49.

these Indians for war. "We cannot expect," said Stoddard, "that either Colonel Johnson or Mr. Lydius should pay this. They have taken a great deal of pains to get the Indians into the war and have effected more than the government did in a course of years. If we let this plan drop now, it would be fatal for our cause. The Indians would despise us and then join the French. For the Indians are of such a humor that if we deal justly and kindly with them, they will put their lives in our hands, but if we deal deceitfully with them, that will soon raise an abhorrence of us. Colonel Johnson and Mr. Lydius are now under a necessity of going forward and fitting out the Indians, so long as they have any substance remaining, and when that is gone, the affair will be at an end."[16]

Governor Shirley then sent a copy of Stoddard's letter to Pennsylvania urging that a sum of money be raised for that purpose. "The General Court of Massachusetts," he said, "had committed their share of the affair into the hands of Mr. Lydius and voted four thousand pounds to Colonel Stoddard to be used to encourage the Six Nations to prosecute the war."

President Palmer, of Pennsylvania, during the adjournment of the Assembly, consulted John Kinsey, the Speaker, and a few members living in or near Philadelphia about the advisability of calling an extra session of the Legislature. Kinsey and his associates told Palmer that they thought it would be very unwise to call the members of the Assembly in from their harvest, that the convening of the Assembly had better be postponed until autumn. It was pretty well known that the Friends, who were in the majority in the Assembly, would vigorously oppose any efforts to utilize Indians and their method of warfare against white men, even if they were French.

Conrad Weiser had been instructed to go to Shamokin and learn what he could of the actions of the Six Nations and, in his report, give his judgment of the affair. Personally, Weiser favored using the Iroquois against the French. And he was jealous of Colonel Johnson and his management of the Mohawk Indian affairs. At the same time, when Weiser interviews Shikellamy, he wavers and appears to favor Iroquois neutrality. "The treaty of Col. Johnson and Mr. Lydius with the Mohawks," he said, "I dislike it. And the Six Nations are offended at the people of Albany because the Mohawks are paid with goods against the opinion of the chief counsel. If these two gentlemen had as much judgment as they have pride, they would never have persuaded the Mohawks into a war in a private way, for it may turn out that both their scalps may be taken and carried to Canada. In short, I don't think it proper our government should countenance such doings, and I hope the counsel will not look upon it

16. *Penna. Archives*, vol. I., pp. 740, 741.

as worthy of their approbation.[17] . . . I would say, if I could without words, that Mr. Lydius cannot be ruined, he has nothing to lose. But Col. Johnson may; but he has neither wife nor children,[18] and Admiral Warren is his uncle, and the Assembly of New York have supplied their Governor, and their Governor him (Admiral Warren)."

After meeting Shikellamy, Weiser wrote: "Col. Johnson and Mr. Lydius did not prevail upon the Council of the Six Nations to declare war against the French, but only upon some straggling poor fellows, to enlist themselves, and take service, by taking the presents and going to war with the Mohawks. I am sorry that Governor Shirley is deceived, but it is like (although he is an honest and capable gentleman) he believes what he wishes to be true, like the rest of our fellow creatures. I never was afraid of the Six Nations engaging against the English, but always doubted whether they would fight the French. When I heard that the Mohawks had actually gone to war against the French, I was sure that the other nations would join them. But when at Shamokin, I was assured that nothing would be done until their people, who are scattered, are called in."

Then Weiser alludes to the projected expedition into Canada, which the colonies had abandoned. It "has done a great deal of hurt" among the Indians.

> No man is able to excuse it with the Indians; they call it downright cowardice that so many hundreds dare not venture to go beyond the inhabited parts of the English settlement, much less to invade Canada. An interpreter must be ashamed to hear them talk of it among themselves or in familiarity with him. The Indians undervalue, or rather make nothing of our valor and think we English will leave them in the lurch. At least a shipload of goods will not engage them into the war if their own reasons don't, for they say the English have goods enough, let us take the presents, and promise a great deal, and do little, according to the custom of the white people. I have known the Indians above thirty-three years now, I have had some warm friends among them. I am not deceived in my mind, and I know also very well how they have been dealt with by the white people, who have frequently learned them to tell lies in public treaties, and to the commissioners and governors that treated with them in particular in a neighboring government. . . . If we send commissioners from all the Northern colonies they can believe Col. Johnson and Mr. John

---

17. *Penna. Archives*, vol. I., p. 751.
18. At this time Col. Johnson was a widower with three children. See Stone, vol. I., p. 189.

Lydius, their report, that the Six Nations have engaged in war against the French if they do not engage before such commissioners meet at New York. I am satisfied that the Six Nations had not declared for war when Col. Stoddard wrote to Governor Shirley. Johnson and Lydius may have known better or have been too credulous, which I am apt to believe for charities sake. They show that their judgment is under age, but if they knew better and with a design gave a false information, I have nothing to say to them. If the commissioners about to meet at New York will undertake some exploit of military, such as taking Crown Point Ford, it will be most instrumental in bringing the Six Nations into open alliance with us, not only by word of mouth as they hitherto have done but by act and deeds, in the meantime let them be assured that they will be supplied by the English with ammunition, etc.[19]

Conrad Weiser favored an Iroquois alliance employing the Six Nations in the war against the French. His influence, in this instance, in directing Indian affairs was weaker than that of the Pennsylvania Assembly. During Palmer's administration, the Legislature was strong, the Executive weak. John Kinsey, the leader of the Pennsylvania Assembly, favored the Iroquois struggle for neutrality. He thwarted the efforts of New York and New England towards securing a general congress of the colonies, which would induce the Iroquois to take sides. He opposed Conrad Weiser's desire that some decisive military blow should be struck as a means to secure the Indians.

The Iroquois adopted the policy of neutrality (1) because they looked upon the war as the white man's quarrel, not theirs; (2) because as long as they remained neutral, they were courted both by the French and the English. . . . Skins brought a higher price, presents were more numerous at public treaties, and rum flowed in a more generous strain.

The Quaker Assembly of Pennsylvania favored the Iroquois policy of neutrality (1) because their peace principles were opposed to war *per se*; (2) because they abhorred the idea of employing the brutal methods of warfare prevalent among savages; (3) because experience had taught that Indian allies were expensive and treacherous.

This remarkable struggle for neutrality lasted until the Treaty of Aix-la-Chapelle, except with a slight English alliance among the Mohawks and a slight French alliance among the Senecas and "Praying Indians," the Iroquois won.

---

19. *Penna. Archives*, vol. I., pp. 761, 762.

The most fruitful result of the struggle to Pennsylvania was winning the great Western tribes of Indians and enlarging the fur trade of Philadelphia until it had no equal on the Atlantic seaboard. The circumstances which led to this signal triumph in trade will be treated in the following chapter.

IX

The First Winning of the West

Rivals in the Beaver Trade—French Monopoly of Trade—The Indian Letter—Croghan's Letter—The Assembly's action upon this letter—Weiser declines to forward the French scalp—The Indians dissatisfied with the French traders—Weiser complains of Frauds practiced by the Indian traders—Laws difficult to enforce among the traders—Weiser demands Justice for the Indians—George Croghan's Influence—Conrad Weiser favors sending a Present to the Western Indians—Weiser begs assistance for Shikellamy—Weiser begins to shape the Indian Policy of the West—Weiser brings the Ohio Indians to Philadelphia—Weiser guides the Indian Policy of the Council—A Council Fire opened on the Ohio—Assembly and Council differ upon the Methods of raising money to meet the increasing Indian Expenses—Shikellamy supports Weiser in his Western Schemes—John Kinsey brings the Assembly to aid Weiser's Plans—Maryland and Virginia solicited for Aid towards the Treaty—A Proclamation issued against the Rum Traffic—The Six Nations opposed to the Ohio Treaty—Weiser suddenly summoned to Philadelphia—Pennsylvania's Appetite for the Western Fur Trade.

THE French and the English had been rivals in the fur trade for many years. The southern peninsula of Michigan was a rich trapping region where, previous to King George's war, the French enjoyed a monopoly of the beaver trade. After the Lancaster treaty of 1744, the Pennsylvania trader grew bolder under the Iroquois promise of protection. The Allegheny River became his halfway place. He built his campfires on the southern shores of Lake Erie and drove his pack-horses over the Scioto. A few of the boldest hunted wild turkeys on the Wabash. The Indians soon learned who paid the best prices for beaver. It took the French traders some time to realize that there were rivals in the woods out-bidding them. As soon as they became aware, they employed Peter Chartiers and his band of disaffected Shawanese Indians to rob the more venturesome traders from Pennsylvania. At the Albany treaty of 1745, when Conrad Weiser was endeavoring- to secure indemnity from the Indians for these losses, we have seen that Canassatego, on behalf of the Iroquois, resented it, saying: "Your traders go very far back into the country, which we desire may not be done because it is in the road of the French."[1]

During Peter Chartiers' successful activity against the traders on the Mississippi and Wabash, the French enjoyed the advantage of an almost exclusive trade in this rich hunting section. The price of furs went down rapidly. The French told the Indians that the war caused it. The Indians, however, entertained their own opinions. They were growing more and more dissatisfied with French rule. Finally, when the price of skins had so far declined that a French trader, one day, offered an Indian only a charge of powder and one bullet for a beaver skin, the savage buried his hatchet in the trader's head and walked away with his scalp.[2] During the spring of 1747, five French traders were killed on the south side of Lake Erie alone. It is more than probable that the Pennsylvania traders incited the Indians to resent their treatment from the French.

The Indians around "De Troit" claimed to be of the Six Nations, and in May 1747, they sent the following letter to Governor Thomas, the spelling and construction of which bear the unmistakable ear-marks of a jealous Pennsylvania trader:

> May Ye 16th, 1747.
> Brother Owass Giaboga:
> Last fall, when our King of ye Six Nations were Down att Albny, you and our Brother of New York gave them ye hatchett to make use of against ye French, which wee very willingly, and with True harts Tuck hould of, and has Naw made use of itt, and killed five of ye French, hard by this fortt which is call'd Detroat, and wee hope in a Little Time to have this fortt in our posesion. We can ashure you Brother, we shall Take all Methods to cutt of all ye French in these parts; we are Likewise Joyn'd by ye Misasaga & Toaways, which are all as one with us; we now take this opertunaty of presenting you by ye berrer, one of those Frenchmen's Sculps, ashuring you itt Shall not

---

1. *Penna. Colonial Records*, vol. V., p. 24.
2. *Penna. Colonial Records*, vol. V., p. 87.

be ye Last of them. You shall see more of them as Soon as we have complated a victory over them in all these parts, which we hope will be very soon done; we hope Brother, you will Consider that wee shall be in need of some powder and Lead, to carry on ye Expedition with a vigor; we hear you have sent an army against Canaday, to reduce itt, which Army wee wish may have as good success as that you sent against Cape Breton, in SLshurance of our Sincear wishes for ye sucksess over all your & our enemies, we present you this string of wampum, and remains ye everlasting Brothers,
Conagaresa
Sunathoaka
Kinnera[3]

Ten days later, George Croghan, the prince of Pennsylvania traders, sent a letter to the governor, with which he forwards the above-mentioned Indian letter and French "sculp." Croghan states that these Indians were always in the French interest until now.

Butt This spring all most all the Ingans in the woods have declared against ye French, and I think this will be a fair opertunity, if purshued by some small Presents, to have all ye French cut off in them parts, for the Ingans are very much led by anything that will Tend to their own self Interest, and will think a great Dail of a Little powder & Lead att this Time, besides it will be a Mains of Drowing (drawing) them, that has not yett Joyn'd
Sr. I remain with respect,
yr. humble Servant to Comm'd
George Croghan.[4]

These letters came into the hands of Anthony Palmer, President of the Council. After being read, it was decided that they should be laid before the Assembly. More than a month elapsing, and the Assembly having taken no notice thereof, the governor again sent a message to that body, saying, "The Indians seated on Lake Erie and on Inomoy Creek, that runs into that Lake, being part of, or in alliance with the Six Nations, said by the Indian traders to be numerous, and people of consequence . . . are desirous to be taken into friendship,

---

3. *Penna. Archives*, vol. I., pp. 741, 742.
4. *Penna. Archives*, vol. I., p. 742.

COL. GEORGE CROGHAN, THE INDIAN TRADER

and it may be of great service to encourage such applications, you will enable us to make them proper presents."[5]

The Assembly, in its reply, does not distinguish the Lake Erie Indians from the other Iroquois but said, "It is, nevertheless, our sentiments, conformable to the practice of this government since its first establishment, that great care should at all times be taken to preserve the friendship and good correspondence which at present subsists between us and the Indians . . . we think a present ought to be made to them, and shall, therefore, before our rising make the provision necessary to this end, as we shall likewise do for payment of the interpreter and maintenance of the Indians expected here during our recess."[6]

Meanwhile, the French scalp sent from the Lake Erie Indians to the governor had gone as far as Thomas McKee's, a trader on the Susquehanna; here it remained several weeks waiting for someone to take it to Philadelphia. Conrad Weiser saw the scalp and met the Indians who brought it down. Said Weiser,

> He pressed very hard upon me to receive the scalp for the government of Pennsylvania, in whose favor the scalp was taken, and at the government of Pennsylvania's request, the Indians of Canayiahagon had taken up the hatchet against the French and that I was the fittest man to receive it. I told him that I had been concerned in Indian affairs these many years, but I never knew that the government of Pennsylvania had given the hatchet or employed anybody to kill Frenchmen and that I was sensible the government had never requested the Indians at Canayiahagon to kill Frenchmen, and, therefore, I could not receive the scalp, and as I was well informed that this scalp had been taken in time of peace I could in no ways receive it; all white people would look upon such actions with contempt, and as my commission for the transaction of Indian affairs did not extend to Ohio or Canayiahagon, but reached only to the Six Nations, I must leave that affair to those that had correspondence that way to inform the government of it and receive an answer, I hoped he would excuse me, and so we parted in friendship.[7]

The scalp never got further east than the banks of the Susquehanna. While Pennsylvania was opposed to using these Western Indians for allies, she was

---

5. *Penna. Colonial Records*, vol. V., pp. 97, 98.
6. *Penna. Colonial Records*, vol. V., p. 102.
7. *Penna. Colonial Records*, vol. V., p. 138.

more than willing to enlarge her area of the fur trade and weaken the strength of the French allies. The governor had already learned through Conrad Weiser that the Zistagechroanu, a powerful tribe of Indians living to the north of Lake Fountenac (Ontario), who had been in the custom of trading at Oswego by going directly across the lake, were growing dissatisfied, and even rebellious against the French. When these Indians learned that their Father Onontio was going to take the English trading station at Oswego into his charge, they sent the following petition to the Six Nations:

> Brethren of the United Nations, we have hitherto been kept like prisoners on the other side of the Lake. Onontio, our Father, told us that if we should treat with the English, he would look upon it as a breach of the peace with him; now we come to let you know that we will no more be stopped from treating with our Brethren, the English; we will join with you to support the House at Oswego, where the goods that the Indians want are so plenty. All the Indians about the lakes will join, and if need take up the hatchet against our foolish Father Onontio, whenever you request it; his goods are very dear, and he is turned malicious because he sees our women and children clothed fine in English clothes, bought at Oswego. We have already let them know that we want none of his advice, as we did formerly when we were young, but we are become now men of age and would think for ourselves, let the consequences be what it will.[8]

This petition from the north of Lake Ontario was an index of the growing discontent among the Indians who had been trading with the French.

Conrad Weiser was quick to see in this an opportunity to enlarge the trade and influence of Pennsylvania. Indeed, his sleepless activity enabled the Indian trade of Pennsylvania to outgrow that of any other province. If unscrupulous traders imposed upon the Indians, which was a common practice then, Weiser was prompt to inform them and tireless in securing justice for the Indians. He reported that one trader at the headwaters of the Joniady (Juniata) River stole forty-seven deer skins and three horses from a "sober, quiet and good-natured" Indian.

> He was down at my house with his complaint a few days before I set out for Shamokin. I sent him back again until I had learned the

---
8. *Penna. Colonial Records*, vol. V., p. 85.

particulars, being I could not talk with him sufficient to find out the truth of the story; he is now (July 1747) with Shikellamy and renewed his complaint. James Dunning is gone down Ohio River and will stay out long; the Indian was content that I should inform the council of his misfortune; he not only lost his skins and horses but pursued James Dunning in vain to the place called Canaviahagon, on the south side of Lake Erie, from thence back again to the place where he left the skins, and from thence again to Ohio, but all in vain: for he could not find or come up with James Dunning.

Weiser's second complaint was against one John Powle, with whom the above-mentioned Indian left several bundles of skins while he was searching for James Dunning. "The Indian," said Weiser, "had sent his brother down Joniady River with the skins that were left after Dunning had rifled his store and desired his brother to leave his two bundles on the island at a certain Indian's house, which this Indian did, and then fell sick at the house of the said John Powle and died there. Before he was dead, John Powle fetched the skins from the island (he said by order of the deceased) and paid himself of what the deceased owed him, who had skins of his own sufficient to answer all his debts and defray his expenses; and would pay what he wanted, notwithstanding the deceased's skins, and his that is alive are all gone, and a very poor account John Powle gives of the whole. The Indians insist upon it that he stole them. The said John Powle had also taken a very fine gun in pawn from the said two Indians for three gallons of liquor (Brandywine). After the deceased paid him, he did not deliver up the gun but alleged that he lent it out and endeavored to cheat the Indian out of it entirely. I sent a few lines to him by the Indians to come to Joseph Chambers' (at Paxton) to meet me and answer to the same complaint. He appeared but laughed at the Indian, but upon examination, I found he was a liar, if not a thief, and offered his oath to confirm a lie of which he was afterward convinced by me. I sent for Justice Armstrong, who did nothing more than order Powle to pay the Indian for the gun. As for the skins, I could do nothing. I, for my part, am convinced that he stole them, or at least the most of them. A great deal of other mischief has been done to some of the Indians. Some horses have been taken on pretense of debt, sometimes skins belonging to a third person, and so on."[9]

The council reported these things to the Assembly, which recommended that if upon "inquiry, the persons against whom the Indians complain appear to be guilty of the crimes laid to their charges, they ought to be prosecuted

---

9. *Penna. Colonial Records*, vol. V., pp. 87, 88.

and punished as the law in such cases directs, besides being obliged to make restitution if they (the plunderers) are able, and if not able, that compensation should be made to them (the Indians) out of the money we intend to provide for presents."[10]

Despite the favorable attitude of the Assembly, which at that time was not only performing the part of a judiciary with appellate jurisdiction but also vigorously absorbing the executive functions, Weiser found it exceedingly difficult to secure the administration of justice locally in Indian affairs. Few magistrates on the frontier would administer law where an Indian was concerned. The class of men holding the commission of Justice on the border was now quite different from what it had been in the early days when the Friends and such Germans as Weiser lived on the frontier and administered the law in the spirit its framers intended. It was useless for the Assembly to insist that the laws be enforced. The magistrates held commissions from the governor, and the gulf between the executive and the legislative was growing broader and broader. For these reasons, Weiser was demanding from the council that justice be extended to the Indians who had lost their horses and peltry. In a few weeks, he wrote again, saying,

> I shall be glad to hear what the President and Council purport to do about the Indian's complaint. . . . Shikellamy is very much concerned about it and did want an answer; he is a feared that no good will come from it if the council don't find a remedy for the Indians lost. I, for my part, am fully satisfied that the Indian's complaint is just in the main, let the particulars fall out as they will; when an Indian in his own judgment thinks himself wronged by somebody, more especially by the white people, he will never forgive, and he is apt to revenge himself, and urged to do it by his country people. John Armstrong,[11] the poor man, had warning sufficient to persuade him to do the Indians justice, but covetousness prevented him, and at last, he paid too dear for his faults. Our people are apt to forget such examples.[12]

A week later, Weiser wrote,

> The Indians must have satisfaction for possible injuries. If we will deal with them according to our public treaties and show that we are

---

10. *Penna. Colonial Records*, vol. V., p. 102.
11. Killed at Jack's Narrows, on the Juniata. See p. 130.
12. *Penna. Archives*, vol. I., pp. 758, 759.

what we pretend to be, that is to say, their friends, people of honor and honesty, the council and Assembly will find a remedy. I own it will be a difficult matter to get at the truth in private quarrels between the white and the brown people, for the former will out-swear the very devil, and the latter oath is not good in our laws. If all come to all, rather than the poor Indians should be wronged, the public ought to make satisfaction if no remedy can be found to prevent it.[13]

These things weighed more and more upon Weiser's mind until he declared more than once that he was sick of Indian affairs. The same summer, he wrote to the council again, the Indians having pressed him to explain why the white people had not kept their promise made at the recent treaties about the illicit sale of rum among the Indians. "Scaiohady," he said, "pressed upon me to put the government in mind of what he said against the traders in rum, that it might be suppressed, for the Indians (said he) will drink away all they have and not be able to do anything against the enemy for want of ammunition; and if rightly considered, death, without judge or jury, to any man that carries rum to sell to any Indian Town, is the only remedy to prevent that trade & a just reward to the traders, for nothing else, will do. It is an abomination before God and man, to say nothing of the particular consequences; it is altogether hurtful to the public, for what little supplies we can give them to carry on the war is not half sufficient, they must buy the greatest part with their hunting, and if they meet with rum they will buy that before anything, and not only drink away their skins but their clothing and everything they may get of us; in short, the inconveniences occasioned by that trade are numerous at this very time, the English and French party (among the Indians) will fall out in their drunkenness and murder one another, and the English will be charged with the mischief thereof."[14]

The rum traffic among the Indians and the traders' disposition to plunder were the hindering things which seriously embarrassed the consummation of those plans leading to the extension of the Indian trade. Yet in the face of these things, Pennsylvania so extended her fur trade into the West during King George's war that all of New France trembled and called for a cessation of hostilities until they could reclaim what was lost. The summer of 1747 developed the plan which brought the Indians of the Ohio Valley into trade relations with Pennsylvania and turned them away from the French posts. The council and Assembly hesitated all summer. The traders urged and importuned the Lake

---

13. *Penna. Archives*, vol. I, p. 762.
14. *Penna. Colonial Records*, vol. V., p. 167.

Erie Indians to be furnished with ammunition and the hatchet placed in their hands against the French.

In September, George Croghan wrote to a council member telling how the Lake Erie Indians were making war briskly against the French in the expectation of a present of powder and lead from Pennsylvania. "If they don't get it," said Croghan, "I am of opinion, by the best accounts I can get, that they will turn to the French, who will be very willing to make up with them again. So, if there be no provision made to send them a present by some of the traders directly, send me an account by first opportunity, for if there be nothing sent, I will not send out any goods or men this year for fear of danger."[15]

Croghan touched the two vital spots, the French and the destruction of Indian trade. Thomas Lawrence laid the letter before the council, which favored sending a present to the value of two hundred and fifty pounds to the Indians on Ohio and Lake Erie.

The secretary was instructed to send a copy of this resolution to Conrad Weiser, requesting his advice and sentiments about the most advantageous manner of laying out the money.[16] Eight days later, Secretary Peters laid before the council "a copy of his letter to Conrad Weiser, Esq. & likewise the draught of a letter to be sent to the Indians on or near Lake Erie; but as no letter is yet come to hand from Mr. Weiser in answer to the Secretary's letter, the council postponed the consideration of Indian affairs to another day.[17] It was over a week before Weiser's letter arrived. He agreed with the council "that a handsome present should be made to the Indians on Ohio and on Lake Erie, who, by their situation, were capable of doing this province abundance of mischief if they should turn to the French."

The council then felt at liberty to consider how to send a present to these Indians. It was decided that two hundred pounds would be sufficient to invest in this project. Many members expressed their fears about entrusting that amount of goods to an Indian trader. They asked what assurance we have that the Indians would ever receive everything. It was finally decided to employ George Croghan to carry the goods to the Ohio River, and in the presence of some reliable man to accompany him, Croghan was to be entrusted with the distribution of the goods. Considerable delay was occasioned in finding a suitable man to go with Croghan to the Ohio. James Logan was opposed to leaving the matter entirely with the traders. In fact, the entire affair was adrift for want

---

15. *Penna. Archives*, vol. I., p. 770.
16. *Penna. Colonial Records*, vol. V., pp. 119, 120.
17. *Penna. Colonial Records*, vol. V., p. 120.

of a man who knew how to push these Western negotiations. Up to October 1747, Western Indian affairs markedly contrasted with those of the Northern Indians. In the latter, Conrad Weiser held a commission as the provincial interpreter, directly or indirectly shaping the Iroquois policy. But with the Lake Erie negotiations, the pushing spirit was George Croghan. James Logan and others in the council opposed trusting or being led by him.

Weiser had been occupied all summer with business relative to the Six Nations. He had been to Shamokin several times, once to notify the Iroquois of the death of John Penn and the departure of Governor Thomas to England. On this journey, he took several dozen silk handkerchiefs that the Indians might have the wherewithal to wipe away their tears of grief. On returning from his October trip to Shamokin, Weiser informs the council that Shikellamy has become a fit object of charity. "he is extremely poor; in his sickness, the horses have eaten all his corn; his cloathes he gave to the Indian doctor to cure him and his family, but all in vain; he has nobody to hunt for him, and I cannot see how the poor old man can live, he has been a true servant to the government, and may perhaps still be if he lives to do well again. As the winter is coming on again, I think it would not be amiss to send him a few blankets or matchcoats and a little powder and lead; if the government would be pleased to do it, and you could send it up soon, I would send my sons with it to Shamokin before the cold weather comes."

The council immediately ordered that a present to the value of six pounds be sent at once to Shikellamy by Weiser's sons.

In the same letter, Weiser again expresses himself upon the Ohio affair. "It is my humble opinion that the Presents intended for the Indians on the Ohio River should be larger. If that what George Croghan is to take with him is intended for the Indians at Canayiahagon (on the south side of Lake Erie), the Indians at Ohio, our much nearer neighbors, should not be passed over without something."[18]

In July, when the council appealed to Weiser for his judgment upon the wisdom of making a present to the Indians on Lake Erie, the far-seeing interpreter replied, "that a small present ought to be made to the Indians on Lake Erie to acknowledge the receipt of theirs, it may be sent by some honest trader. I think George Croghan is fit to perform it. I always took him for an honest man and have as yet no reason to think otherwise of him."[19]

---

18. *Penna. Colonial Records.*, vol. V., pp. 138, 139.
19. *Penna. Archives*, vol. I., p. 762.

In November, after Weiser had been pondering for some time upon this western problem, he concluded that the important quarter for Pennsylvania to expend her energies is not in the Lake Erie region but at the forks of the Ohio. In this conclusion, Weiser's keen insight into the future marks him as the only man outside of the French who, up to that time, grasped that the Ohio basin would be the seat of the future struggle between the French and the English. Indeed, it is probable that Weiser was in advance of the keenest of the French leaders. Only after Weiser won this region for Pennsylvania did the French awaken to its real value, and Virginia became a jealous rival of the Keystone traders.

A few days after Weiser reported that he considered the Ohio Indians were equally or more worthy of a present than the tribes on Lake Erie, the provincial Secretary received a letter from George Croghan stating that his wagon was in Philadelphia waiting to carry the goods to the Lake Erie Indians. The council then decided that since they had not found a suitable man to accompany Croghan, the goods should be taken no further than John Harris' Ferry. James Logan was instructed to direct Croghan to hold them there until he received further orders. And Secretary Peters was directed "to dispatch an express forthwith to Mr. Weiser to let him know that the goods are sent there. . . . And that the council will proceed no further without consulting him, and as the season was far advanced they desired he would not fail to come and attend the board as soon as possible."[20] This virtually placed these Ohio negotiations entirely in the hands of Conrad Weiser.

Three days later, Secretary Peters informed the council that he had heard from Weiser and would be in Philadelphia in a few days. He sent a letter with the messenger saying that in Lancaster, he had met ten of these Ohio Indians who were on their way to Philadelphia. And Weiser promised that he would arrive as soon as they.

On November the 13th, Weiser and these Ohio Indians were called before the council. Their leader addressed himself not only to the governor of Pennsylvania but also to the governor of New York.

"We who speak to you," he said, "are warriors living at Ohio and address you on behalf of ourselves and the rest of the warriors of the Six Nations."

After explaining the cause of their coming and alluding to the ancient friendship existing between the Six Nations and English, and after reviewing the stand taken by the Iroquois for neutrality, he called attention to the fact that he represented warring and hunting tribes of the Ohio Valley living in alliance with the Six Nations, that the young men could no longer remain neutral.

---

20. *Penna. Colonial Records*, vol. V., p. 139.

We, the young Indians, the warriors, and captains, have consulted together and resolved to take up the hatchet against the will of our old people. We will lay aside the counsel of our old people as of no use except in time of peace. We have done this only after repeated applications from our brethren, the English. And we are now come to tell you that the French have hard heads and that we have nothing strong enough to break them with. We have only little sticks and hickories and such things that will do little or no service against the hard heads of the French.

They then asked for better guns and a supply of powder and lead, saying,

when once we, the young warriors, engaged, we put a great deal of fire under our kettle, and the kettle boiled high, and so it does still (meaning that they carried the war on briskly), that the Frenchmen's heads might soon be boiled; but when we looked about us to see how it was with the English kettle, we saw the fire was almost out, and that it had hardly boiled at all, and that no Frenchmen's heads were like to be in it. This truly surprises us, and we are come down on purpose to know the reason of it. How came it to pass that the English, who brought us into the war, will not fight themselves? This is not a good appearance, and therefore we give you this string of wampum to hearten and encourage you to desire that you would put more fire under your kettle.[21]

The council members decided that before a reply could be framed to this speech, it would be necessary to learn from Conrad Weiser "the particular history of these Indians, their real disposition towards us, and their future designs." Weiser was called before the council. He told them that the Indians had only told a portion of their mission and would see what he could learn from them in conversation.

The council also believed it would be best to find out James Logan's sentiments on this subject. Since Logan had previously retired from the council, Richard Peters and Conrad Weiser were appointed to wait on him. In two days, Weiser came before the council with a policy. His purposes were clearly defined. He told the council that,

---

21. *Penna. Colonial Records*, vol. V., p. 147.

Last summer, the governor of Canada had sent the hatchet to the Indians about the lakes and on branches of the Ohio; that one nation took it up; and that these Indians and the Indians in those quarters, consisting principally of warriors, being afraid others would do the like, to prevent this took up the English hatchet and proclaimed war against the French, which had a good effect, no more daring after this to meddle with the French hatchet. That these Indians on Ohio had concluded to kindle a Fire[22] in their town and had invited all the Indians to a considerable distance around about them to come to their fire in the spring and that they had consented to it.

Weiser also declared that these Ohio Indians numbered five hundred warriors "and as many allies more numerous than themselves. That it was always the custom in wartime to put the management into the hands of the young people and that it would be of the most pernicious consequences at this time if the council did not approve the action of these Indians in taking up the hatchet in the English interests and encourage them in their work." Weiser went further and told the council that "he thought Providence had furnished this province with a fine opportunity of making all the Indians about the lakes their friends, and warm friends too."

The council then asked Weiser what kind of a present he thought should be made to these Indians. He replied,

> that the value of one hundred pounds would appear but small, that they should have as much given them at least, and half as much to the Canayiahaga Indians; not that this was by any means sufficient, but would be a good salutation present, and preparatory to a larger, to be sent in the summer. This he judged necessary to be done, and that they should be told of the future present. And tho' he had never been in those parts, yet he judged the attaching these Indians and their friends to the English cause to be so necessary that he would, if the council pleased, and his health should permit, go with the present himself, and see with his own eyes, what number of Indians were there, and in what disposition.

Weiser also reported that in consultation with James Logan, they had outlined a reply to be made to the Indians. The council caused this to be read, and

---

22. A council.

after a few unimportant changes, it was considered suitable to be presented to the Indians. The reply complimented them for listening to the English and for the ready concurrence of their allies.

"You live," said the speaker, "in small tribes at a distance from one another. Separate, you will be easily overcome; united, it will be difficult, if not impossible, to hurt you. Like the strings on which you put your wampum, a single thread is soon snapped, but if you weave them into a belt and fasten them tight together, it must be a strong hand that can break it. We are pleased to hear that the pressing instances of the governor of New York and New England, you have taken up the hatchet against the French, who you know, notwithstanding their fair speeches, have been, from the beginning, your inveterate enemies. And in confirmation that we approve of what you have done, we give you this belt. In reference to the English kettle not boiling, you gave your wampum string to all the governors; therefore, we must send it to the other provinces before we can reply. But to lessen your concern on this account, we are to apprize you that the French were sending large forces in big ships, well-armed with great cannon over the seas to Canada, that the English pursued them, attacked them, took their men-of-war, killed a number of their men and carried the rest prisoners to England. This victory put a stop for the present to the expedition intended against Canada. You are, therefore, not to judge by the appearance things make now that the English Fire is going out but that this is only accidental, and it will soon blaze again."[23]

The Indians were then told of the warm friendship "the sons of Onas" had for them, and a present worth over one hundred and forty-eight pounds was waiting for the Ohio Indians at John Harris' Ferry. Also, a present worth over forty-six pounds was there for the Lake Erie Indians. The Indians were highly delighted with their treatment and danced the war dance as evidence of their approbation. The Lake Erie Indians never knew that Conrad Weiser divided the two hundred pounds voted as a present to them, giving the Ohio Indians three parts and leaving one part to them. By this movement, Conrad Weiser set on foot negotiations, giving Pennsylvania a fur trade monopoly as far west as the Mississippi River. He went with these Indians to John Harris' Ferry and distributed the goods. At the same time, the council promptly began arranging for the expedition in the spring.

The president and council sent a message to the Assembly, saying:

> Gentlemen:—You will see by the papers which are ordered to be laid before you that we have had a treaty with some Indian warriors from

---
23. *Penna. Colonial Records*, vol. V., pp. 149, 150.

Ohio, who came to town for that purpose. By them, we are given to understand that this tribe of Indians, being a mixture of the Six Nations, to whom these warriors belong, have actually resolved to adhere to their brethren, the English, against the French and propose to kindle a great Fire at Ohio in the spring, to which they have invited the Indians living around about them to join with them in these resolutions. This is an extraordinary event in our favor, which ought to be improved to the greatest advantage. From the situation of these people, being mostly within the limits of this government, they are capable of doing or preventing the greatest mischiefs; and from what passed at conversation between them and the interpreter, there is reason to apprehend that without encouragement from this province they may be seduced by the French to go over to their side, whereby the lives of the back inhabitants will be in the utmost danger. These considerations have induced us to give them the goods mentioned ill the account delivered you herewith and to promise to send the interpreter with a larger present to their Fire at Ohio in the spring. You will therefore take care at this session to come to such resolves as will enable us to make good our engagements.[24]

Several weeks elapsed before the Assembly came to any conclusion on this matter. Most members vigorously opposed bribes to persuade the Indians into war against the French. Moreover, there was a growing difference between the council and the Assembly about raising money for the war. The Assembly was willing to add to the five thousand pounds already voted for the King's use any necessary sum provided it could be raised by issuing bills of credit. The President of the Council refused to sanction any such measure, saying that his instructions forbade him from signing any acts providing for the issue of bills of credit. This difficulty very much embarrassed the Assembly in providing funds for encouraging the Ohio Indians in their warlike schemes against the French.

While the Assembly was vainly trying to frame a measure that would provide for these Indians, Conrad Weiser sent a letter to the council telling how well pleased Shikellamy was with the present that had been sent to him. Shikellamy, it appears, heartily approved of Weiser's schemes with the Western Indians. He told of the Twightwees, the Janontady Havas (Juniata Ohios), and other tribes who had made war with the French, having "seized all the French goods they could meet with" and having killed several French traders they sent

24. *Penna. Colonial Records*, vol. V., pp. 156, 157.

others stripped and naked to their father Onontio to acquaint him "that his children the Indians were angry with him."

Weiser also reported that two strong nations of French Indians, living west of the Great Lakes, were on their way during the past summer to attack the frontier inhabitants but were turned back by the Twightwees, who told them that such an attack would be equivalent to declaring war with the Six Nations and their allies. It was well known to Weiser that all such information was valuable in securing the appropriation bill from the Assembly.

On November 28, 1747, Weiser reported that he had accompanied the Ohio Indians on their homeward journey as far as "Paxton," where the goods that had been sent on were divided among them. "This day," said Weiser, "I delivered the goods to them, and they were well pleased for my adding two half barrels of powder to the four which they were to have. George Croghan was present and undertook to find men and horses to carry the powder and lead, with two casks of liquor, for them to Ohio. I was obliged to allow them the liquor because they all followed my advice and did not get drunk, neither in town nor by the way."

The Assembly adjourned and took no action upon the Ohio Indian appropriation. Finally, during the next session of the House, John Kinsey, the Speaker, sent a message to the council saying the importance of our alliance with the Western Indians, which we observe from the treaty, depends very much upon their own report of themselves.

> However, as they are a part of the Six Nations, who very probably in these calamitous times are often in want of necessaries to acquire their livelihood, we approve of the present you have thought fit to make them and also of the account you have sent the Six Nations of a larger present intended for them in the spring; and we shall take the care which is necessary to enable you to fulfill that engagement. Permit us, however, to add that we think it will be necessary to press their union among themselves and that they will do well to have due regard to the opinions of their old and experienced men; whose advice from the account they give seems to have been laid aside; most of us, you are sensible, are men of peaceable principles, and the presents we give (and those formerly given on behalf of this government, so far as we understand), were to supply them with necessaries toward acquiring a livelihood and to cultivate friendship between us, and not to encourage their entering into war. This we think most for the

King's interest and the peace and safety of his colonies in America; it being well known that wars once begun amongst them are not to be ended without great difficulty and are attended with so much bloodshed and cruelty as usually excite revenge and like inhumanity from the Indians in the French interest against those in amity with us, and against others, the King's subjects. We observe from Conrad Weiser's letter, which you were pleased to order to be laid before us, the Indians continue their complaints of the injuries they have received by the carrying of rum amongst them, and we, therefore, hope you will endeavor to prevent this for the future by directing the laws provided against this abuse, duly put in execution.[25]

The council was now at liberty to go on with its plan. President Palmer wrote at once to the governors of Virginia and Maryland, telling them how important an alliance with the Western Indians was and urging the necessity of these colonies' making a considerable addition to the present, which was to be sent to Ohio in the spring. And to see that this present was delivered, Palmer invited each colony to send commissioners with Conrad Weiser to Logstown. Maryland gave no attention to the appeal, it having been reported that she had no more money to spend on Indian affairs. Governor Gooch of Virginia was in hearty sympathy with the suggestion and urged his Legislature to make an appropriation for the same.[26] The council was exceedingly anxious to send a large present worth at least a thousand pounds into Ohio as early in the spring as possible. Promptness was urged to anticipate the French. The Virginia Legislature already contained members who were entertaining growing jealousy of the Pennsylvania fur trade, and they feared that Virginia might lose a portion of her Western claims if she assisted Pennsylvania in holding a treaty with Ohio Indians; consequently, they declined to appoint commissioners. Governor Gooch, however, sent word that he would furnish whatever sum Pennsylvania thought necessary.

The president and council, influenced by Conrad Weiser and the Assembly, concluded to issue a proclamation against the Indian rum traffic and have Conrad Weiser take it with him to Ohio and thus see if the sale of rum to the Indians could not be confined to the licensed traders. This proclamation provided that any unlicensed person found carrying more than one gallon of rum among the Indians should forfeit said liquor, and even Indians were empowered to stave the casks and destroy the rum when they found it.

---

25. *Penna. Colonial Records*, vol. V., pp. 184, 185.
26. *Penna. Colonial Records*, vol. V., p. 222.

By the middle of February, Conrad Weiser was called before the council to assist in selecting goods to be sent to Ohio. It was decided to furnish one ton of lead, eighteen barrels of powder, forty guns, and the other usual merchandise to the value of eight hundred and twenty-eight pounds, eight shillings, and one-half pence. Over twenty-two more pounds were considered necessary to pay the cost of transportation, in which a list of expenses, a trunk, and a hammock were set apart for the use of Conrad Weiser. All arrangements now appeared to be made for the expedition, which only awaited the opening of the spring season. But during the winter, unforeseen difficulties had been brewing. Doubtless, they started among the Iroquois, who would most naturally feel jealous of the Ohio Indians treating directly with Pennsylvania. The Six Nations' policy was that all tributary nations should affect their negotiations through them. Before spring, Shikellamy developed a determined opposition to Conrad Weiser's Western journey. He came down to see him early in March and arranged things to delay the interpreter's departure for Ohio. He soon convinced Weiser that nothing material would come from the Ohio mission. Since Shikellamy had always been the source of all of Weiser's information about Indian affairs, it is easy to understand why this change of attitude would strongly influence Weiser. Shikellamy insisted that these Western Indians had not gone to war against the French and could not do this without the permission of the Six Nations since they were subjects of the Confederacy. Therefore, he saw no reason for the expedition and declined Weiser's invitation to accompany him. Shikellamy went still further and said that at the Great Council Fire of the Six Nations, it was decided to send deputies to Philadelphia early in the spring to fix upon a chief for the Delawares and other important business which would make it necessary for Weiser to attend since he was the official interpreter for the Six Nations as well as for Pennsylvania. Weiser hurried his son off to Philadelphia with this news and desired an immediate reply. "If the journey should be delayed or given over," he asked, "what must be said to the Indians by George Croghan? His own cargo is already gone, and he must follow in a few days. I will undertake to ride to George Croghan's, let things go as they will before he goes to the woods. I reckon he will be greatly disappointed, he having kept about twenty horses in readiness to carry the goods. I am ready to do whatever the president and council will be pleased to signifie to me."[27]

The council immediately called for Weiser's former letters, and since "there appeared to be an inconsistency between them and this present letter," it was decided to summon Conrad Weiser and Shikellamy before the council with all possible dispatch, the council not being able to come to any decision among

---

27. *Penna. Colonial Records*, vol. V., pp. 212, 213.

themselves. The Secretary in his letter said: "It is expected that neither of you will make any excuses nor the least delay, since not to come, or not to come forthwith, as the matters under consideration affect this province, and, indeed, all Indian nations in a very sensible manner, would be equally dangerous."[28]

With this summons, Richard Peters sent a letter to George Croghan, asking Conrad Weiser, by postscript, to add anything he thought necessary, "for I am sensible," wrote Peters, that "more may be said to him, and it will come better from you."

In Croghan's letter, he is told that the expedition must be delayed, "but he will be generously remunerated for any extra expense which it may occasion."

When Shikellamy with his son and Conrad Weiser arrived in Philadelphia in April 1748, the old Indian repeated the same story he told Weiser in the winter, insisting that Conrad must remain and act as interpreter when the Iroquois should come down. The council, therefore, decided to postpone the Ohio expedition until after the Six Nation deputies had accomplished their business at Philadelphia. This decision was the more easily reached since it was not yet known what Maryland and Virginia intended to do toward aiding in the expenses of the treaty.

Pennsylvania had now learned from Conrad Weiser that the Ohio Valley was a vast fur trading section capable of drawing rich tributary currents from the region around the Great Lakes. These reasons, more than any hope of allies, influenced Pennsylvania to secure the friendship of the Ohio Indians. If Maryland and Virginia should furnish no help, Pennsylvania could do it alone. If the Six Nations, through Shikellamy, should endeavor to persuade Conrad Weiser from the mission, Pennsylvania could go on with the treaty. Conrad Weiser was shrewd enough to see this, and to a man who loved a dollar as devotedly as he, this opportunity should not be lost nor his share of provincial patronage put in jeopardy. At that time, Weiser and Secretary Peters were both buying land with the money received from public service. These circumstances may explain why Weiser was not wholly a convert to the views of the Six Nations. In the previous autumn, he had defined the province's policy and created the appetite for the Western trade; he now held himself neutral. If the expedition fails or is entrusted to George Croghan, Weiser will have faithfully served the Six Nations. If the council insists upon delaying the mission and having Weiser conduct it, he will have served his State to his honor and profit. Whatever his motives, the interpreter kept his lips closed and permitted events to take their course. Six months earlier, his policy was in the active voice; now, it was in the passive.

---

28. *Penna. Colonial Records*, vol. V., p. 213.

X

The Ohio Mission

Croghan goes to Ohio—The Indians appreciate the Proclamation against the Selling of Rum—The Twightwees or Miami Indians are won over to the English—Weiser introduces Andrew Montour to the Council—The Twightwees at Lancaster—The Twightwees make a Speech—The Twightwees describe their Country—Flattering Prospects of increased Trade—Weiser starts for Ohio—Weiser received at Logstown—The Wyandot Indians won over to the English Cause—Weiser restores to Carolina her lost Prisoners—Weiser destroys the Traders' Rum Stores—The Indians at Logstown receive their Presents—Results of the Logstown Treaty—Organization of the Ohio Company—Results of this Organization.

THE council of Pennsylvania decided to send George Croghan to the Ohio country early in the spring of 1748 with presents to the value of two hundred pounds, which was to be an earnest of a more valuable present to be sent later in the summer by Conrad Weiser. Croghan went out in April. He told the Indians assembled in council that he was sent by the president and council at Philadelphia "to return . . . thanks for the French sculp you sent down last spring." He then told them of the great present that Mr. Weiser would bring them in the summer. After distributing the goods, he read the proclamation against rum selling among them. The Indians expressed their thanks for the presents and rejoiced over the coming of Conrad Weiser especially, saying that he could not come in a more suitable time since a number of their tribes would be in from the hunt and very destitute of ammunition.

"You tell us," they said, "that you have put a stop to the traders carrying out strong liquors, which we approve of very well, for we have suffered considerable from such abuses—for there is many people who bring nothing else but liquor, and so cheats us of our skins, and many of our people have lost their lives. But brothers, we have one thing to acquaint you with, and that is there is a great nation of Indians come from the French to be your brothers as well as ours, who say they never tasted English rum yet but would be very glad to taste it now, as they are come to live with the English, so we hope you will order some of your traders to bring them some, for which request we send you this string of wampum."[1]

These Indians who were said never to have tasted English rum were the Twightwees, whose hunting and trapping grounds extended to the Mississippi River. They had been allies of the French, but when they heard of Conrad Weiser and the big Pennsylvania present, they became interested in the English. The Twightwees realized by experience that the French fur market was very poor in sections with no rivalry. They had heard of the Six Nations and their profitable conferences held in Pennsylvania. Accordingly, with characteristic Indian business enterprise, they sent word that their deputies were coming eastward with the hope of kindling a Council Fire at Lancaster. Conrad Weiser urged that a delegation be sent at once to meet these Indians and conduct them to Lancaster.

Weiser then presented Andrew Montour to the council and recommended him as a "person who might be of service to the province in quality of Indian interpreter and messenger . . . Andrew Montour was the son of the celebrated French woman, Madame Montour, who married an Iroquois chief. Andrew was a prominent man among the Delawares and sufficiently familiar with English to serve well as an interpreter.

For some years, there had been jealousy and bad feeling between Weiser and Montour, growing out of Andrew's efforts to secure the position of the interpreter for Virginia in her negotiations with the Six Nations. Now, however, when Weiser realized the necessity of having a man like Montour to secure the alliance of the Indians in the Ohio Valley, all past differences were healed. He was invited to Weiser's house and handsomely entertained. Weiser ceased writing letters to Secretary Peters complaining of him and his crafty methods. In introducing Montour to the council, Weiser said that he had frequently employed him in numerous affairs of importance and had "found him faithful, knowing, and prudent." During the previous winter, Weiser had sent Montour to Ohio and Lake Erie, desiring him "to observe what passed among the Indians" and gather what they said when the deputies returned from Pennsylvania.

---

1. *Penna. Colonial Records*, vol. V., p. 289.

This was Weiser's method of preparing himself for a mission into strange lands. He then recommended the council remunerate Andrew for his journey. This was promptly and cheerfully done.

Montour was directed to go to the woods and meet the Twightwees' deputies and, if possible, persuade them to come to Philadelphia. He was not to press this last point should the Indians be unfavorable. And in no case was Andrew to fail to send word to Conrad Weiser about the number of Indians, their purpose, etc. When Andrew met the Ohio Indians, he found persuading them to come to Philadelphia impossible. They were sure that the city was "sickly" and were determined to hold their conference at Lancaster. The council discussed this for a long time, but finally, it was decided to appoint four commissioners[2] to meet the Indians. Andrew Montour was the interpreter for the Western Indians and Conrad Weiser for the Six Nations. Scaroyady, an Oneida chief living on the Ohio, and exercising for the Six Nations jurisdiction over the Western tribes similar to that held by Shikellamy in Pennsylvania, was to have been their speaker on this occasion but was disabled by a fall. Andrew Montour then became a speaker for the Western Indians.

They said they came from the banks of the "Ouebach (Wabash), a great river running into the Ohio . . . last fall." Pennsylvania sent "a message addressed to all the tribes of Indians at Ohio and elsewhere in amity with the English, which the Six Nations' hunting tribes delivered to the Shawanese, and by them, given to us. Since you have opened the door for us, we are glad to come to you and grasp firmly the chain of friendship, praying that it may never grow dull and that the road between us and you may never grow over with briers. We have not come to this conclusion hastily. We thought many nights and days of this affair. We weighed everything well before we took the resolution of seeking your friendship. We repeat it; our request does not come from the mouth only; no, it comes from the heart.[3] This is what we said last winter to the Ohio Indians, we say it now to you, and in confirmation thereof, we now present you these thirty beaver skins."

A calumet pipe with a "long stem curiously wrought and wrapped round with wampum of several colors" was then filled with tobacco and smoked by the Indians and commissioners. A peace treaty was drawn up with the Twightwees on the condition that they would have no more communication with the French. An exchange of presents then took place. Pennsylvania gave the Indians goods to the value of one hundred and eighty-nine pounds and eight pence.

---

2. Benjamin Shoemaker, Joseph Turner, Thomas Hopkinson, William Logan.
3. *Penna. Colonial Records*, vol. V., p. 309.

The Indians gave the commissioners: "White wampum worth 1 pound, 4s; fifty-five pounds of beaver skins worth 22 pounds; seven and one-half pounds of ordinary beaver, worth 2 pounds, 5s.; forty-one deer skins, worth 7 pounds, 17s., 8d.; fifteen dressed leather skins, worth 5 pounds, 16s." This was deducted from the cost of the treaty, making the net expense amount 149 pounds, 18s.

The Twightwee chief then took a piece of chalk and drew the courses of the Ohio and Mississippi Rivers on the courthouse floor, marking the Ouebach (Wabash). They represented this river as rising in a little lake "at a small distance from the west end of Lake Erie, from which it runs southwesterly four or five hundred miles and falls into the Ohio about three hundred miles from the Mississippi." On this river and another called the Hatchet, the Twightwees located twenty Indian towns where they claimed they had one thousand fighting men. The Twightwees also located two French forts on the Mississippi River "whereby it is manifest," write the commissioners, "that if these Indians and their allies prove faithful to the English, the French will be deprived of the most convenient and nearest communication with their forts on the Mississippi, the ready road lying through their nations, and that there will be nothing to interrupt an intercourse between this province and that great river."[4]

At the close of the treaty, the Twightwees said that they had brought along a few skins to begin trade. They requested the commissioners to order the traders to put fewer stones in their scales so that the skins might weigh more. They promised that if the prices for furs were good, it would encourage them and other tribes to trade more generally with the Pennsylvania traders. In writing to the proprietary in England of this treaty, the council said, "we hope it will be productive of considerable advantages to the people of this province by enlarging our Indian trade and extending our friendship to Indians hitherto unknown to us."[5]

Before the Twightwees departed from Lancaster, they were told by the commissioners that there was a prospect of peace between England and France. To this important statement, the Indians made no answer. The value of this new relationship with the Twightwees was pretty generally appreciated. The governor wrote to the Assembly that such an alliance would not only enlarge the Indian trade but would seriously interrupt the communications of the French, in Quebec, with their settlements on the Mississippi River; since the Twightwees' town lies on the route followed by the French in going from the lake country to New Orleans.

---

4. *Penna. Colonial Records*, vol. V., p. 315.
5. *Penna. Colonial Records*, vol. V., p. 322.

On the 11th of August 1748, Conrad Weiser started his journey to the Ohio. His route lay from Tulpehocken to James Galbreath's and George Croghan's, at which places he found lodgings. After the third day out, Weiser camped at night in the woods and slept in the hammock he had provided. In his declining years, the province had made this purchase to protect Weiser from cold and exposure incidental to lying on the ground at night. The Tuscarora Path and the Black Log Sleeping Place marked the trail which guided Weiser's party to the Juniata River, where they camped two miles below Standing Stone (Huntingdon), called by the Indians "Onojutta Haga," meaning standing stone people.

At Frankstown, they overtook Croghan and his train of pack horses laden with the Indian presents.

Leaving Frankstown, where Weiser remarked that he saw neither a house nor a cabin, they crossed the mountains to "Clearfields."

After traveling one hundred and eight miles from Frankstown, they crossed the Kiskiminitas Creek and came to what was then called the Ohio River, now known as the Allegheny. They hired a canoe for 1000 of black wampum and, leaving their horses, paddled down the river.

At the different Indian villages, they were received with sincere joy. Guns were fired, and feasts were spread. They reached Logstown on the evening of August 27th and were greeted by firing one hundred guns. This Indian village, with its corn fields on the opposite side of the river, was eighteen to nineteen miles from the forks of the Ohio. It stood on the land now the property of the Harmony Society, at Economy, a short distance below the town, on the north bank of the river.

That evening all the old and wise men among the Indians met and shook hands with Weiser. Arrangements were also made to send boats to Chartier's Old Town, where the horses were left and get the goods.

While waiting for the present to arrive, Weiser visited some neighboring Indian towns and gathered the current news of the clay. The Indians of Coscosky wanted the council held there instead of in Logstown. Weiser told them that last spring, when they feared that their corn crop was going to be small, they desired that the council might be held at Logstown, but now since the crop was large, they wanted to change the location of the council. Weiser insisted that they must stand by their word, especially since the notice had been given out at Lancaster, and the other tribes would be offended if the seat of the council was changed.

The secret of Weiser's success with the Indians was a desire to furnish them with a reason for the things he wanted and what he denied them. Now that we find him a stranger among strange Indians, we can better examine the fertility of his resources. Not being a trader, the Indians realized that he had no mercenary motives and imposed large confidence in his words. Weiser thoroughly knew the things which pleased the heart of an Indian. On the day when the deputies from the distant nations were expected, he caused the English flag to be raised upon a long pole and the King's health to be drunk by all the Indians and white men present. Towards evening, while the deputies in a long delegation were arriving, all the Indians and traders in the town kept a constant firing of salutes. To what extent these festivities were the cause of Weiser's severe attack of colic that night is not known. For several days he was confined to his couch and was visited by the leading chiefs, who were very concerned about his recovery.

Various rumors of an Indian war with the French were afloat. When Weiser sent his secret agent, Andrew Montour, to inquire into the truth of this report, he found that it was without foundation. The Wyandots, a powerful group of Indian tribes, at one time in the French interest, and recently avowed friends of the English, were reported to Weiser as weakening in their new resolution and inclined to return to the French. These Wyandots, said Weiser, were called Ionontady Hagas and were an exceedingly influential body of Indians. He at once called a council of their chiefs and asked them why they had left the French. They replied that it arose from their hard usage. The French had treated their young men in the wars as they would slaves. And for some years, French goods had been so dear that the Indians could not buy them. They further said that all the Wyandot tribes were dissatisfied with the neutral action of the Six Nations and desired that they would take a decided stand against the French. They reported a treaty having been made over fifty years previous with the governor of New York, showing in confirmation thereof a large belt of wampum, which they believed had been sent to them by "the Great King across the water"; Weiser describes this belt as follows: It "was 25 grains wide and 265 long, very curiously wrought; there were seven images of men holding one another by the hand, the first signifying the governor of New York (or rather as they said the King of Great Britain); the second, the Mohawks; the third, the Oneidas; the fourth, the Cayugas: the fifth, the Onondagas; the sixth, the Senecas; the seventh, the Owandaets [Wyandots] and two rows of black wampum under their feet, thro' the whole length of the belt to signify the road from Albany thro' the Five Nations to the Owendaets." Weiser gave these Indians some tobacco and whiskey and made them the warm friends of the English.

A few days after Weiser had left Berks County upon this mission, the governor of Pennsylvania received word from Governor Gooch of Virginia that

Governor Glenn of South Carolina had informed him that sometime in July, a party of Northern Indians had been on a war excursion against the Catawbas, and had carried off a white man, Mr. Haig, and his servant. Haig, it appears, was a captain of the militia and a justice of the peace, a much-valued man among the German inhabitants. When this news reached Governor Thomas, a dispatch was sent to overtake Conrad Weiser and place the solution to the affair in his hands.

While Weiser was firing salutes and treating the Indians at Logstown, his secret agents were not idle, and they learned that the Seneca Indians were responsible for this crime. Weiser immediately held a council with the Seneca chiefs on the Ohio and, after charging them with the deed, demanded the return of Mr. Haig. The Senecas took three days for consideration. Weiser was well aware that of all the nations of the United Confederacy, the Senecas were closest to the French interests and their cause, and to call these proud warriors to account for their misdeeds was dangerous. During these three days, the emissaries of the Pennsylvania interpreter were vigilant. How they accomplished their work is not known. But Weiser secured the Seneca influence on the Ohio for the English cause. After three days, the chiefs told him that the woods were full of evil spirits, and they gave him a belt of wampum "to clear his eyes and mind and remove all bitterness of spirit."

Their speaker then reviewed the ancient friendship of the Six Nations for the English and finally brought his discourse to the capture of Mr. Haig.

"We are very sorry," he said, "that at your coming here, we are obliged to talk of the accident that lately befell you in Carolina, where some of our warriors, by the instigation of the Evil Spirit, struck their hatchet into our own body like, for our brethren, the English and we are of one body, and what was done we utterly abhor as a thing done by the Evil Spirit himself. We never expected any of our people would ever do so to our brethren. We, therefore, remove our hatchet, which by the influence of the Evil Spirit was struck into your body, and we desire that our brethren, the governor of New York and Onas, may use their utmost endeavors that the thing may be buried in the bottomless pit that it may never be seen again, that the chain of friendship which is of so long standing may be preserved bright and unhurt."

The Indians then gave Weiser a belt of wampum and, taking up another which was almost black, said, "Brethren, as we have removed our hatchet out of your body, or properly out of our own. We now desire that the air may be cleared tip again, and the wound given may be healed, and everything put in good understanding, as it was before, and we desire that you will assist us in making up everything with the governor of Carolina. The man that has been brought as a prisoner we now deliver up to you; he is yours."

The speaker then laid down his wampum and, taking the prisoner by the hand, delivered him to Conrad Weiser. Some time afterward, it was discovered that the prisoner was one Brown, the servant to Mr. Haig and that the Indians had murdered the master. Nothing further was done since Weiser was informed that there were certain English traders among the Catawba Indians who not infrequently betrayed the position of the Iroquois to the Catawbas, and for this reason, the Iroquois warriors were prone to take revenge.

During the delay occasioned by the tardy arrival of the goods, Weiser was very much annoyed by a Maryland trader who appeared with thirty gallons of whiskey and opened a profitable business. Weiser tried to persuade him to desist and hide the liquor in the woods. The trader was not to be put off but pushed his trade briskly. Of course, this was an injury to Croghan, who felt that he was the only trader who should be allowed to sell at that time. Furthermore, Croghan was a licensed trader, while Nolan was a "detested Marylander." Accordingly, Weiser and Croghan availed themselves of the laws of Pennsylvania and staved Nolan's store of liquor.

After two weeks of embarrassing delay, the presents finally arrived. Weiser called a full council and repeated all that had transpired at the recent treaty at Lancaster. The goods were laid out before the eyes of the Indians in five piles. One pile, Weiser told them, was sent by the governor of Virginia. He continued that these goods have been sent to you so that the chain of friendship may be made bright.

> A French peace is a very uncertain one; they keep it no longer than their interests permit.... The French King's people have been almost starved in old France for want of provisions, which has made them wish and seek for peace; but our wise people are of opinion that after their bellies are full, they will quarrel again and raise another war. All nations in Europe know that their friendship is mixed with poison, and many who trusted too much on their friendship have been ruined.

The goods were then uncovered, and the Indians were given to understand that they were all for them. Weiser then complimented these Western Indians on their location and avocation, saying they came here for hunting.

Our traders followed you at your invitation. Since then, some of your young men have robbed our traders. You, no doubt, have lived here long enough to have some wise men among you who will control your conduct in the future, that you may be more upright than in the past when only a few hunters lived here. You have recently made loud complaints about the traders who carry rum among you. You ask that it may be stopped. I will read you the laws made by the governor and wise men of Pennsylvania, but it seems to me that it is not in your white brethren's power to stop this trade entirely. You send down your skins by the traders to buy rum for you. You go yourselves and fetch horseloads of strong liquor. Only the other day, an Indian came to this town out of Maryland with three horseloads of liquor, so it appears you love it so well that you cannot be without it. You know very well that the country near the Endless Mountains (Blue Mountains) affords strong liquor, and the moment the traders buy it, they are gone out of the inhabitants and are traveling to this place without being discovered; besides this, you never agree about it—one will have it, the other won't (tho' very few), a third said he will have it cheaper; this last we believe is spoken from your hearts (here they laughed). Your brethren, therefore, have ordered that every _____ of whiskey shall be sold to you for five bucks in your town, and if a trader offers to sell whiskey to you and will not let you have it at that price, you may take it from him and drink it for nothing.[6]

Before distributing the goods, Weiser called up a trader saying, here is a sober, honest man whom you have "robbed of the value of three hundred bucks, and you all know by whom. Let, therefore, satisfaction be made to the trader."

The five piles of goods were distributed as follows, one pile to the Seneca nation, which was very powerful in that region; the second pile to the remaining nations of the Iroquois Confederacy, not including the Tuscaroras. The third pile was given to the Delaware Indians. A fourth pile to the Shawanese tribes, and the fifth and sixth piles to the Wyandots and other extremely Western tribes.

The Indians seemed very thankful for these presents, saying through their speaker, "Our brethren (the white men) have indeed tied our hearts to theirs. We at present can but return thanks with an empty hand till another opportunity

---

6. *Penna. Colonial Records*, vol. V., p. 357.

serves to do it sufficiently. We must call a great council and do everything regularly; in the meantime, look upon us as your true brothers."

After giving a few individual presents, Weiser hurried home.

This treaty left Pennsylvania in possession of the Indian trade from Logstown to the Mississippi River and from the Ohio to the Michigan region. The unorganized condition of the English fur trade put the colonists at a great disadvantage compared with the French. The success of Weiser's Ohio negotiations opened up new and exceedingly profitable lines of trade.

Although Maryland refused to furnish any aid toward the expense of the Logstown treaty, her traders were now eager to avail themselves of the profits resulting from the recently developed opportunities. Accordingly, many Maryland traders pushed into Logstown and the Ohio country. Virginia, on the other hand, had paid for one-fifth of the presents, and when she fully realized that trade on the Ohio was safe, that Conrad Weiser and Pennsylvania enterprise had unlocked a mine of wealth, she became aware of new values belonging to these Ohio lands.

The Logstown treaty aroused Virginia's jealousy of the professed boundaries of Pennsylvania. It was claimed that the Ohio Valley was a part of Virginia by virtue of the King's charter and certain explorations made in the Shenandoah Valley by Governor Spottswood in 1723. Moreover, this region had been bought from the Iroquois Indians at the Lancaster Treaty in 1744. Did not the deed say, "extending west to the setting sun"? Did not Pennsylvania hear this and enter no protest? Therefore, reasoned Virginia, these lands are ours.

About the time that Virginia paid one-fifth of the expense of this treaty and her council read the report of Conrad Weiser, Thomas Lee, a member of the King's council in Virginia, conceived the idea of organizing a land company to be known as the Ohio Company. It was represented to the English Board of Trade that there were no English residents in those regions.

"A few traders," wrote Lee, wander "from tribe to tribe and dwell among the Indians, but they neither cultivate nor occupy the land." Thomas Lee then proposed organizing for settlement. He accordingly associated himself with twelve other persons in Virginia and Maryland, of whom Lawrence and Augustine Washington were two. With the aid of Mr. Mamburg, a London merchant, the Ohio Company was put into operation. The King of England approved their petition and granted them 500,000 acres of land on the south side of the Ohio River, between the mouth of the Monongahela and the Kanawha Rivers. The company, however, held the privilege of occupying lands north of the Ohio River if found desirable. Two hundred thousand acres were to be selected at once and held for ten years free from quit rents or any tax to the King, on condition that the company should, at its own expense, seat one hundred families on the land within seven years, and build a fort, and maintain a garrison sufficient to protect the settlement. Arrangements were made with Mr. Mamburg to send over goods valued at four thousand pounds for Indian trade. The first cargo was to arrive in November 1749 and the second in March 1750.

As a result of this movement, a vigorous and bitter rivalry sprang up among the English traders. All manner of stories were told to the Indians by the traders of Pennsylvania to prejudice them against the traders of Virginia and Maryland. The lack of organization was the weak spot in the English trade. Local contention and jealousy began destroying the fruit of what Conrad Weiser gained at Logstown in the summer of 1748.

On the other hand, the French used the peace of Aix-la-Chapelle to their advantage. With their system of trade thoroughly organized and controlled, they began a careful method of regaining the lost friendship of the Western Indians. No horde of rum traders and Indian debauchees were permitted to follow the regular French traders.

George Croghan wrote from Ohio in July 1749, recounting the rumors of the French intention to prevent English settlements on the Ohio. He tells of two Maryland traders who brought word to the Allegheny country that the Virginians would settle the following spring along the Youghiogheny and that their traders would furnish the Indians their goods cheaper than the Pennsylvania traders could. He informs that the Western Indians are averse to having any white people, especially the Virginians, settle west of the Allegheny Mountains. He realizes the distracted and divided state of Indian trade among the colonists, and since the French had, by Conrad Weiser's treaty, lost the Twightwee or Miami trade, Croghan insists that the French will spare no trouble and expense in their efforts to regain what had been lost during the war.

"No people," he wrote, "carries on ye Indian trade in so regular a manner as the French. I wish with all my heart ye government of this province would take some method to regulate ye Indian trade and to prevent many disorders which arise from ye carrying of Spirits in ye Indian Cuntrys."

Croghan had sent Andrew Montour to Lake Erie as a spy to learn if there were any French in that region and what their intentions were. "I make no doubt butt the French will make use of unfair methods to bring over all the Indians they can to their interests."

Croghan believed that the Indians were so well "grafted in ye English interests that they will not be easy deceived by the French." He offered to remain on the Ohio with Andrew Montour and keep the Indians true to the interest of Pennsylvania if such action should be found necessary.

Croghan's postscript describes a drunken spree among the Indians near his Carlisle farm at a still house, where one of the Indians was killed. "I cannot find out," he wrote, "whether he was killed by one of the Indians or by a white man. But I shall secure all the white men that was at the place till I find out ye truth of ye affair, and I will let you know more fully ye truth of ye matter. Butt, I think all stillers and tavernkeepers should be fined for making ye Indians drunk, and especially warriors."[7]

Thus, rumors of Indian outrages were increasing, and the temper of the frontier people was growing more sensitive. Adam Furney, of Conewago, west of the Susquehanna River, was shot by an intoxicated Indian. The native had been importuning Furney for more rum, and the trader persistently refused until the infuriated Indian shot him. This deed occurred very near the disputed boundary line. It was uncertain which province should apprehend the murderer. It was finally decided that Cumberland County, Pennsylvania, should administer justice. The "Indian was captured and lodged in jail to await his trial when contrary to all expectations, Furney recovered. It was then thought best to release the Indian. This act added to the excitement and prejudice of the frontier people.

The peace of Aix-la-Chapelle filled western Pennsylvania's forests with unlicensed traders eager to avail themselves of the protection offered by the Logstown treaty and reap profit from the uncontrolled appetite of the Indians. As a result, numberless outbreaks occurred, especially among those traders who drank with the Indians. These things made it difficult for the wise men among the Indians to restrain their voting men.

In addition to these troubles, the provinces which had borne the brunt and expense of the recent war were now anxious to reduce all Indian expenses to a minimum. Indeed, they were desirous of hearing no more of the Indians for some time. While the colonists were resting in this indifferent attitude, the French made renewed and well-planned schemes to regain all that had been lost during the war.

---

7. *Penna. Archives*, vol. II., pp. 32, 33.

XI

Turning the People Off

TROUBLE WITH THE JUNIATA SQUATTERS—TROUBLE ON THE SOUTHERN BORDER—THE IROQUOIS INTERCEDE FOR THE DELAWARE HUNTING GROUNDS—WEISER ASKS DAMAGES FOR INDIAN DEPREDATIONS—INDIAN INSOLENCE—THE DEATH OF SHIKELLAMY—WEISER EXPLAINS WHY THE SQUATTERS CAME—WEISER CLAIMS THAT THE INDIANS DEFY THE LAWS OF THE PROVINCE—THE SENECAS COMPLAIN TO GOVERNOR HAMILTON—THE GOVERNOR PROMISES TO DRIVE OFF THE SQUATTERS—A PROCLAMATION ISSUED—WEISER TOLD TO KEEP BACK THE INDIANS—A SECOND BLOODLESS INVASION—CANASSATEGO OFFERS TO SELL LAND—HAMILTON KEEPS HIS PROMISE WITH THE INDIANS—THE INDIANS GIVE ADVICE—WEISER AND THE MAGISTRATES SENT TO DRIVE OFF THE SQUATTERS—THEIR CABINS BURNED—WEISER ABANDONS THE UNDERTAKING—WHY DID WEISER WITHDRAW FROM THE PROJECT?—INVADING THE PATH VALLEY, THE BIG AND LITTLE COVES—THE CUMBERLAND COUNTY MAGISTRATES ABANDON THE ENTERPRISE.

THE white squatters west of the Susquehanna River had been causing trouble for thirty years. As early as 1721, the governor ordered the magistrates of Lancaster County to burn and destroy the squatters' cabins west of the Susquehanna. After the purchase of 1736, when all the land southeast of the Blue Mountains had been bought from the Indians, the squatters soon appeared beyond those mountains.

About 1740 or 1741, Frederick Star and two or three more Germans settled on the Juniata about twenty-five miles from its mouth. Probably these were the first settlers in the valley. The Delaware Indians reported this action of Star and his companions to the Six Nations' representative at Shamokin, and at the treaty of 1742, the Iroquois chiefs demanded that these settlers be "thrown over the Big Mountain." Governor Thomas promised to have them removed and immediately issued a proclamation to that effect. The following year, 1743, the governor's secretary was commissioned to remove these Juniata settlers, which was done.

While it was comparatively easy to drive a few German families out of the Juniata Valley, it was not so easy to dislodge the squatters whose rude cabins soon appeared in both the "Big and Little Cove" and in the "Big and Little Conolloways," all of which places were on or near the temporary and disputed boundary line between Maryland and Pennsylvania. Since the two governments were not then on good terms, the governor of Pennsylvania, in opposition to the strict orders of the proprietaries, who were then in England, deemed it more prudent not to molest the squatters. The Iroquois Indians then threatened to make war upon Maryland unless these intruders were removed. Conrad Weiser planned the Lancaster Treaty to avoid an open irruption, at which Maryland bought out the Iroquois claims within Lord Baltimore's jurisdiction. This transferred the responsibility for the squatters in the Coves and the Conolloways from Maryland to Pennsylvania. Since the boundary line was in dispute, the Six Nations agreed to suspend their action against these people until it could be determined in which province they were located. The war immediately followed, and during these years, the squatters increased rapidly because of the confusion in the executive matters of the province. Not only in the Coves and the Conolloways but on the Juniata and Sherman's Creek, numerous settlers appeared. Their cabins and patches of stump land spotted the trail to Allegheny. During this time, the nearest magistrates issued notices warning them of the danger and advising them to remove, or the laws of the province would be enforced. These things had no effect whatever.

After the treaty of Aix-la-Chapelle, the Delaware Indians complained loudly to the Six Nations, who at once determined to demand justice. On July 1st, 1749, deputies from the Senecas and Onondaga nations, with Indians from the tributary tribes, arrived in Philadelphia and requested an audience with the governor. These Indians said that at the Big Council Fire at Onondaga in the spring, it was decided by all the nations to send deputies to Philadelphia to return an answer concerning the peace between the Catawba and the Iroquois Indians and also to shake hands with the new Governor (Hamilton), whom they had heard had arrived from England. It was agreed at the council that the deputies should meet at Wyoming in May. These Indians said that they had been at the place of rendezvous for over a month waiting for the others, and when they could hear nothing from them, they were undecided whether to return or proceed to Philadelphia. Finally, it was decided for reasons to be explained during the conference to come and meet the governor. These Indians did not tell Governor Hamilton how they loitered along the way; how they stopped at Conrad Weiser's, and a number of the Tortuloes injured and destroyed a large amount of his property; they did not mention how Conrad Weiser expostulated and tried to influence them until he finally secured aid from the Senecas and drove them off.[1]

Governor Hamilton, writing to the Assembly of this affair, said that Conrad Weiser had spent sixty pounds defraying the expenses of these Indians to and from Philadelphia. "He must by this time have laid out a considerable sum more, which you will be pleased to order payment of; And tho' from your long knowledge of his merit, it might be unnecessary for me to say anything in his favor, yet as the last set of Indians did damage to his plantation, and he had abundance of trouble with them, & is likely to meet with much more on this occasion, I cannot excuse myself from most heartily recommending it to you to make him a handsome reward for his services."[2]

The Indians were more indifferent after the war and more fully realized their importance now that the English and French vied against each other for Indian alliances and Indian trade. Another cause of their insolence was, without doubt, the death of Shikellamy, which had but recently occurred. Weiser's solicitude for this Indian is indeed pathetic. As Shikellamy grew old and feeble, Conrad kept starvation from his door. Five years before his death, with eight young German carpenters, Weiser went to Shamokin and built a house for Shikellamy. During the autumn of 1747, he went to Shamokin and found the old chief very sick with a fever.

"He was hardly able," wrote Weiser, "to stretch forth his hand to bid me welcome. In the same condition was his wife; his three sons not quite so bad but very poorly. Also, one of his daughters and two or three of his grandchildren all had the fever. There were three buried out of the family a few days before, viz., Cajadis, Shikellamy's son-in-law, that had been married to his daughter above fifteen years, and reckoned the best hunter among all the Indians; also his eldest son's wife, and grandchild. Next morning, I administered the medicines to Shikellamy and one of his sons, under the direction of Dr. Groeme, which had a very good effect upon both. Next morning, I gave the same medicines to two more (who would not venture at first), it had the same effect, and the four

---

1. See manuscript letters of Conrad Weiser, in the collections of the Pennsylvania Historical Society, July 16, 1749.
2. *Penna. Colonial Records*, vol. V., p. 396.

persons thought themselves as good as recovered. But above all, Shikellamy was able to walk about with me, with a stick in his hand, before I left Shamokin."

During the winter of 1748-49, the scarcity of food in Shamokin overcame Shikellamy, and he died. Weiser went up early in the spring to condole with his sons, which he did to the extent of fifteen pounds worth of presents, which was charged to the account of the province. The death of this old Indian was a material loss to the country. Weiser's power over the Indians declined from that hour. Although he gave presents to Shikellamy's eldest son and urged him to take his father's place, the younger Shikellamy never did what his father did for Weiser.

Conrad sent a messenger to Onondaga apprising the council of what he had done for Shikellamy's sons. "There was a necessity for my so doing," he said. "The Indians were very uneasy about the white people settling beyond the Endless Mountains on Juniata, on Sherman's Creek, and elsewhere. They tell me that above thirty families are settled upon the Indians' land this spring, and daily more go to settling thereon. Some have settled almost to the head of Juniata River, along the path that leads to Ohio. The Indian said (and that with truth) that that country is only hunting ground for deer because further to the north, there was nothing but spruce woods and ground covered with palm bushes. Not a single deer could be found or killed there. They asked me very seriously whether their brother Onas had given the people leave to settle there. I informed them of the contrary and told them that I believe some of the Indians from Ohio that were down last summer had given liberty (with what right I could not tell) to settle. I told them of what passed on the Tuscarora Path last summer when the sheriff and three magistrates were sent to turn off the people there settled, and that I then perceived that the people were favored by some of the Indians above mentioned, by which means the orders of the governor came to no effect."

This reply of Conrad Weiser's satisfied the Indians at Shamokin for the present. They said they would let the matter rest until the chiefs of the Six Nations came down when they would hold a council. It must be remembered that when Conrad Weiser went to Ohio the previous summer, he had been instructed to "turn off the squatters," which he found in the Juniata Valley. Writing from the Tuscarora Path, August 15th, 1748, to Secretary Peters, he said, "The proclamation has this minute been read to the people, who for the most part (I believe every one), are willing to go off next spring, if not a more favorable order comes from the government. The Indians have desired me not to join to turn the people off until I come (return) from Ohio. I promised them I would not.... When the Indians here had been informed that the squatters were to be turned off by the government, and I suppose the people used the Indians well on their coming by and informed them of the design. . . . The Indians asked me about them, and desired that at least two families, to wit, Abraham Schlechl and another might stay; that they, the Indians had given them liberty, and that they thought it was in their power to give liberty to such as they liked."

Weiser represented the Juniata Indians as being partial to certain settlers and declared that it was not the fault of the magistrates or sheriff that the governor's orders had not been literally obeyed. While on his Logstown journey, Weiser was visibly influenced by the Juniata Indians and, with the above excuse, did not fulfill his instructions from Governor Hamilton about the squatters.

Such was the condition of affairs in the summer of 1749 when a portion of the Six Nation deputies opened their conference at Philadelphia. With considerable skill, a Seneca chief asked Governor Hamilton by what right the white people were building cabins on the Juniata. "The governor will be pleased to tell us," he said, "whether he brought any orders from the King or the proprietors for those people to settle on our lands, and if not, we earnestly pray that they may be made to remove instantly with all their effects. To prevent the sad consequences which will otherwise ensue and to enforce this request, we present you this belt of wampum."[3]

They then congratulated the province upon the arrival of Governor Hamilton and, with the usual apologies, presented him with a small bundle of skins "to make him a pair of shoes." Then, with genuine Seneca sincerity, they advised Governor Hamilton "to walk in the footsteps" of his predecessors who were "good and kind to the Indians."

"Do Brother," they said, "make it your study to consult the interests of our nations; as you have so large an authority, you can do us much good or harm; we would, therefore, engage your influence and affection for us."

When the Indians withdrew, the council consulted with John Kinsey, the Speaker of the Assembly, and agreed that a present of not less than one hundred pounds value should be given to the Indians. After two days of consultation, the governor's reply was agreed upon. He told the Indians that Pennsylvania stood bound by a treaty not to suffer any people to settle on the unpurchased lands. The proprietors have endeavored to observe this promise faithfully. Proclamations with the severest penalties have been sent to these people, and whenever any have been so audacious as to disobey these orders, "they have been forcibly removed, and their plantations broken up and destroyed." Governor Hamilton emphatically denied that he had ever received directions from the

---

3. *Penna. Colonial Records*, vol. V., p. 389.

GOVERNOR JAMES HAMILTON

King or proprietors to settle men on land beyond the Blue Mountains. He also promised to do all in his power to protect the interests of the Indians on the Juniata. After expressing* his sincere friendship for the Indians, the presents were distributed, and their guns were ordered to be mended. The Indians and their thieving retinue started home well pleased with their visit. The Assembly quietly paid the settlers for all damages sustained by these pilfering visitors.

The governor promptly issued a broadside and had it posted on the trees and public places along the frontier and the banks of the Juniata, warning all squatters to remove before November 1st, under penalty of the law. Hamilton went a step further and issued another proclamation against the unlicensed sale of rum to the Indians, under penalty of twenty pounds fine to be paid to the informers.

About a month after this, Conrad Weiser sent word to the governor that the deputies of the remaining tribes of the Iroquois were at Shamokin on their way to Philadelphia. Hamilton immediately sent an express to Conrad Weiser with directions to exert every possible means to divert these Indians from their purpose. The council and Assembly were by no means desirous of having another peaceful Indian invasion this summer. We are told Weiser did all he could to dissuade the Indians from their proposed visit, but this was resented with so much spirit that the patient and weary interpreter was obliged to turn his protests into invitations and make the best of circumstances. The Indians were not slow to remember the day when the authorities of Pennsylvania would have been only too willing to receive them. Indeed, they recalled the time when they had been bribed to come. Therefore, on they came "not only these deputies, but the Seneca delegates, and with them, Mohicans, Tortuloes, Delawares, and Nanticokes, amounting in number to two hundred and eighty."[4]

Canassatego was the speaker for this delegation. He had been spokesman at many treaties and was among the last of that group of Iroquois chiefs who entertained a personal friendship for Conrad Weiser. He was the last of the great Iroquois diplomats, who yielded not to the allurements of the white man's strong drink, who knew his people and could hold the conflicting interests of the Six Nations in hand.

Canassatego explained that his deputies came to pay a friendly visit, brighten the friendship chain, and clean the brush out of the path. He would have the governor remember that during the late war, the Iroquois lived on the frontier country between him and his enemy, the French. During that time, "we were your guard, and things were so well managed that the war was kept from your

---

4. *Penna. Colonial Records*, vol. V., p. 399.

door. And tho' we have been exposed to many calamities, and blood has been shed among us," we have not troubled you with any mention of our hardships. Then desiring to speak only to the governor and his council, Canassatego referred once more to the squatters on the Juniata. He told the governor that while the Indians appreciated the efforts to remove those settlers, they knew it was all to no effect. "We see," he said, "that white people are no more obedient to you than our young Indians are to us."

To relieve the governor of the embarrassment which must follow an unsuccessful effort to keep a treaty, Canassatego, on behalf of his people, offered to sell a strip of land east of the Susquehanna River, parallel with the Blue Mountains. He thought this would furnish a place for the Juniata squatters because, said the astute Indian, if these men are not effectually removed, there will be serious trouble.

> The valley of the Juniata is our hunting ground, and we must not be deprived of it. Indeed, this will be a hurt to you, for all we kill goes to you, and you have the profit of all the skins. For these lands which we have offered, we are willing to leave it entirely to the honor of the governor and council as to remuneration. People tell us that the proprietors receive immense sums for the lands we have sold to them, and those lands are now worth a great deal of money. You know this better than us, and we trust you will have a regard to this when you fix the price to be paid for them.[5]

Again, the governor appealed to the Assembly about the size of the present which would be proper to make to the Indians, and it was decided that goods to the value of five hundred pounds be given to them. The governor then spoke to them in the usual congratulatory style and presented the goods. After this generous present had been made, the governor replied to their last offer. He told them that all the land they proposed to sell "is mountainous, poor and broken, you must know that it is not worth our acceptance. If you will extend your offer up the Susquehanna as far as Shamokin and permit that tract to carry its breadth to the Delaware River so that we could in any manner justify ourselves to the Proprietor, we will close and give you a just consideration for the lands."

The Indians held a council and agreed to a compromise between their offer and Governor Hamilton's demands. They concluded to sell all the land between the Susquehanna and Delaware Rivers, northwest of the Blue Mountains,

---

5. *Penna. Colonial Records*, vol. V., p. 401.

back to a straight line running from where the Mahony Mountains touch the Susquehanna River to the north side of the mouth of Lackawaxen Creek, where it enters the Delaware River. For this large tract, the governor, on behalf of the proprietors, paid the Indians five hundred pounds and agreed to turn the people off from the Juniata and send them to this region. The Indians were told plainly that they must not permit any of their people to do as they did last summer when they interfered with Conrad Weiser and prevented him from removing the squatters. The governor promised that the Juniata settlers would be removed to the new purchases east of the Susquehanna. The Indians were reprimanded for their rude behavior in coming to the treaty, and it was agreed that Pennsylvania should intercede between the Catawba and Iroquois Indians and determine a time and place for a peace conference. Several quarrels between traders and Indians, where, in most cases, some lives were lost, were adjusted. Then Conrad Weiser conducted the deputies and their associates out of the city.

Governor Hamilton was a man prompt to act. He immediately consulted with Conrad Weiser upon the advisability of removing the settlers on the Juniata. Weiser insisted that there would be an Indian war unless this was done effectively. More proclamations were sent west of the Susquehanna River and directed to be posted by the magistrates. The squatters gave them no attention. The spring of 1750 opened with an increased population. The governor sent Richard Peters and Conrad Weiser to Cumberland County, empowered to summon the magistrates and the sheriff and remove every squatter.

At George Croghairs farm, they all met and held a preliminary meeting with the Indians. "We have thought a great deal," said an old chief, "of what you imparted to us, that you were come to turn the people off who were settled over the hills. We are pleased to see you on this occasion, and as the council of Onondaga has this affair exceedingly at heart, and it was particularly recommended to us by the deputies of the Six Nations when they parted from us last summer, we desire to accompany you, but we are afraid, notwithstanding the care of the governor, that this may prove like many former attempts. The people will be put off now and come next year again, and if so, the Six Nations will no longer bear it but do themselves justice. To prevent this, therefore, when you shall have turned the people off, we recommend it to the governor to place two or three faithful persons over the mountains who may be agreeable to him and us, with commission empowering them immediately to remove everyone who shall presume after this to settle there."[6]

---

6. *Penna. Colonial Records*, vol. V., p. 436.

The Indians were assured that the removal work would be effective. On May 22, the party arrived on the Juniata at a place not far west of the present site of Thompsontown. Here they found four log cabins in possession of William White, George Cohoon, George and William Galloway, and Andrew Lycon. A fifth cabin owned by David Hiddleston was in the process of construction. The Cumberland County magistrates, Matthew Dill, George Croghan, Benjamin Chambers, Thomas Wilson, John Finley, and James Galbreath, called these settlers out of their cabins and asked them by what authority they took possession of these lands and built their cabins. They replied by no right or authority. They recognized the land as belonging to Penn's heirs. The magistrates then asked them if they were not aware that they were acting contrary to the laws of the province and in contempt of the governor's frequent proclamations. They replied that they had only seen one such proclamation and begged that the officers would have mercy upon them. The magistrates then declared that these men were convicted of unlawful trespass and ordered the deputy sheriff of Cumberland County, who was present, to take them into custody. The sheriff got possession of White, Hiddleston, and Cohoon, but the Galloway brothers resisted, and after escaping to some distance, they stopped and called to the officers, saying, "you may take our land and houses and do what you please with them, we deliver them to you with all our hearts, but you shall not carry us to jail."

The following morning the officers and their prisoners went to the cabin of Andrew Lycon. They found no one at home except the children, who said their father and mother would return soon. The magistrates experienced some embarrassment about the proper course to pursue when the prisoners offered to go security for Lycon's prompt appearance at court. Accordingly, a bond calling for five hundred pounds bail was then and there executed. The officers went to the house of the Galloway brothers, who had made good their escape the evening before. All their goods and belongings were taken out and piled upon the ground, and the empty cabin was given into the possession of Richard Peters, the agent of the proprietors. The officers then held a council to decide what disposition should be made of the cabin. They appealed to Conrad Weiser for his judgment. Without any hesitation, Weiser replied that it was his firm opinion that if all the cabins were left standing, the Indians would have such contempt for the government that they would come themselves during the winter and murder the people and set the houses on fire. Based on this opinion, the magistrates gave the order, and the deputy sheriff burnt the Galloway cabin. After this, the company went to the unfinished house of Hiddleston, who voluntarily took out all his things and, without a murmur, saw his house burned.

The next day the sheriff, with Conrad Weiser and James Galbreath, called at Lycon's house to tell him that his neighbors had gone his bail to appear at court and to caution him not to bring trouble upon himself by a refusal. But Lycon evidently felt that his rights as a free citizen were being infringed upon. He met them at his door with a loaded rifle and swore that he would shoot the first man who came toward him. After a short struggle, he was disarmed and made a prisoner. A party of Indians were camped near and saw the capture. They came up at once, and the sons of Shikellamy demanded that Lycon's cabin be burned, saying that if the white men did not destroy it, they would. The attitude of the Indians cooled Lycon's anger considerably. He assisted the sheriff in carrying out the goods. The house was burned, and he was sent to jail.

In the meantime, George Croghan and Benjamin Chambers had gone over on Sherman's Creek, then called Little Juniata, and found eleven families: James Parker, Thomas Parker, Owen McKeib, John McClare, Richard Kirkpatrick, James Murray, John Scott, Henry Gass, John Cowan, Simon Girty, and John Kilaugh. Simon Girty's reputation as the white man's enemy and an Indian abettor was not yet earned. All these people were bound over to appear in court to be held at Shippensburg. Their personal property was pledged as security for prompt removal, and then a number, but not all of their cabins were burned.

The party then repaired to Shippensburg, where an additional number of magistrates were pressed into the service preparatory to removing the squatters from the Tuscarora Path and Big and Little Cove and Aughwick. At this point, Conrad Weiser, for reasons which are not clear, "earnestly pressed that he might be excused from any further attendance, having an abundance of necessary business to do at his home."[7] The other magistrates reluctantly consented, but Weiser finally left the party and returned to Tulpehocken.

Since Weiser had been the leading and guiding spirit of this singular expedition, it is exceedingly difficult to account for his sudden determination to abandon the project. In sending a report of these proceedings to Governor Hamilton, Richard Peters speaks of Weiser as the one in whom the governor had placed the same confidence that he did in the provincial Secretary. The "one whom I principally consulted about executing your commands." And again, when Peters attempted to justify their actions in burning the cabins, he said, "I leave it to Mr. Weiser, as he was joined with me by your Honor, to make his own report, and shall only observe that in all our consultations he, who is Indian interpreter for Virginia and Maryland, as well as this province, and must be supposed to know the minds of the Indians best, proceeded on this as

---

7. *Penna. Colonial Records*, vol. V., p. 443.

a certain truth, that if we did not in this journey, entirely remove these people, it would not be in the power of the government to prevent an Indian war; and as the neighboring provinces were as much concerned in this event as ourselves, he recommended it to the magistrates either not to go or to act with the utmost spirit, and his arguments were so convincing that all the magistrates determined to go in a body."

At the very moment when Weiser succeeded in getting all the magistrates of Cumberland County enlisted into this service, he astonished them all with a sudden determination to go home. He may have realized that his official position as the Indian interpreter for Maryland might be jeopardized should he take an active part in removing the squatters from Big and Little Cove, a territory that was claimed by Maryland as well as Pennsylvania. While he earnestly advised, he seems to have arranged that others should be the apparent agents of removal. The governor appointed Richard Peters and Conrad Weiser, empowering them equally to do this work. Weiser devised the means and aroused the local magistrates, but Peters remained to finish the work and report to the governor.

To what extent Weiser realized that the native Indians might resent too zealous participation in this work is unclear. He well knew the changeableness of the Indian heart and recognized that if a squatter was harshly used, there were Indians to sympathize with him and hold with him a semi-smothered sense of revenge toward the perpetrator. Among the squatters removed from Sherman's Creek was Simon Girty, who, from this experience, imbibed his first lesson of unrelenting hatred toward the white men and all government. To what extent Conrad Weiser was cognizant of these things and deemed it the more prudent course to keep his own hand away from direct contact with this work is uncertain. But when Big and Little Cove became the immediate districts of invasion, the shrewd and diplomatic interpreter for three provinces seems to have concluded that his presence would somehow injure his future and withdrew. The excuse he offered of having urgent business at home would have no convincing force with one familiar with his life habits. A man accustomed to being from home would have everything arranged so he could leave without loss or inconvenience.

After Weiser's departure, the party proceeded to Path Valley. They summoned the eighteen scattered settlers in that valley into one place and convicted them upon their confessions. These people promised to remove all their goods and drive their cattle and other stock away. They assisted the officers in carrying out the rude furniture. Eleven of these houses were burned. At Aughwick, four settlers were found,[8] and two of their cabins burned. At Big Cove, twenty families[9] were removed. Here only three houses were destroyed. Secretary Peters reported them as waste cabins and said their occupants fired them.

The only places remaining to be visited were the Little Cove and Big and Little Conolloways. Since these places were on or near the disputed boundary line with Maryland, the Cumberland County magistrates refused to go and returned home.

The next day Peters and the sheriff received a petition from the people in the Little Cove, and Big and Little Conolloways, in which they acknowledged being within the limits of Pennsylvania but claimed that they were west of the temporary line and then asked that they might be allowed to remain until that line had been extended further west. Since only a few settlers signed this petition, Richard Peters returned it with the explanation that his sole purpose was to prevent an Indian war, which concerned Maryland and Pennsylvania. Peters did all in his power to conciliate the settlers and even offered them his own land east of the Susquehanna. Pennsylvania was becoming uncomfortably aware that the frontier was swarming with a hardy, independent, and more or less lawless crowd of people whose roaming and unstable habits more and more embarrassed the Indian policy of the province.

---

8. Peter Falconer, Nicholas DeLong, Samuel Perry, and John Carleton.

9. Andrew Donaldson, John MacClelland, Charles Stuart, James Downy, John MacMean, Robert Kendall, Samuel Brown, William Shepperd, Roger Murphy, Robert Smith, William Dickey, William Millican, William MacConnell, Alexander MacConnell, James Campbell, William Carrell, John Martin, John Jamison, Hans Potter, John MacCollin, Adam MacCollin, James Wilson and John Wilson.

XII

Rival English Traders

CURTAILING INDIAN EXPENSES—QUARREL BETWEEN ASSEMBLY AND PROPRIETARIES—JEALOUSY OF THE PENNSYLVANIA TRADERS—BEGINNINGS OF THE PENNSYLVANIA AND VIRGINIA BOUNDARY DISPUTE—PENNSYLVANIA ORDERS A MAP TO BE SECRETLY MADE—PENNSYLVANIA'S STRUGGLE FOR THE FUR TRADE—WEISER DECLINES TO ACT AS A SPY—CUMBERLAND COUNTY WANTS A NEW COUNTY SEAT—THE PROGRESS OF THE OHIO COMPANY RETARDED—DID VIRGINIA BUY THE OHIO COUNTRY AT LANCASTER IN 1744?—A DESIRE FOR THE UNION OF THE COLONIES—THE MARYLAND TRADERS BID FOR PATRONAGE—WEISER'S ADVICE—WEISER'S OPINION OF COLONEL JOHNSON—WEISER HAD NO PERSONAL INTEREST IN THE FUR TRADE.

DURING King George's war, little or no complaint was made about the expense of conducting Indian affairs, although the outlay had been rapidly increasing. After peace had been declared, the treaties and conferences of 1749 added materially to the provincial expenses, which everyone hoped would be curtailed. Immediately, loud and persistent complaints were made, especially was this the case in the Assembly. The governor writing to the Legislature in July 1749, just after the departure of the Indians, said: "The committee of Assembly appointed to take care of the Indians, conceiving that they had no authority to make any further provisions for them than during their stay in the city, the interpreter, at my request, defrayed the expenses in their return, which you will please order to be defrayed to him."[1]

John Kinsey, Speaker of the Assembly, replied to the request: "We shall take the necessary care to discharge the remainder of the money due for the maintenance of the Indians in their return homewards. We observe their frequent visits

---

1. *Penna. Colonial Records*, vol. V., p. 413.

put the province to considerable charge, whereas part of their business often is either for the sale of land to the Proprietor or other matters relative thereto. We, therefore, hope the governor will take an opportunity of recommending it to the proprietaries that they may bear a share of the expense, who receive so great a part of the benefit by the coming of the Indians."

This was the beginning of a growing controversy between the Assembly and the proprietors about an equitable division of Indian expenses. The proprietors claimed that if they paid for the land purchased, they did enough, and the province should bear all expenses incident to conferences, presents, and Indian entertainments. This increasing division of purpose within the very councils of the then most important province connected with Indian affairs materially embarrassed its future policy. The weakening influence of a divided purpose grew increasingly manifest as the circumstances leading to the French and Indian war deepened. The second division in Indian affairs arose between the rival trade interests of Virginia and Pennsylvania.

The formation of the Ohio Company aroused the jealousy of the Pennsylvania traders. These men, who were in large measure outside the pale of the law, resorted to every possible means to prevent the agents of the Ohio Company from securing a foothold in the Ohio Valley. The Pennsylvania traders told the Indians, who brought peltries to Logstown, that the Virginians wanted the Indians' land and that, under the guise of trade, they were coming with the intent of driving them out in a few years. As a result, the first Virginia traders on the Ohio were roughly handled, so much so that Thomas Lee, Governor of Virginia, writing to James Hamilton as early as November 1749, said:

> His Majesty has been graciously pleased to grant to some gentlemen and merchants of London, and some of both sorts of inhabitants of this colony, a large quantity of land west of the mountains, the design of this grant and one condition of it is to erect and garrison a fort to protect our trade from the French, and that of any of the neighboring colonies, and by fair, open trade to engage the Indians in affection to his Majesty's subjects, to supply them with what they want, so they will be under no necessity to apply to the French, and to make a very strong settlement on the frontier of the colony, all which his Majesty has approved and directed the governor here to assist the said company in carrying their laudable design into execution; but your traders have prevailed with the Indians on the Ohio to believe that the fort is to be a bridle for them, and that the roads

which the company are to make is to let in the Catawhas upon them to destroy them, and the Indians, naturally jealous, are so possessed with the truth of the Insinuations that they threaten our agents, if they survey or make these roads that they had given them leave to make, and by this, the carrying the King's grant into execution, is at present impracticable. Yet these lands are purchased of the Six Nations by the treaty of Lancaster. I need not say anything more to prevail with you to take the necessary means to put a stop to these mischievous practices of those traders. We are informed that there is measures designed by the Court of France that will be mischievous to these colonies, which will, in prudence, oblige us to unite and not divide the interests of the King's subjects on the Continent. I am with esteem and respect, sir,

Your obedient, humble servant,
Thomas Lee

James Hamilton disavows for Pennsylvania any responsibility for the acts of her traders and promises to examine and punish anyone found guilty of such charges. Hamilton then suggests the advisability of applying to the Crown for commissioners to run the boundary between Pennsylvania and Virginia. It was generally believed in Maryland that the King's grant of five degrees of length for the province of Pennsylvania would not extend further west than the extreme western limits of Maryland. The governor of that province wrote, if your boundary should go further west than the head of the Potomac, we will be out of the affair, "and you and Virginia will have the point to settle between you."

Governor Ogle wrote about the five degrees of longitude: "I apprehend that the gentlemen of Virginia have very different sentiments upon the subject."

So that the government of Pennsylvania might more thoroughly comprehend the boundary problem and understand the trade conditions on the Ohio, Lewis Evans was instructed to travel through that country and collect material for the construction of a map. He was directed "to carefully examine the southern and western bounds of Pennsylvania, where they were not then settled, to ascertain if the temporary boundary line would in any way touch the Potomac River, to examine the limits of the Lord Fairfax grant in Virginia, and look carefully into the designs of the Ohio Company, noting definitely what advantages and disadvantages it might labor under in prosecuting trade compared with Pennsylvania."

Evans was expected to describe all the rivers, "noting the soil and prospect of minerals, and marking probable quarries of limestone, grindstones, and millstones." If he could not reach the Ohio by the branches of the Potomac and Monongahela, he was to choose his own route. Lake Erie was to be "closely examined in order to locate the site for a future trading station," which he was instructed "to do in such a manner as to prevent any suspicion that he was employed by the government of Pennsylvania."

He was, therefore, directed to travel in the disguise of a trader and to employ traders for any purpose he deemed necessary. For personal protection, Evans had a contract with the province in which he was promised one hundred guineas for his services, including all traveling and incidental expenses. In case of death, his heirs were to receive the above sum, and in case of being captured and sent a prisoner to Canada, Louisiana, or France, the proprietors were to use all reasonable efforts to secure his release and were to bear all expenses and pay damages for time lost.[2]

The purpose of the province is manifest in these instructions. The design was the extension of the Indian trade beyond either Virginia or New York. Since Pennsylvania had already been enjoying a lucrative fur trade for two years, gathered from the larger part of what was subsequently known as "The Old Northwest," she did not intend to stand calmly by and see either Virginia or New France deprive her of it.

The fruit of Conrad Weiser's treaty at Logstown must be defended. Yet since there was an immediate prospect of a favorable boundary settlement from the Crown, Pennsylvania was not desirous of openly antagonizing other provinces. Settling the Maryland dispute before opening the Virginia one was deemed wise.

It is more than probable that it was the primary intention of the governor to send Conrad Weiser on this secret mission of half spy and half surveyor. In a letter of Mr. Parson's, of Lancaster, to Richard Peters, dated more than a year previous to Evan's instructions, he said:

> Upon my opening to Mr. Weiser, the affair you gave me in charge, it affected him pretty much, as he looked upon it as a matter of great importance but did not hesitate obedience. He is entirely of opinion that it will be best to proceed from south to north and that it will be impracticable to prosecute the business till sometime in August next, as well upon account of subsistence, which will not be met with in

---

2. *Penna. Archives*, vol. II., pp. 47, 49.

those parts before that time, as upon account of gnats, mosquitoes, flies and other vermin, which are intolerable in the summer season, and especially to horses. It will be necessary, he thinks, to have at least two Indians, Shikellamy's sons, with us. And these may be necessary even in extending the temporary lines. The number of persons necessary cannot yet be determined because if we go at a time when provision is not to be had in the desert woods, a greater number will be wanting then, as it must all be carried with us.[3]

Just how Conrad Weiser managed not to go on this mission does not appear. It would seem that the matter was taken out of Parson's hands and given a year later to Lewis Evans. Weiser, no doubt, hesitated about going. He was now fifty-four years old and increasingly reluctant to undertake any Ohio journeys. The difficulties and dangers of such a journey grew in his mind with increasing years. Mosquitoes and famine, with the possible disapproval of Maryland and Virginia, are not attractive to him. Even in 1748, when on his way to Logstown, Conrad Weiser wrote to Richard Peters, "It is possible I may be obliged to pay the debt of human nature before I get home."[4]

The degree of jealousy entertained by the council toward Virginia as a rival in the Indian trade does not seem to have so deeply impressed the frontier magistrates who were thoroughly familiar with the currents of the fur trade. Thomas Cookson, commissioned in 1749 to locate a site for a county town for Cumberland County, opposed the arguments advanced by the settlers on Conococheague Creek. These settlers wanted the county seat along or near this stream because if Lord Fairfax of Virginia were going to establish a trading station on the Potomac River, this new county seat of Cumberland County would be able to draw aside that trade. Cookson insisted that it would be a great disadvantage to the merchants of Philadelphia to have another trading station near the Virginia post. "It would only give the people concerned," he wrote, "the choice of two markets, and in which we cannot possibly be any gainers, having already the bulk of the trade in our hands, but may risk the losing some part of it."[5]

The attitude of the Pennsylvania traders toward those from Virginia as they met on the Ohio materially retarded the progress of the Ohio Company. After the goods the company had ordered from Europe arrived in November 1749 and March 1750, it was found impossible to use them with profit until the

---

3. *Penna. Archives*, vol. II., p. 41.
4. *Penna. Archives*, vol. II., p. 15.
5. *Penna. Archives*, vol. II., p. 43.

roads were opened to the Ohio and friendly relations were established with the Indians. Accordingly, while work was progressing on the road, Christopher Gist was sent out to explore the country. He spent nearly two years examining both sides of the Ohio Valley as far south as the mouth of the Kanawha. In the meantime, Virginia arranged for a general conference of the Indians to be held at Logstown. But through the influence of the French, and more especially of the Pennsylvania traders, the Indians did not assemble. For this reason, the Virginia treaty was delayed until June 1752.

When Virginia claimed all the Ohio lands by the purchase made at Lancaster in 1744, in which it was stated that the western limit of the Iroquois sale was the setting sun, Conrad Weiser told the governor of Pennsylvania that the Six Nations never contemplated such a sale. To the setting sun was understood to be the water divide between Mississippi and the Atlantic drainage.

At the Logstown treaty of 1752, an Iroquois chief told the Virginia commissioners that they were mistaken in their claim, "You acquainted us yesterday with the King's right to all the lands in Virginia, as far as it is settled, and back from thence to the sunsetting, whenever he shall think fit to extend his settlements. You produced also a copy of his deed from the Onondaga Council at the treaty of Lancaster, 1744., and desired that your brethren of the Ohio might likewise confirm the deed. We are well aware that our chief council at the treaty of Lancaster confirmed a deed to you for a quantity of land in Virginia, which you have a right to; but we never understood before you told us yesterday that the lands then sold were to extend further to the sunsetting, than the hill on the other side of the Alleghany Hill, so that we can give you no further answer."

These things retarded the Ohio Company's movements. In 1750, Virginia, urged by Governor Glenn of Carolina, arranged for a conference of Catawba and Iroquois deputies to be held at Williamsburg. The purpose of this conference was to arrange for long-deferred peace between these two Indian confederacies. Weiser went again to Onondaga on Virginia's behalf but accomplished very little. Governor Glenn wrote to Thomas Lee of Virginia: "The French are united in all their councils, which gives them advantages that they could not have if the King's Governors on the Continent were to act on the same principle."

Richard Peters, in replying on behalf of Pennsylvania to Governor Glenn's letter, said: "The larger the trade is & ye more of the colonies who reap the benefit of it, the more it strengthens the general interest, and at the same time there is more than ever required a union of hearts as well as purses to defeat ye indefatigable industry of the French."[6]

---

6. *Penna. Archives*, vol. II., p. 59.

At the Indian conference at George Croghan's in June 1750, three chiefs from Ohio, Seneca George, Broken Kettle, and The Stone, asked Conrad Weiser and Richard Peters for advice. They reported that Colonel Cresap,[7] a Maryland trader, had invited them to come and trade with him. he had a large quantity of goods, "and from the true love he bore the Indians, he would sell to them much cheaper than the Pennsylvania traders did. The people of Pennsylvania," said Cresap, "call you brethren, and pretend to have great affection for you, but this is all from the mouth and not from the heart. These men constantly cheat you in all their dealings."

Cresap claimed that he and Parker, another Maryland trader, touched with pity for the much-abused Indian would sell below cost and quoted the following rates: "A match coat for a Buck, a Stroud for a Buck and a Doe. A pair of stockings for two Racoons. Twelve bars of lead for a Buck."

Weiser and Peters replied to these Indians:

> Trade is of a private nature. The Indians ought to buy their goods where they can be best served. The people of Virginia and Maryland, who deal in this trade may serve you as well as any others from Pennsylvania or elsewhere, and I advise you, by all means, to go to Captain Cresap's and to cultivate a good understanding with everybody who can supply you with goods, for it is equal to this government from whence the Indians are supplied so that there be good harmony kept up between them and all the King's subjects. It is no part of my business to give you advice, but I cannot help repeating to you my sentiments that you do well to trade with the good people of Virginia and Maryland, as well as with those of Pennsylvania, and to give the preference if you find they treat you better than our people; and as I am now at the house of an Indian trader, I charge you, Mr. Montour, to tell them truly what I say, and that it will be agreeable to the proprietors and this government that the Indians trade wherever they can be best supplied.[8]

There was a vast difference, however, between the attitude of the Colonial governments and their officers and the actions of their respective traders who were removed from the arm of the law by many months of travel. In his more confidential correspondence, Conrad Weiser rarely fails to express his contempt

---

7. Col. Thomas Cresap, who was formerly at a ferry on the Susquehanna, now Wrightsville.
8. *Penna. Colonial Records*, vol. V., pp. 439, 440.

for Colonel Johnson and the management of Indian affairs in New York. In a letter to Governor Hamilton, Weiser wrote: "I positively believe that Warraghiyage[9] squanders a great deal of money in a year, which the public must pay, and I am satisfied he has not wit enough to know the Indians thoroughly, but I hope he does not fall short of honesty."[10]

Doubtless, Johnson had a very poor opinion of Weiser since some years later, when it became necessary for the Crown to centralize Indian affairs in the colonies, and Johnson, who was placed at the head, needed a deputy in Pennsylvania, he did not choose Weiser, who was by far the best fitted but took George Croghan. Like Johnson, Croghan had an eye for his profit and is not clear of the implication that he worked secretly against Weiser.

Andrew Montour had remarkable influence with the Ohio Indians and, through these conferences, became prominent in the province. He was subsequently given a large plantation in the Juniata Valley and commissioned to keep the squatters away from that district. Viewed by the standards of that day, Andrew was a man of immense wealth. In his public acts, he also found ways to add to his fortune that would not bear investigation. Weiser stood alone. He was no Indian trader. Colonel Johnson, Croghan, Montour, the Ohio Company, and a host of little traders were all bent on their gain and consequently jealous of each other. During the later years of his life, Weiser was crowded aside. English centralization in Indian affairs was a name, not a fact. The colonies were unable to control the fur trade. They became the dupes of an army of mercenary traders. And in proportion as the Colonial interests were divided, the French, by centralization, won. In 1750 the English controlled the trade on the Ohio, the Scioto, and the Wabash and shared it with the French in the lake region. By 1755 this trade was all lost, and the Delaware Indians of Pennsylvania had taken up the hatchet against the "sons of Onas."

---

9. Indian name for Col. Johnson.
10. *Penna. Archives*, vol. II., p. 45.

XIII

The French Traders in the Ohio Valley

New York gratified over the increased Western Trade—Rumors of the French Soldiers on the Ohio River—Celoron's Letter—Montour reported Indian Outrages on the Ohio—The Laws of Pennsylvania are too weak to operate on the Ohio—The Miami Indians resent the French Overtures—The Miami Indians remain true to Pennsylvania—The governor urges the Miamis to protest to the Pennsylvania Traders—The Miamis seek English Protection—New York neglects the Indians—Hamilton begs Aid from the other colonies—The colonies Reply—Pennsylvania left alone—Weiser goes once more to Onandago—Weiser calls on Sir William Johnson—The Councils of the Onandagos changed—The old Sachem's Song of Lamentation—The Unanswered Wampum buried with Canassatego—Iroquois Corruption—The French capture two Pennsylvania Traders—The Pennsylvania Assembly favors a union of the Ohio Indians—Weiser declines to go to Ohio—Joncaire endeavors to locate a Fort on the Allegheny—The Leaden Plates are discovered—Joncaire's Speech—Croghan and the proprietaries want a Fort at Logstown—The Pennsylvania Assembly opposed to a Fort at Logstown—The Indians reply to Celoron's Request of 1749—Croghan's doubtful Construction thereof.

AS has been seen, King George's war made it possible for Conrad Weiser at the Logstown treaty of 1748 to deprive the French of their cherished trade in the Ohio Valley and around the lakes. In writing to the governor of Pennsylvania in May 1749, Governor Clinton said:

> We have gained a considerable influence over these nations to the westward, and who before knew but little of the English, while the French have at the same time lost theirs. We ought, I think, not to be negligent in using all the means in our power to preserve these advantages which we have got. I shall be well pleased with every information and advice which your honor shall think proper to give for this purpose. And as your traders go among the Indian traders to the westward, I do not doubt that you will take care to employ the means you may have thereby of promoting the British interest among them and of defeating the designs of the French.[1]

Clinton said further that he had sent his interpreter to Oswego with presents to confirm former friendships. Scarcely three weeks later,[2] Clinton sent Hamilton a report, brought to Albany by Captain Marshall, saying that a thousand French soldiers were already on their way to Belle River (Ohio) to prevent the English from settling there.

Governor Hamilton immediately apprised the Pennsylvania traders that they might be on their guard. These rumors were not entirely without foundation since in August of the same year, 1749, the traders on the Ohio and the Wabash met a French officer, Celoron, with three hundred soldiers and some Indian allies. Celoron told the traders that he had been sent out by the governor of Canada "to reprove the Indians" for forming an alliance and opening trade with the English. Captain Celoron gave these traders three copies of the following letter to Governor Hamilton, dated August the 6th, 1749.

> From our camp on Belle River, at an ancient village of the Chonanous, 6th of August 1749.
>
> SIR:—Having been sent with a detachment into these quarters by Monsieur the Marquis de La Galissoniere, commandant general of New France, to reconcile among themselves certain savage nations, who are ever at variance on account of the war just terminated, I have been much surprised to find some traders of your government in a country to which England never had any pretensions.
>
> It even appears that the same opinion is entertained in New England since in many of the villages I passed through, the English who

---
1. *Penna. Archives*, vol. II., p. 29.
2. June 23, 1749.

were trading there have mostly taken flight. Those whom I first fell in with and by whom I write you, I have treated with all mildness possible, although I would have been justified in treating them as interlopers and men without design, their enterprise being contrary to the preliminaries of peace signed five months ago. I hope, sir, you will carefully prohibit for the future this trade, which is contrary to treaties, and give notice to your traders that they will expose themselves to great risks in returning to these countries and that they must impute only to themselves the misfortunes they may meet with. I know that our commandant general would be very sorry to have resource to violence, but he has orders not to permit foreign traders in his government.

I have the honor to be, with great respect, sir, your humble and obedient servant, Celoron.

Governor Hamilton reported to the council that these letters were extraordinary. One was sent to the proprietaries in London and the other to the governor of New York. Celoron's surprise in finding Pennsylvania traders on the Ohio was carefully feigned diplomacy. The French were thoroughly aware of the Logstown treaty and its blow to their trade. Celoron was sent out to repair these losses. He had not been in the Ohio country long before Andrew Montour sent word to Governor Hamilton that the Indians had killed two or three traders and that nothing had been done to apprehend and punish the murderers. No complaints having been made by the other traders, Montour was uncertain whether this crime had been committed on Virginia or Pennsylvania soil, but of one thing he was sure, and that was unless the instigators were promptly brought to punishment, it would cause the loss of much innocent blood, and lead to fatal consequences.

Governor Hamilton immediately sent a proclamation to the Shawanese, Delaware, and Six Nation Indians living on the Ohio, calling upon them to look promptly and vigorously into the nature and cause of the offense. The Indians were informed that they must not expect the governor of Pennsylvania to treat with them on friendly terms until the murderers were brought to justice. "I have been informed," he wrote, "that some of you said one of the persons killed was a Virginian, and this would not draw on you the anger of the government of Pennsylvania, but I must tell you that to hurt or kill any of the inhabitants of that province will give us equal concern, equal offence, as if it was one who lived in my government, we are all one people; there is no difference between us, and if anyone is hurt all ought to resent it, and will do it, you may depend upon it."[3]

It is doubtful if the Indians ever did anything more than listen to the reading of this proclamation. The laws of Pennsylvania, which had been so successfully enforced in the Delaware and Susquehanna region, were too weak now under the rapidly changing Indian conditions to be enforced on the Ohio and Wabash. There is no evidence that these murderers were ever brought to trial.

There were influences at work in those distant forests, which made it impossible for Pennsylvania to extend the arm of the law beyond the Alleghanies. Hugh Crawford, one of Pennsylvania's bold traders on the Wabash, reported that as early as July 1749, scarcely four months after the treaty of Aix-la-Chapelle and before Celoron's letter was written to Governor Hamilton, a party of two hundred French soldiers, and thirty-five Indian allies, came to a Twightwee, or Miami town to persuade these Indians away from their English affiliations. Crawford reported that the French were determined to use force if fair means did not succeed. These Indians were upbraided for joining the English, who, the French said, had never shown the Miamis any affection or given them any presents.

When the French attempted to use force, they found that the Miamis were numerous and determined to resist. Then the French became quite friendly again and offered the Indians a present of four half barrels of powder, four bags of bullets, and four bags of paint, with a few needles and some thread. This present the Miamis indignantly refused. The French became frightened and hurried away, leaving their goods scattered about on the ground. These same Indians, in their message to Governor Hamilton, insisted that their friendship with the English was constant and enduring, and they hoped it would last while "the sun and the moon ran round the world."

The governor sent a message to these Indians by Hugh Crawford, expressing his appreciation of their friendship and alliance, which he hoped would be strong as the strongest mountain and endure while the sun shines and the rivers run. "I have proposed it," he wrote, "to some of our best traders to carry on commerce with you, and to sell you their goods at as easy a price as they can afford, and by all means to cultivate a good understanding with you, and they seem willing to do it; but as your towns are at a great distance from the Six Nations, and that several of your tribes seem to be firmly attached to the French, the traders cannot help expressing their apprehensions of the great danger there

---

3. *Penna. Colonial Records*, vol. V., p. 450.

is in being intercepted either in their passage to or return from your country; and unless some measures be concerted to preserve the road safe and commodious for their persons and effects it will not be possible to extend their trade into countries so remote to any great degree. I mention this with the more earnestness as I have lately received information that two of our traders going from Logstown to the Twightwees, about three hundred miles from the first place, were either killed or taken by the French or Indians and that a party of French Indians have killed fourteen of our people belonging to Carolina. I say our people, for the inhabitants of Carolina, Virginia, Maryland, and this province, and New York, are all one people; all of us are equally affected and must resent it alike. Some other stories are likewise told us, which, if true, make it evident that the road is by no means safe to travel."[4]

The governor also assured these Indians of the hearty friendship of all the Colonial Governors, whom he expected to join in sending a handsome present to the Twightwees this season; if not, they could depend upon its arrival next spring.

The summer of 1750 opened with numerous rumors from Colonel Johnson of New York and the Pennsylvania traders that the French were coming out from Canada with a strong force to take possession of the Ohio Valley and to alienate the Indians from the English cause.

At the Indian conference held at George Croghan's in May 1750, previous to turning the squatters off from the Juniata lands, the Miami deputies from the Wabash brightened the chain of friendship and told Conrad Weiser that they wanted the road to the Wabash made clear and safe so that the Pennsylvania trader might go among them. They said,*

> Onontio, the governor of Canada, has kept us poor and blind,"* they said, "now we are under the care of the Six Nations and the English, and declare by this string of wampum, that the Twightwees have entirely laid Onontio aside, and will no more be governed by his advice, nor any longer hearken to what he shall say.[5]
>
> The Six Nations have taken all the Ohio and Wabash Indians by the hand and placed it in the hand of the English Governors. During the late war, we were persuaded by Corlear (Governor of New York) to strike the French. When peace was made, we expected that we were included in that peace, but we don't find it so. The French

---

4. *Penna. Colonial Records*, vol. V., pp. 450, 451.
5. *Penna. Colonial Records*, vol. V., pp. 432, 433.

are always threatening us and put us in much fear by their menaces, that we dare not suffer our people to go into the hunting places, at a distance from .us, lest we should meet a party of French. This was the case all last summer, and we have received intelligence from the Six Nations that the French of Canada are now making military preparations and intend to attack us this summer.

Brethren, you ought to have included us in your peace, but since you did not, we now request that the English Governors would jointly apply to have us included in the peace, that we may not be subject to the insinuations and resentment of the French, but be in quiet as well as you.[6]

About this time, Conrad Weiser learned through some of his former Mohawk acquaintances that since peace had been established, the governor of New York never spoke to the Indians, nor offered them any presents, that the Mohawks had received no thanks for the blood they lost in the late war. The English had badly treated their warriors, and when some of their stoutest Indians had the misfortune to be taken prisoners by the French, no effort was made to have them exchanged until June 1750. During the absence of these prisoners, nobody cared for their wives and children. In addition to these complaints, an old chief asked Weiser why the governor and Assembly in New York could not agree. Weiser very prudently replied that he did not know.

Being cognizant of these things, Governor Hamilton wrote to Clinton of New York, telling him that at the suggestion of the Pennsylvania Assembly, he had just sent a present to the Miami Indians as a reward for their attachment to the English cause. He calls Clinton's attention to the importance of retaining the friendship of these Wabash Indians and to the fact that a large number of Six Nation Indians have recently gone out of New York into the Ohio country and are more numerous there than they are in the home district. Hamilton insists that this westward migration of the Iroquois will "give a remarkable turn to Indian affairs, and must draw the attention of his Majesty's Governors into those more remote parts. If my information be true and I have it from persons of undoubted credit," chief among whom was Conrad Weiser, "these refugees of the Six Nations, if I may use the term, the Shawanese, and Delawares, with their new allies, the Wyandots and the Miamis, make a body of fifteen hundred, if not two thousand men, and, in my opinion, these different nations are now upon the balance. If a prudent management and seasonable liberality

---

6. *Penna. Colonial Records*, vol. V., p. 534.

be exercised, they may be retained in our interest. But if no notice be taken of them, nor suitable presents made to them, the French may justly reproach the Twightwees for their defection, and they will cast these reproaches upon our Indians who persuaded them into our alliance, and thereupon they may not only leave us themselves, but draw off our Indians with them, and if we fall into these unhappy circumstances 'tis not probable we will retain the Six Nations at Onondaga long, for when these are stripped of their allies and of those westward Indians, they will be despised, or to avoid contempt, will go over to the French with the other Indians."[7]

Hamilton then called attention to the expense that Pennsylvania had always cheerfully borne but had become too great for any colony. He accordingly asked Clinton to share this expense, saying he would urge Maryland and Virginia to do likewise.

The Maryland Assembly, in answer to this request, declines to have anything to do with Indian affairs. In the interests of the Ohio Company, Virginia evades a direct reply and attempted to manage Indian affairs alone. Governor Clinton is fully aware of the prophetic truth in Governor Hamilton's words and lays the matter forcibly before the New York Assembly, saying: "I must . . . earnestly recommend to you to take this matter into your serious deliberation, that the mischiefs which threaten all the colonies in North America may be prevented before it is too late." The New York Assembly declined to furnish any money "on the plea of poverty," claiming that during the late war, "New York, without any aid from other colonies, was at great expense in defending her borders, and by so doing protected Pennsylvania. The Assembly claimed that it was nothing more than just and reasonable now, since peace existed, that Pennsylvania should bear the expense of retaining the fidelity of the Indians."

This falling away of the sister colonies left Pennsylvania too weak to cope single-handed with the centralized French schemes, which aimed to draw away the Indian alliances which Conrad Weiser had so skillfully won. The old interpreter was beginning to realize that Indian affairs had outgrown him, that unless all the colonies could agree upon a united policy, the French must eventually win. And yet confident of his former influence at the councils of the Iroquois, Weiser once more consented to go among them and carry a message from the governor of Virginia, who was extremely desirous of making peace between the Iroquois and the Catawbas. Weiser's chief purpose, however, was to try and prevent French disaffection.

---

7. *Penna. Colonial Records*, vol. V., p. 463.

He left Reading about the middle of August 1750 and went to Albany by way of the Delaware and Hudson Rivers. He was extremely social with all the Indians he met. His first interview was with two old Mohawks who had just returned from the French prisons.

"I spent the evening with them in a public house," he wrote, "and treated them with several bottles of wine. At another place, I bought a quart of rum here for me and my companions to drink at six shillings, but the company being too great, I was obliged to buy two other quarts."

Weiser called on Sir William Johnson, the sole commissioner of Indian affairs in New York. "I staid twenty-four hours with him," wrote Weiser, "and was kindly received and hospitably entertained."

Johnson told Weiser that the governor of South Carolina had written him to arrange for a treaty with the Catawbas and that his negotiations were already well underway. "We both agreed," he wrote, "that it was best for me not to say anything about the Catawbas because he had made, it is hoped, a good beginning."[8]

Why Weiser gave up his commission on behalf of Virginia without a more vigorous protest is unclear. The sturdy old German was doubtless growing discouraged. He found great changes taking place among the Iroquois. Henry, a Mohawk chief, who had well learned the arts of political craft, told Weiser in strict confidence that he did not believe that Colonel Johnson could bring about peace with the Catawbas, but if the governor of Carolina would make him a handsome present, or pay him well for his trouble, he could bring about the much-desired peace. Henry divined that Weiser had the thing in commission and hinted that he would be willing to avail himself of aid practically. Weiser, however, seems to have given up the Virginia part of the mission with very little remonstrance.

Canassatego, Weiser's warmest Indian friend next to Shikellamy, was dead, and Canassatego had been the leader in the Iroquois Confederacy. He was the chief speaker at all the great treaties for thirty years.

Weiser wrote to Secretary Peters, "Our friend, Canassatego, was buried today before I came to Onondaga, and Solconwanaghly, our other good friend, died sometime before. He that is at the head of affairs now is a professed Roman Catholic and altogether devoted to the French. The French priests have made a hundred converts of the Onondagas, that is to say, men, women, and children, and they are all clothed and walk in the finest clothes, dressed with silver and gold, and I believe that the English interests among the Six Nations can be of no

---

8. *Penna. Colonial Records*, vol. V., p. 472.

consideration anymore. The Indians speak with contempt of the New Yorkers and the Albany people, and much the same of the rest of the English colonies."[9]

These things seem to have broken the spirit of Weiser in intercolonial affairs. From this point, the sturdy interpreter, who once fashioned the course of Indian affairs from a national standpoint, gradually sinks back until his influence is bounded only by his province.

While Weiser was on his way to a village, at one time celebrated among the Onondagas for the wise men who lived there, an old Indian, a member of the council, joined him and began singing a song of lamentation, which signified in an allegorical sense that the town toward which they were journeying was not inhabited by such good friends as formerly. And now, especially since the "word"[10] died "the evil spirits would reign and bring forth thorns and briers out of the earth." At the resting place, Weiser treated the old sachem with "a dram of good rum and told him that nothing was certain in the world and that the Great Being, who had created the world knew how to govern it, . . . and would order everything well," to which the old Indian in his way said, amen.[11]

Weiser's apparent optimism had a heavy burden to bear during this visit. On good authority, he had learned that all the belts of wampum, which remained unanswered in Canassatego's hands at the time of his death, wampum which had been given him by various English Governors, and which stood for all the unfulfilled Iroquois negotiations with the English, were by Canassatego's orders buried with him. Indian gossip said that Canassatego's family had stolen the wampum, thereby corrupting themselves by putting public treasure to private use. Others said that Canassatego's will made him a thief after his death, but in his own heart, Weiser knew that all future negotiations between the Iroquois and the English were jeopardized with the loss of those wampum belts. This fact, combined with the evidence of a change of heart among the Iroquois, discouraged him.

He learned that the French had built a fort further up the St. Lawrence River, not far from Lake Fountanac[12] Here, Piquet, a French missionary, was located. He instructed the Indian children in the Catholic religion, cleared land, and built houses for them at the French King's expense. When Weiser was at Onondaga, Piquet was reported to have had over one hundred converts. These were handsomely clad in garments laced with silver and gold and sent

---

9. *Penna. Colonial Records*, vol. V., p. 467.
10. "Word"—in place of Canassatego. Indians decline to mention a man's name after his death.
11. *Penna. Colonial Records*, vol. V., p. 475.
12. This and the fort at Detroit were all that the French had at that time that were considered encroachments on the English claims.

down to see the French Governor at Montreal. Here they were most hospitably entertained and given many presents. Weiser, whose hatred for anything French or Roman Catholic was deep-seated, reported that many of these converts came "back to Onondaga and drank away their fine clothes. They reported that the missionary's words were not true and that he was seeking to enslave the Indians. They were sure of this since they were asked to renounce their own form of government and come under control of a guardian appointed by the French King, who always professed to protect the Indians against their enemies. Many of these Indians, in mockery, derided the more susceptible ones, saying, 'Go and get baptized again by your father, and bring home fine clothes that we may get some drink.'

"'No,' said another, still joking, 'he will be hanged now if he goes again for fine clothes; his father is angry because his holy water is of no force with the Indians.' So many such discourses I have heard, by which I saw plain that they do not pay any respect to any religion, let it come from where it will if they do not get by it."[13]

Having put out the council fire at Onondaga, as was the custom, Weiser came home disheartened and discouraged. The future looked dark and threatening to him. He had not yet read the depositions of Morris Turner and Ralph Kilgore, two men belonging to John Fraser, a Lancaster County trader. Sometime in May 1750, these two men, who had bought more skins from Miami Indians than their horses could carry, were returning from Logstown for a second load when seven Indians came into their camp one evening a little before sunset. They asked for victuals, and when meat was given to them, they dressed and ate it in a friendly manner. After their appetites were satisfied, they examined the traders' guns, apparently from curiosity; one picked up a tomahawk, and others asked for knives to cut their tobacco. Immediately the two traders were seized and securely tied. The Indians then hurried their prisoners off towards Detroit, which contained about one hundred and fifty houses, securely stockaded. The prisoners were delivered to the commander, and the Indians received a ten-gallon keg of brandy and one hundred pounds of tobacco as a reward. The commander placed these two traders with a farmer living about a mile from the town. Here they were compelled to hoe corn and reap wheat. The Indians frequently came to see them and acted very insolently, taunting them, calling them dogs, and declaring that they were going down to the Wabash after more traders. The prisoners were detained for three months at this farmer's house when the commander at the fort was changed, and they were sent to Canada. At

---

13. *Penna. Colonial Records*, vol. V., p. 476.

Niagara, they met the chief French interpreter, Joncaire. He was taking a large present to the Indians in Ohio. The prisoners saw the goods spread out on the riverbank and estimated them to be worth fifteen hundred pounds. They also heard that in the spring (1751), a French army of five hundred men was going to invade the Ohio country and drive out the Shawanese and the Wyandots, who they believed were contaminating the resident Indians and persuading them over to the English. If these Indians did not go east, the French would kill them. The prisoners also learned that a reward of one thousand pounds had been offered for the scalps of George Croghan and James Lowery, whom they considered the most influential and injurious among the Pennsylvania traders. While following the shores of Lake Ontario, the prisoners made their escape.

The evidence of these two traders and the report of Conrad Weiser's Onondaga visit alarmed Governor Hamilton. He immediately laid the subject before the Assembly at its opening session in October 1750. Hamilton went on to say that as soon as he heard of the unaccountable actions of the French, he desired George Croghan and Andrew Montour to go to Ohio with the small present provided by the Assembly during its last session. He had hoped that his envoys would arrive among the Miami Indians in time to frustrate the schemes of the French, but unfortunately, Croghan and Montour could not go at that time because of sickness. The governor then asked the Assembly for advice. This body promptly replied with the statement that they had decided to add to the present already made up and to include within their generosity not only the Miami Indians but the Wyandots, Shawanese, Delawares, and such other nations as were in that region, with the suggestion that all these Indian nations be urged to form a union like the Six Nations.

The Assembly again beseeched the governor to petition the proprietaries to share the burden of Indian expenses with the people. Shortly after the Legislature had made this unusually liberal appropriation for Indian presents, the governor reported that it would cost two hundred and fifty pounds alone for the transportation of this present; while he considers this an extravagant sum, he cannot find anyone to do it for less. Therefore, the Assembly directed Conrad Weiser to go across the Susquehanna and arrange their transportation for economic purposes. All autumn, winter, and spring go by before the goods can be forwarded. Croghan wrote from Logstown in December 1750, urging all possible haste. He insisted that unless a large present arrived promptly, it would be impossible to hold the Indians to the British interest. He then told of the staunch friendship of the Ohio Indians and outlined his plans for future negotiations. The council and Assembly became distrustful of Croghan's sincerity and expressed suspicions that he might be secretly in league with the French and complained that he was an exceedingly expensive agent in Indian affairs. Accordingly, the governor, secretary, council, and Assembly were unanimous in urging Weiser to go to Logstown and superintend the distribution of this present.

Weiser replied to this request,

> You ask me to distribute this present on the fifteenth of May at Logstown and expect me to be back in time to attend the Indian conference at Albany (1751). With submission, I would say that it is now (22nd of April 1751) impossible. Time will show that what I here say is true; and besides this, the Indians cannot be sent for until the goods are on the spot because this is a hungry time with the Indians, and the few that live in Logstown cannot provide for the rest that come from other towns. Should the goods be delayed, no explanations will satisfy the gnawing appetite of the Indians. I have experienced something of this in the year 1748 when the goods could not come to Logstown according to the time appointed.

Weiser insisted that this present could not arrive in time and urged the governor to commission Croghan and Montour to distribute it. "They must act according to your instructions. If Mr. Croghan's integrity is questioned, some of the traders at Ohio might be required to be present and see that the goods are delivered article for article. I am satisfied that there are some men in Ohio who will not spare or favor him; as for my own part, I believe he will do all in his power to act according to your Honor's commands. Moreover, all these Ohio Indians are subservient to the Six Nations whom we will treat with at Albany." For these reasons, Weiser asked to be excused from the Ohio journey.

The governor, council, and Assembly acquiesced, and minute instructions were drawn up for Croghan and Montour. The importance of these instructions can only be appreciated by recalling the events of autumn and winter (1750 and 1751). In December, Joncaire, a French commander and interpreter, was seen by some Iroquois chiefs examining the upper waters of the Alleghany River, searching for a site for a fort. He had five canoes loaded with goods and was very generous with his presents. He was reported to have said that if he could get the permission of the Ohio Indians, the fort would be built at once. It is quite probable that Joncaire was in the vicinity of Venango. Croghan reported that the French had recently attacked a Shawanese town about three hundred miles from Logstown, killing a man and taking a woman and two children prisoners. The Shawanese pursued them, taking five French men and some Indian prisoners. The Miami Indians also warned the French that they would make them prisoners if they found any of them in the Miami country. For these reasons, Croghan said, "I expect nothing less than an Indian war in the spring."

In January 1751, Governor Clinton sent Governor Hamilton a copy of an inscription found on a lead plate[14] stolen from Joncaire some months previous in the Seneca country. A number of these lead plates had been buried at various points along the Ohio River by Celoron the summer previous. The Six Nation chiefs were curious to know what was on them, and they induced some of the young Senecas to steal one and bring it to the council. When they learned the contents of this plate from Colonel Johnson, like faithful allies, they reported Joncaire's speech made to them that summer.

"Children," he said, "your Father (Governor of Canada) having, out of a tender regard for you, considered the great difficulty you labor under by carrying your goods, canoes, etc., over the great carrying place of Niagara, has desired me to acquaint you that in order to ease you all of so much trouble for the future, he has resolved to build a house at the other end of the said carrying place, which he will furnish with all necessaries for your use."

Joncaire also told these Indians that he was sent to remain in this Ohio country for three years and intended to build a house at the carrying place between Lake Erie and the Alleghany River, where the Western Indians could secure all the goods they needed without the trouble of going to Oswego. Joncaire then asked the Indians their opinion of this and permission to build the two forts, one at Niagara and the other on Lake Erie or the Allegheny River. The Seneca Indians asked the advice of Colonel Johnson. He told them that by fine speeches, the French sought to rob the Indians of their land and cut them off from their English brethren in New York, Pennsylvania, and Virginia.

This effort made by Joncaire to secure the Indians' permission to build two forts alarmed George Croghan, who, as early as December 1750, urged the authorities of Pennsylvania to build a fort at Logstown. Croghan's plea for a fort purported to be the desire of the Indians in that region, who insisted that

---

14. Translation of the inscription found on the leaden plate. "In the year 1749, during the reign of Louis XV., King of France, we Celoron, commander of a detachment sent by the Marquis de La Gallissoniere, commander-in-chief of New France, to restore tranquility in some savage villages of these districts, have buried these plates at the confluence of the Ohio ("Alleghany"), and Tch-a-da-koin, this 29th of July, near the River Ohio, alias 'Beautiful River,' as a monument of our having retaken possession of the said river, and of those that fall into the same, and of all the lands on both sides as far as the source of the said rivers, as well as of those of which the preceding kings of France have enjoyed possession, partly by force of arms, partly by treaties, especially by those of Ryswick, Utrecht and Aix-la-Chapelle."

the English trade would not be secure, and the roads safe for travel until there was an English fort on the river. When the proprietary of Pennsylvania read Croghan's letter, he immediately sent a message to the governor, saying:

> Your report alarms me. I have sent your report to the Duke of Bedford and Lord Halifax, and I think something should be done immediately if it can, by consent of the Indians, to take possession. This, I think, you should advise with the council and Assembly about, as it is of great import to the trade of the province to have a settlement there and a house a little more secure than an Indian cabin. I make no doubt that the Indians would readily consent to such a settlement; and if there is stone and lime in the neighborhood, I think a house with thick walls of stone, with small bastions, might be built at no very great expense, as it is little matter how rough it is within side; or a wall of that sort perhaps fifty feet square, with a small log house in the middle of it, might perhaps be better. The command of this might be given to the principal Indian trader, and he be obliged to keep four or six men in it who might serve him in it, and the house be his magazine for goods. If something of this kind can be done, we shall be willing to be at the expense of four hundred pounds currency for the building of it, and of one hundred pounds a year for keeping some men with a few arms and some powder, this, with what the Assembly might be willing to give will in some measure protect the trade, and be a mark of possession. However, few the men are they should wear a uniform dress, that tho' very small it may look fort-like.[15]

During the winter and spring of 1750, the governor, again and again, consulted the speaker and the leading members of the House upon the proposals made by the proprietaries. For nearly two years, the Assembly had urged that the proprietaries bear a share of the Indian expenses. And now, when they offer four hundred pounds towards building a fort at Logstown and one hundred pounds a year towards its maintenance, the Assembly refused to vote one dollar for any such purpose.

For seventy years, Indian affairs in Pennsylvania had, through the influence of William Penn and the Friends, been conducted in peaceable channels, and now when the sons of Penn are the first to advocate the establishment of a fort

---

15. Penna. Colonial Records, vol. V., p. 515.

garrisoned by an armed force and are arranging things so that the people of Pennsylvania shall bear the major part of the expense, the peace-loving element among the Friends and Germans say "No, this will be warfare. It will not only offend the Indians, but it will embroil England ill a border war with France."

The Assembly was perfectly willing to furnish presents, more presents than any other colony had given, to hold the Indians in the English interests and retain the fur trade, but to take the initial step which must necessarily lead to a long and bitter war, Pennsylvania refused, even after Penn's sons had arranged it in a tempting form. Furthermore, the Assembly was not sure, at that time, that Logstown was a part of Pennsylvania. If a fort were built there, it would foment a quarrel with Virginia, and since arrangements were then being made for a peaceful settlement of the disputed boundary between Virginia and Pennsylvania, the Assembly positively refused to support the proprietaries' Indian Policy. The Assemblymen were well aware of the effect of the "Walking Purchase" upon the Indians on the Delaware. Numerous murders had occurred above the mouth of the Lehigh. Just recently (1751), Scull, the provincial surveyor, had been prevented by the Delaware Indians from running the line in the purchase of 1749. These Indians insisted that the Iroquois had no right to sell any land on the Delaware River, that William Penn never recognized any Iroquois claims to land in this basin, and that the new policy of his sons since the Walking Purchase had brought about all these changes. The Assembly had the same opinion and never agreed with the governor and Conrad Weiser in allowing the Iroquois to spread a pretended claim into the Valley of the Delaware. For these reasons, Governor Hamilton, in his private instructions to George Croghan, forbade his saying anything about a fort. He was to do nothing more than to sound the Indians privately and learn their opinions.

On the 18th of May 1751, Croghan and Montour arrived at Logstown with the long-delayed Pennsylvania present. Joncaire held a council with the Indians three days later at the same place. He asked them for a reply to Celoron's request made in 1749, which was that all the Indians turn away from the English traders and forbid them from ever coming to trade anymore on the Ohio. The Indians replied to this in Croghan's presence.

> Fathers, I mean you that call yourselves fathers, hear what I am going to say to you. You desire that we may turn our brothers, the English away, and not suffer them to come and trade with us again; I now tell you from our hearts we will not, for we ourselves brought them here to trade with us, and they shall live among us as long as there is

one of us alive. You are always threatening our brothers what you will do to them, and in particular to that man (pointing to me [George Croghan]); now, if you have anything to say to our brothers, tell it to him, if you be a man, as you French men always say you are, and the head of all the nations. Our brothers are the people we will trade with and not you. Go and tell your Governor and ask the Onondaga Council if I don't speak the minds of all the Six Nations.[16]

There is not the least doubt about the thorough loyalty of the Ohio Indians to the Pennsylvania government at that time. Their reply to Joncaire may have been as reported. Still, Croghan, like Colonel Johnson, was bent on his own interests and had evidently exaggerated his translation since the Onondagfo Councils had not at that time determined to trade only with the English. These councils had endeavored to play an even game with the French and English for many years. But since the treaty of Aix-la-Chapelle and the death of the old Iroquois leaders, the Onondaga Councils, as Weiser's visit there in 1750 revealed, were sadly divided. Croghan may have been misinformed, but he did not grasp Indian affairs with anything like Weiser's clearness. Croghan's friends on the Ohio were loyal, his enemies bitter. The Assembly of Pennsylvania was loath to trust him, especially since they believed that his advocacy of the fort on the Ohio was to enhance his own profits.

---

16. *Penna. Colonial Records*, vol. V., p. 531.

XIV

Who Shall Take the Initiative?

WHO SHALL STRIKE FIRST?—CROGHAN TREATS WITH THE OHIO INDIANS—THE INDIANS' REPLY—THE OHIO INDIANS ASK FOR AN ENGLISH FORT—THE PENNSYLVANIA OPPOSED TO A FORT—A DESIRE FOR A UNION OF THE COLONIES UPON INDIAN AFFAIRS—THE PENNSYLVANIA OPPOSED TO A UNION—WEISER AT ALBANY—FRENCH ACTIVITY—CLINTON'S LETTER TO THE GOVERNOR OF CANADA—THE FRENCH COMMANDER'S REPLY—ANDREW MONTOUR—MONTOUR'S COMMISSION—PENNSYLVANIA LOSES THE INFLUENCE OF MONTOUR AND CROGHAN—THE PETITION OF THE SHAWANESE FOR HELP—HAMILTON TELLS THE SHAWANESE TO GET HELP FROM VIRGINIA—THE MIAMIS BEG FOR HELP—MONTOUR'S ONANDAGO MISSION—THE FRENCH AND INDIANS ON LAKE ERIE—PENNSYLVANIA OFFERS EIGHT HUNDRED POUNDS—HAMILTON FAILS TO USE THIS MONEY—THE INDIANS TURN FROM PENNSYLVANIA TO VIRGINIA—THE PENNSYLVANIA TRADING POST AT VENANGO DESTROYED—THE CARLISLE CONFERENCE—THE FRENCH AT LE BCEUF WARNED OFF BY THE INDIANS—THE FRENCH REPLY—THE INDIANS DECLARE WAR AGAINST THE FRENCH—WEISER FAVORS A GENERAL PRESENT—THE INDIANS' STATEMENT AT CARLISLE—THE INDIANS INSIST THAT RUM IS THE CAUSE OF THEIR RUIN—WEISER'S POWER LIMITED BY JEALOUS INFLUENCES—VIRGINIA TAKES THE INITIATIVE.

THE treaties of 1751 on the Ohio and at Albany revealed the unanswered question of who should first take possession of the Ohio Valley. It was well understood that whoever did, whether New France, New York, Pennsylvania, or Virginia, it would be necessary to defend the land, that the rival claimants would not give it up without a struggle. The English colonies, therefore, realized the necessity of union in Indian affairs but could not agree upon the disposition of the Ohio country should they succeed in driving off the French. These disagreements retarded the prompt action of the English provinces and allowed France to gain a foothold.

Croghan busied himself on the Ohio while the goods arrived in visiting Indians of note, making presents and gaining friendships. To one old Indian, a Shawanese chief, he gave a full suit of clothes. When the treaty opened, Croghan told the Shawanese that their troubles and scattered condition as a people were occasioned by the French. The Indians were then assured that the English forgave all their former treachery. To the Wyandots, he said:

> I understand that the French, whom you call your father, won't let you rest in your towns in peace but constantly threaten to cut you off. How comes this? Are you not a free and independent people? Have you not a right to live where you please on your own land and trade with whom you please? Your brethren, the English, always considered you a free nation, and I think the French, who attempt to infringe on your liberties, should be opposed by one and all the Indians.

To the Twightwees or Miamis, he urged all their tribes to ally themselves with the English and abandon the French. To the Six Nations on the Ohio, he showed the necessity of a strong Western confederacy of Indians. To all the Indians, he said, "you do wrong to allow the French among you to permit them to build houses on your land. It makes it dangerous for English traders and will, in time, force you to pay more for your goods."

When the Indians replied, they first spoke to Joncaire in open council, saying,

> How comes it that you have broken the general peace? Is it not three years since you as well as our brothers, the English, told us that there was a peace between the English and French, and how comes it that you have taken our brothers as prisoners on our lands? Is it not our land [stamping on the ground and putting his finger to Joncaire's nose]? What right has Onontio to our lands? I desire that you may go home directly off our lands and tell Onontio to send us word immediately what was his reason for using our brothers so, or what he means by such proceedings, that we may know what to do, for I can assure Onontio that we, the Six Nations, will not take such usage.

You hear what I say, and that is the sentiment of all our nations; tell it to Onontio that that is what the Six Nations said to you.[1]

The Indians all appeared duly thankful for their present but declined the Virginia invitation sent by Christopher Gist to go and receive the King's present offered by that colony. According to George Croghan's report, all the Indians on the Ohio united with the Six Nations of the West in making the following reply to Croghan's complaint about the treatment of English traders.

Brother; as to what you mention of the traders being taken by the French, we, your brethren of the Six Nations, have a true sense of the ill-usage you have received from the French, and we can assure you we will take a method to oblige the French to make satisfaction. Brother, we have discharged the French from amongst us and told them that they should not build upon our land. Now, brothers, we have been considering what the French mean by their behavior and believe they want to cheat us out of our country, but we will stop them, and brother, you must help us. We expect that you, our brother, will build a strong house on the River Ohio, that if we should be obliged to engage in a war, we should have a place to secure our wives and children, likewise to secure our brothers who come to trade with us, for without our brothers supply us with goods we cannot live.[2]

The Indians said they would take two months to select a site for a fort, and then they would expect the governor of Pennsylvania to order such a house to be built.

When Governor Hamilton laid this matter before the Assembly, that body consulted Conrad Weiser and Andrew Montour and was informed that George Croghan misunderstood or misinformed the governor.[3] The Assembly advised Hamilton of this and said further, "We have seriously considered the offer made by our proprietors of contributing toward building such a house, [meaning the fort,] but as we have always found that sincere, upright dealing with the Indians, a friendly treatment of them on all occasions, and particularly in relieving their necessities at proper times by suitable presents have been the best means of securing their friendship, we could wish our proprietaries had rather seen fit to join with us in the expense of these presents, the effects of which have at

---

1. *Penna. Colonial Records*, vol. V., p. 536.
2. *Penna. Colonial Records*, vol. V., p. 538.
3. *Penna. Colonial Records*, vol. V., p. 547.

all times so manifestly advanced their interest with the security of our frontier settlements."[4]

This became the policy of the Pennsylvania Assembly, so far as taking the initiative in possessing the Ohio Valley was concerned. The governor complained loudly to the other provinces and the proprietaries but to no purpose.

From then on, it became more and more evident that either New York or Virginia would have to come to the front if the French were to be excluded from the disputed territory. Early in 1750, the governors of Virginia, Pennsylvania, and New York suggested a union of colonies so far as Indian affairs were concerned. Nothing came of these suggestions save a general polite agreement on the part of all the governors that such a union would be desirable, but no one seemed inclined to make the first move. The necessities of such a union pressed hardest upon New York. Governor Clinton wrote to Governor Hamilton in December 1750 and emphasized the impossibility of any one colony being able, financially, to cope with the French by keeping the Indians in the English interests. A union of colonies, he said, would inspire the Indians and remove their fear of the French, who were threatening them from all sides; Clinton then invited all the English Governors to attend an Indian conference to be held at Albany in 1751. Here he suggested they might agree upon a report to be sent to the Crown upon Indian affairs. Clinton then called attention to the terrible suffering on the border if the French won over the Indians. Many of the colonies paid no attention whatever to Clinton's invitation. Governor Hamilton entered the plan with his usual vigor, and arrangements were made to send Conrad Weiser to Albany in 1751. It was the general opinion that this would be an exceedingly important conference, Weiser himself must have thought so when he declined to go to Logstown, lest he might not be able to return in time to go to Albany.

The Pennsylvania Assembly distinctly recalled the experiences during King George's war and looked suspiciously upon all efforts toward union, especially those in New York and New England. The Assembly sent word to Governor Hamilton that they did not consider it necessary for them to take part in the intended treaty at Albany. But advised him to send Conrad Weiser with a small present and a message of condolence for the death of Canassatego, and if Conrad Weiser should learn that anything more was necessary, the Assembly would "cheerfully concur in doing what may be most conductive to the peace and tranquility of the province."[5] As a result, the importance of the Albany Con-

---

4. *Penna. Colonial Records*, vol. V., p. 574.
5. *Penna. Colonial Records*, vol. V., p. 526.

ference was materially diminished. Weiser alone must represent his province, and the conference upon a union of colonies was deferred. New York rapidly absorbed the management of the Six Nation Indian affairs, which Weiser fully realized when he reached Albany on June 27th, 1751.

During the first eight days after his arrival, the Indians constantly came and went from his headquarters. Weiser then called on Governor Clinton to deliver his message. "I had not the honor to see his Excellency," wrote Weiser, "but one Mr. Askew carried my request to him, who brought back answer, to wit, that his Excellency must have it in writing in order to lay it before the council."[6]

This was the first time the governor of New York had interfered with Pennsylvania Indian affairs since Weiser had been conducting them. Whether the cause was due to some unwise conduct on Weiser's part during his eight days of Indian receptions, the budding boundary dispute between Pennsylvania and New York, or the secret jealousy of Col. Johnson is unclear.

Weiser informed Governor Clinton that he could not deviate from his instructions, which he immediately furnished. These were read in council, where it was determined that Weiser should not confer with the Indians until after Governor Clinton had interviewed them. Weiser replied that he had been instructed not to treat with the Indians without Governor Clinton's permission. "As for the Indians coming to see me," he said, "I could not lock up my door upon them."[7]

The previous year Sir William Johnson had thwarted Weiser's Virginia negotiations, and it is quite probable that Governor Clinton's attitude toward Weiser was due to Johnson's subtle influence. One thing, however, is quite certain, New York was beginning to impose limitations upon Pennsylvania's conferences with the Iroquois. Weiser accomplished little on this mission save to put a few Indian leaders in temporary good humor and to arrange for his son "Sammie" to remain and study the Maqua dialects.

The autumn of 1752 was full of rumors of a French invasion. Sir William Johnson reported twelve hundred French soldiers and two hundred Indian allies going to the Ohio to attack the Indians who were in the British interests "and to stop the Philadelphians building at or near Ohio, or anywhere else." It was also rumored that the French were building a three-masted vessel on one of the Great Lakes and carrying cannons toward the Indian country. A trader wrote that the French were going to attack the big stone trading house in the principal Miami village where Croghan traded. It is not improbable that Croghan had

---

6. *Penna. Colonial Records*, vol. V., p. 541.
7. *Penna. Colonial Records*, vol. V., p. 541.

built this fort on the Wabash at his own expense and concealed the fact from the authorities of Pennsylvania.

The French ordered the English to desist from finishing this stone house and peacefully leave the country. If they refused, force was to be used. These things led Governor Clinton to write to the governor-general of Canada on June 12th, 1751, asking him if the fort the French had recently erected at Niagara was by his order. "Surely, if the treaties of Utrecht and Aix-la-Chapelle be not broken, the existence of this fort must be unknown to you." This was the first message of an English Governor questioning the right of the French to build forts on the disputed boundary lines. Clinton also apprised the French commander that the Six English traders (Pennsylvanians) had been captured while trading peacefully on the Wabash and carried off as prisoners. These Governor Clinton demanded to be returned and the damages paid.

The French general, in his reply, said:

> You claim this land because it is owned by the Iroquois, whom you call your subjects. If this is true, then your claim is good. But it is very well known that the Six Nations are subject to no white man. If they sought allegiance anywhere, they would, from natural inclination, prefer the French to the English. Since we were the first people here, the Indians call us father. The traders, which you claim, we arrested because they were found to be traitors to France. They were found on French soil stirring up the Indians against us, and we could do no more than arrest them. They had been warned to leave the country but chose to remain and face the consequences.

The rising power and influence of Andrew Montour at this time reached such proportions as to embarrass Pennsylvania's management of Indian affairs seriously. During the early part of Conrad Weiser's public life, he and Andrew Montour were best friends. Andrew was the interpreter for the Delawares and Conrad for the Iroquois. After the Lancaster treaty of 1744, Andrew attempted to poison the mind of the governor of Virginia against Weiser to secure the management of Virginia's Indian affairs. At this time, 1746-48, he extolled George Croghan and execrated Conrad Weiser. In a letter to Richard Peters in 1747 or 1748, Weiser wrote,

> I am glad that the governor of Virginia has seen fit to send Andrew Montour to Onondaga. I could have wished that Andrew had come

by my house, but I know very well that his guilty conscience won't admit him. His signing a paper for the Pennsylvania Assembly in favor of George Croghan and against me, his friend, that is what troubles him. And, perhaps, he wishes me dead to have the management of Indian affairs all to himself without contradiction. But I am sure his great pride will soon render him odious to the Onondaga Council, without he has mended of late. I know he aims of having a piece of ground over the hills and a good number of settlers on it to pay contributions to him, but how he will bring it about is a mystery to me. Though he may give us some trouble, I think it is best to give him some rope till matters come to a crisis. I don't think it safe to meddle with him until he has run his length.[8]

That which was a mystery to Conrad Weiser was no mystery to Andrew Montour. There was enough white blood in his veins to aid his schemes. He soon won back Weiser's friendship and secured the governor's confidence. He made himself indispensable to Pennsylvania and Virginia in the affairs of the Delaware Indians. He knew how to save and how to invest.

Before the Logstown treaty of 1748, Weiser and Montour had another disagreement. In a letter from Weiser to Peters, dated August 4th and written from Lancaster, we learn that "Andrew Montour has pitched upon a place in the proprietor's manor, at Canataqueany. He expects that the government shall build him a house there and furnish his family with necessaries. In short, I am at a loss what to say to him. I am very much concerned about him. He seems very hard to please. I should think myself happy if I had nothing to do in public affairs and could turn farmer entirely."

At this time, many capitalists of Philadelphia and the East were eager to invest in Western land across the Susquehanna River. Weiser and Peters were making extensive purchases there, and when Montour secured the influence of the Assembly and picked out the best piece of land west of the river, Weiser was astonished. Montour's plantation was in Cumberland County, about ten miles north of Carlisle. In 1752 the council of Pennsylvania recorded that Andrew Montour having earnestly and repeatedly applied for permission to live in some plantation over the Blue Hills in Cumberland County, the governor declined to give him leave till he should have conferred with Mr. Weiser and Mr. Peters on the subject. In fact, ever since the squatters had been driven out of the Juniata

---

8. Manuscript letters of Conrad Weiser, 1746 or 1747, vol. I. Collections of the Pennsylvania Historical Society.

Valley in 1749, Andrew Montour had been petitioning both Governor and Assembly for a commission to live there and keep out all invaders. Weiser's influence upon Secretary Peters had been the restraining force that prevented Montour from accomplishing his purpose. But Andrew bided his time and became especially active in Ohio negotiations, and in proportion as the province recognized his merit and trusted him and Croghan with the distribution of public presents, Andrew became better able to secure the surrender of Weiser and the commission to guard the Juniata lands.

The much-coveted commission was dated April 18th, 1752, and authorized Montour "to go and reside in such place over the Kittochtinny Hills, as you shall judge most central and convenient, in order that you may by your personal care and vigilance preserve the lands from being settled as well as warn off all who have presumed to go there, and do whatever is in your power to discourage others from attempting it, letting all know what an offence it is against this government, and how injurious to the Six Nations."

Montour was further required to report all the names of squatters, so they might be punished.[9] Andrew grew in wealth from this time, and when he traveled to Philadelphia, it was with a retinue of servants clad in regal splendor.

But back of an Indian's love of display was the keen man of business. Montour soon advised Governor Hamilton of the great treaty Virginia proposed to hold that summer (1752), at Logstown, with the Ohio Indians and asked the governor's advice should Virginia invite him to act as interpreter.

Hamilton replied without committing himself but took this occasion to urge all the Ohio Indians to come to Logstown and receive the King's present, thankfully, even if the Virginia people dispensed it. Hamilton went further and urged the Indians to treat the men of Virginia kindly if they wished to please Pennsylvania. However, as Montour and Croghan found that the King's bounty could flow more freely through Virginia than Pennsylvania, their zeal was changed from the Keystone to the Old Dominion. Weiser's influence on the Ohio was discounted, and Pennsylvania came ere long to realize that her Southern rival for Indian trade and land claims was stronger than her Northern one [New York].

For some time, Croghan and Montour were successful in drawing sustenance from both States, but the dawn of Virginia supremacy dates with Montour's commission to reign as monarch of the Juniata.

The application of the Shawanese for help after the French had killed thirty of the Miamis warriors started another train of events that tied Pennsylvania's

---

9. *Penna. Colonial Records*, vol. V., p. 567.

hands and placed Virginia more prominently in the front. The Shawanese, on behalf of their injured brethren, the Miamis, sent by Conrad Weiser the following message to Governor Hamilton.

> It is a great while since you and we, your brothers, were made by one God, that made all things. You gave us books and told us to pray, and we thought we would do so, but in a short time, we got into debt, and the traders told us we must pay them, so we quitted praying and fell to hunting, and the God that made us, gave us all the beasts of the field for our food, and water for our drink, and wood for our fire, and threw down fire from Heaven to kindle our wood. Our white brothers setting on the seaside has obliged us to move back here in search of game. And now we are in fear always. The French are behind us. They are directed by the evil spirit and not God. They trouble us much. They cheat us with advice. They have killed thirty of our brothers, the Twightwees. We must fight. Will our English brothers help us? We need help.

Hamilton wrote Croghan that he could do nothing since the Assembly, which held the purse strings, was averse to any war-like measures. To the Shawanese, he professed the warmest kind of friendship and referred them to Virginia for a direct answer to their request. This action of Hamilton's, resulting from his embarrassment, turned the attention of the Western Indians to Virginia as a source of succor. If the Great King beyond the Ocean spoke through Virginia, now, instead of Pennsylvania, they would apply to Virginia first. In writing to Governor Clinton, Hamilton said, "It is a great mortification to me to find myself so embarrassed in that respect by the religious scruples of one branch of our Legislature, that I fear it would not be in my power [whatever necessity there might be for it] to afford our Indian allies that assistance and protection my own inclination leads me to."[10]

The injured Miami Indians retaliated and killed fifteen Frenchmen. This act brought down on their tribe the anger of the French General at Montreal. A large force was at once sent out against these rebellious Indians. The Miamis immediately sent messengers to Virginia and Pennsylvania, begging for aid. The deputy who came to Philadelphia carried a French scalp and five belts of wampum as credentials. He declared that his people were more grieved for the loss of some English traders than their own men.

---

10. *Penna. Colonial Records*, vol. V., p. 575.

"We are still loyal to the English interests," he said, "and are willing to die for them, and will never give up to this treatment, although we saw our Great Piankaskaw King[11] taken, killed, and eaten within a hundred yards of the fort before our faces. We now look upon ourselves as lost people, fearing that our brothers will leave us, but before we will be subject to the French or call them our fathers, we will perish here."

This appeal, supplemented by Andrew Montour's report when he returned from Onondaga, set the Assembly to thinking. Montour had been to Onondaga to urge the Six Nations to come to Winchester and hold a treaty with Virginia. The Iroquois declined the invitation on the plea; the times were too full of danger to permit them to leave their houses. But Montour did learn that the French were raising a large army to punish the Miamis and drive all the English traders out of the Ohio Valley. Although the Six Nations had sent a message to Canada sternly forbidding the French from invading their Ohio lands, Montour reported that the Iroquois were thoroughly frightened and that the strong French party in their midst had sadly divided their councils. When the governor laid these reports before the Assembly, he called attention to the evil results of having French forts within our province and a hostile army among the Indians. The governor of New York had ordered the French from the Niagara River, but his Assembly did little, if anything, for him. That body was bent on securing the expense of Indian affairs from the Crown and determined that in the future, no other provinces should treat with the Six Nations, except at Albany, in the presence of a representative of New York. The governor of Virginia, on the other hand, was determined that all Indian negotiations in the future should be held at Winchester, and with the aid of the Ohio Company, he had the promise of material assistance from the Crown.

About the latter part of May 1753, news came from the Ohio by John Fraser, a trader, that since March, a party of one hundred and fifty French and Indians had been near Lake Erie, building canoes and making preparations to receive a large party of French soldiers in the summer, who were expected to bring eight brass cannon and a large quantity of provisions and ammunition. Forts were to be built at the carrying places, and two strong ones were to be located on the Ohio River. All the English traders were to be removed, and if they did not go peaceably, they would be driven off by force. This news especially excited the Ohio Company; it appealed at once to Virginia and Pennsylvania for aid and support. It would order the French out of its country and defend its land with its last drop of blood if it could count upon aid and support from

---

11. Known to the English traders as "Old Britain," to the French traders as the "Demoiselle."

Virginia and Pennsylvania. Virginia, backed by the Ohio Company, or most probably the Ohio Company acting through Virginia, promptly sent the Indians word that if the French attempted to settle on the Ohio lands or build any forts, Virginia would supply the Indians with arms and ammunition.

Governor Hamilton immediately laid these reports before the Pennsylvania Assembly. This much-maligned body which had during the past seventy years given to the Indians more gold and presents than any other colony and had never spent a dollar in Indian warfare within its borders, now when real danger threatened, and an enemy was about to invade the borders of the province, promptly voted eight hundred pounds to Governor Hamilton, to be laid out by him and distributed in such manner as he shall think most suitable to their (the Indians') present exigencies.[12]

This appropriation was voted on May 31st, 1753. For two months, Governor Hamilton held the money and then wrote to Governor Dinwiddie, explaining his tardy actions as caused by an Assembly which would do nothing to defend the province. He acknowledged the reception of the eight hundred pounds but said: "I cannot allow myself to dispose of it till some application be first made by the Indians for assistance, and I am well assured of their real friendship and hearty goodwill to the English."[13]

A month later, the governor apologized to the convening Assembly for not having sent a portion of this money as a present of condolence to the Miamis, as the Legislature directed in May. He said there was a danger of the present being stolen by the French while transported.

This delay of Hamilton's, which was laid upon the shoulders of a long-suffering Assembly, was a source of disappointment to the Indians. Since no reply came from Philadelphia, they turned to Virginia, who had promised them arms and ammunition. A convention of Indian deputies was sent to Winchester to arrange for aid and supplies. While there, they heard, doubtless through Governor Dinwiddie, that the Pennsylvania Assembly had voted eight hundred pounds to their support. Thereupon these warriors determined, although no invitation had been received, to send a portion of their deputies to Carlisle to ascertain if these rumors were true. To meet these Indians, Governor Hamilton sent to Carlisle, Conrad Weiser, Richard Peters, Isaac Norris, and Benjamin Franklin.

Before starting, this commission read a letter from John Fraser, a Lancaster County trader who had maintained a gun shop at Venango for some years. Fraser

---

12. *Penna. Colonial Records*, vol. V., p. 617.
13. *Penna. Colonial Records*, vol. V. p. 633.

reported that scarcely any furs had been bought that year because the Indians had not been hunting but had been living upon French bounty. Fraser's man escaped from the French who attacked this gun shop and, with great difficulty, reached home. His associate, John Trotter, was captured and carried to a fort, which had recently been built on French Creek, soon to be called "Le Boeuf."

When the commissioners reached Carlisle, they immediately applied to George Croghan and Andrew Montour to explain why the Indians had been to Virginia. Montour said that the Western Indians had gone to Virginia to hold a peace treaty and urged them to come to Pennsylvania, insisting that the governor was anxious to see them.

When the Indians arrived, it became necessary to condole them with presents since a number of their people had been killed during the summer by the French. No public business could be done with the Indians until their tears were wiped away by a generous gift. The commissioners had gone to Carlisle without presents. They had Conrad Weiser interview an old Oneida chief and asked him if it were not possible to go through the forms of condolence on the promise to pay when the goods arrived. The chief replied frankly that his people would not proceed with any public business while the blood of their tribe remained upon their garments, and nothing would wash it out unless the presents, intended to cover the graves of the departed, were actually spread on the ground before them.

While all concerned were waiting for the goods to arrive, Conrad Weiser learned from the Indians that when the message from Pennsylvania arrived in the spring advising them of the threatened invasion of the French, the Indians sent a warning to the invaders, who were then at Niagara, forbidding them to come any further west; this notice did not deter the French in the least. The Indians then held a conference at Logstown and sent a second notice to the French, who had recently left Lake Erie and were approaching the headwaters of French Creek. In this message, the Western Indians said,

> Your children on Ohio are alarmed to hear of your coming so far this way. We at first heard that you came to destroy us. Our women left off planting, and our warriors prepared for war. We have since heard that you came to visit us as friends without design to hurt us, but then we wondered, you came with so strong a body. If you have had any cause of complaint, you might have spoken to Onas or Corlear (meaning the governors of Pennsylvania and New York) and not come to disturb us here. We have a Fire at Logstown, where

are the Delawares and Shawanese and Brother Onas; you might have sent deputies there and said openly what you came about if you had thought amiss of the English being there, and we invite you to do it now before you proceed any further.

To this notice, the French replied:

I find you come to give me an invitation to your Council Fire with a design, as I suppose to call me to account for coming here. I must let you know that my heart is good to you; I mean no hurt to you. I am come by the Great King's command to do you, my children, good. You seem to think I carry my hatchet under my coat; I always carry it openly, not to strike you but those that oppose me. I cannot come to your Council Fire, nor can I return or stay here. I am so heavy a body that the stream will carry me down, and down I shall go unless you pull off my arm. But this I will tell you, I am commanded to build four strong houses, viz., at Weningo (Venango), Mohongialo Forks (present site of Pittsburgh), Logstown, and Beaver Creek, and this I will do. As to what concerns Onas and Assaragoa (meaning the governors of Pennsylvania and Virginia), I have spoken to them and let them know they must go off the land, and I shall speak to them again. If they will not hear me, it is their own fault. I will take them by the arm and throw them over the hills. All the lands and waters on this side Allegheny Hills are mine; on the other side theirs. This is agreed on between the two Crowns over the waters. I do not like you selling your land to the English; they shall draw you into no more foolish bargains. I will take care of your lands for you. The English give you no goods but for land. We give you our goods for nothing.

This peculiar form of metaphor so common with the French pioneers had a certain fascination for the natives, who admired people who knew their own minds and could speak quickly without consulting assemblies or disagreeing.

This reply from the French softened the hearts of many of the younger Indians at the conference. The old men, however, saw clearly their course and replied as follows:

You say you cannot come to our Council Fire at Logstown; we, therefore, now come to you to know what is your heart. When you tired of Queen Anne's war, you plead for peace. You begged to talk with us. You said, 'We must all eat with one spoon out of this silver bowl and all drink out of this silver cup. Let us exchange hatchets. Let us bury our hatchets in this bottomless pit hole.' Then we consented to make peace, and you made a solemn declaration, saying, 'Whoever shall hereafter transgress this peace, let the transgressor be chastised with a rod, even tho' it be I, your father.' . . . Now, Father, notwithstanding this solemn declaration of yours. You have whipped several of your children. You know best why. Of late, you have chastised the Twightwees very severely without telling us the reason, and now you are come with a strong band on our land and have, contrary to your engagement, taken up the hatchet without any previous parley. These things are a breach of the peace; they are contrary to your own declarations. Therefore, now I come to forbid you. I will strike over all this land with my rod; let it hurt who it will. I tell you in plain words; you must go off this land. You say you have a strong body, a strong neck, and a strong voice, that when you speak, all the Indians must hear you. It is true you are a strong body, and ours is but weak, yet we are not afraid of you. We forbid you to come any further; turn back to the place from whence you came."[14]

These three warnings were equivalent to a declaration of war. The Indians had sent deputies to Virginia and Pennsylvania to learn what assistance they might expect. Virginia agreed to furnish a suitable quantity of ammunition to be distributed by Christopher Gist, Andrew Montour, and William Trent. The Pennsylvania commissioners at Carlisle were at a loss for what to do. Conrad Weiser was consulted. He gathered all possible information from the Indians and then urged that the entire appropriation recently made by the Assembly be expended at once.

"Only by a generous donation could we expect to hold the friendship of those Indians," he said. Goods were accordingly bought, the forms of the condolence observed, and the conference commenced. The commissioners expressed their friendship for these Indians in the warmest possible terms and told them of the generous supplies awaiting them.

The Indians were profuse in their thanks and expressed their deep affection for the English, and then made the following statement:

---

14. *Penna. Colonial Records*, vol. V., pp. 667, 668.

GEORGE WASHINGTON, THE MESSENGER

The governor of Virginia desired leave to build a strong house on the Ohio, which came to the ears of the governor of Canada, and we suppose this caused him to invade our country. We do not know his intent because he speaks with two tongues. So soon as we know his heart, we shall be able to know what to do and shall speak accordingly to him. We desire that Pennsylvania and Virginia would at present forbear settling on our lands over the Allegheny Hills. We advise you rather to call your people back on this side the Hills lest damage should be done,' and you think ill of us.

To keep trade and friendship open with Pennsylvania, they advised placing George Croghan and someone else to be chosen by the governor at Aughwick, to guide and control Indian affairs. They demanded that all traders be withdrawn from the Ohio because the French looked upon them with envy, which would be a constant source of trouble. The Indians requested that all trade be restricted to three centers only, the mouth of the Monongahela, Logstown, and the mouth of the Kanawha. Here goods could be brought in public, and traders would not be allowed to go among the Indians in their villages.

A bitter complaint was made about the unregulated trade in rum. "The rum ruins us," they said, "We never understood the trade was to be for whiskey and flour. We desire it may be forbidden and none more sold in the Indian country, but that if the Indians will have any, they may go among the inhabitants and deal with them for it. When the whiskey traders come, they bring thirty or forty kegs and put them down before us and make us drink and get all the skins that should go to pay the debts we have contracted for goods bought of the fair traders, and by this means we not only ruin ourselves but them too. These wicked whiskey sellers, when they have once got the Indians in liquor, make them sell the very clothes from their backs."

The commissioners expressed profound sympathy for all these requests and complaints and promised to lay them before the governor. The Indians went home pleased with their presents and promises. But the traders were not recalled, the rum traffic was not stopped, and the squatters multiplied in the Juniata Valley.

Governor Dinwiddie, in a letter to Hamilton on September 3rd, 1753, complimented Conrad Weiser, saying, "I am very sensible of his capacity, and do not doubt of his inclination in serving this government, or more properly, the English interests."

Weiser, who felt Croghan and Montour were absorbing his Virginia business, had asked Governor Hamilton to recommend him to Governor

Dinwiddie. Sometime before the Carlisle treaty Weiser was sent to Onondaga on important business for Virginia and Pennsylvania. Governor Dinwiddie was especially anxious to learn the attitude of the Six Nations toward peace with the southern tribes.

When Weiser arrived in Albany, he found it necessary to lay a copy of his instructions before Governor Clinton that the council might consider them. Weiser consulted with several Indians privately at his headquarters before Clinton permitted him to go on to Onondaga. For some reason, most probably the persuasions of Sir William Johnson, Clinton declared that Weiser had acted disrespectfully and should not be allowed to go any further among the Indians or in any way deal with them on behalf of either Virginia or Pennsylvania.

Weiser called upon the governor, begged his pardon, and then returned home without accomplishing the purpose for which he had been sent. Both Governors Hamilton and Dinwiddie resented this action of Clinton's. It weakened the English cause with the Indians and took out of Conrad Weiser's hand his strongest instrument in Indian affairs, the influence of the Six Nations.

The Western Indians were largely left to their own resources. They were not as skillful in public affairs as their better-trained brothers in New York and were more easily changed in their minds than the Iroquois. When Conrad Weiser's hands were tied, the colonies lost a councilor and a guide at the most critical moment. Pennsylvania was not, owing to the waning influence of the proprietors with the Crown, in a position to take as prominent a part in Indian affairs as Virginia or New York. The Crown attempted to work through Virginia and, in a measure, used New York, instructing them to commit no act of hostility but to hold the Crown's land. Aid was offered to Virginia, and she immediately did by messenger what New York had done by letter a year or more before, warn the French to depart from the Ohio lands. The messenger sent was George Washington, a brother of two of the leading members of the Ohio Company. Although the Pennsylvania donations made to the Indians at Carlisle included a large quantity of powder and lead, and as much encouragement toward resistance had been given to the Indians as Virginia had furnished, the King's action enabled Dinwiddie to take the initiative, and Virginia became what she had for some years hoped to be, the leading English colony in Indian affairs.

XV

The Ohio Indians Go Over to the French

THE FRENCH FAIL IN THEIR PLANS, 1754—THE COUNCILS OF THE IROQUOIS ARE DIVIDED—THE DELAWARES CEASE TO BE WOMEN AND BECOME MEN—DISPUTES OVER THE LANCASTER LAND SALES OF 1744—THE PROPRIETORS WANT LAND FROM THE INDIANS, 1754—COMMISSIONERS TO THE ALBANY TREATY—WEISER OBJECTS TO BEING CHIEF INTERPRETER AT ALBANY—WEISER COMPLIMENTED ON HIS SKILL IN THE MAQUA TONGUE—THE INDIANS CHARGE THE ENGLISH WITH COWARDICE—THE COMMISSIONERS DENY THESE ALLEGATIONS—WEISER DEFENDS THE ACTION OF VIRGINIA AND PENNSYLVANIA—WEISER TELLS OF THE FIRST ENGAGEMENT AT FORT DUQUESNE—CONCLUSIONS OF THE ALBANY COMMISSIONERS—PREPARING THE INDIANS TO SELL SOUTHWESTERN PENNSYLVANIA—CONNECTICUT MEN TRYING TO BUY LAND IN THE WYOMING VALLEY—WEISER EMPLOYS AN AGENT TO AID HIM—THE GOVERNOR OF NEW YORK REFUSES TO HAVE PENNSYLVANIA LAND PURCHASES PLACED ON THE MINUTES—THE INDIANS WILL SELL LAND IF THEY WILL BE ALLOWED TO REMAIN THERE—THE CONNECTICUT AGENTS MAKE TROUBLE—WEISER FORCES A PURCHASE—INDIANS OPPOSED TO SELLING WYOMING LANDS—WEISER EMPLOYED TO OBSTRUCT THE CONNECTICUT PURCHASE—THE HALF-KING COMPLAINS OF WASHINGTON—WEISER WINS BACK THE HALF-KING'S GOOD-WILL—THE INDIANS AT AUGHWICK WANT TO HEAR ABOUT THE ALBANY PURCHASE—JOHN SHIKELLAMY RESENTS THE OCCUPATION OF WYOMING VALLEY BY THE MEN FROM CONNECTICUT—HENDRICKS COMPLAINS OF BAD TREATMENT FROM NEW YORK—THE INDIANS PREVENT WEISER FROM RUNNING THE PURCHASE LINE—THE EFFECTS OF THE ALBANY PURCHASE—THE DEATH OF THE HALF-KING—RELUCTANCE OF THE WESTERN INDIANS TO MAKE WAR UPON PENNSYLVANIA—ILL-TREATMENT OF THE INDIANS.

THE OHIO INDIANS GO OVER TO THE FRENCH

The loss of the Indian alliance, and the savage cruelty which fell upon Pennsylvania, were caused by several circumstances which grew out of jealousies between the colonies and difficulties between the Assemblies and their Governors. During the autumn of 1753, the greater part of the French army returned to Canada, complaining that their schemes had all been defeated because the Indians remained true to the English interests.[1]

The French spent the winter preparing with renewed vigor to secure an Indian alliance in 1754. Pennsylvania and New York changed governors this year, which considerably crippled the management of Indian affairs in those two important colonies. Sir William Johnson, the head of Indian affairs in New York, was not even trusted by his governor. Conrad Weiser realized that Johnson's jealousy closed to him the Onondaga Council. The French quickly availed themselves of Johnson's inability and hastened to divide the councils of the Iroquois. Johnson, in self-defense, used the governor of New York to debar all the English colonies from any intercourse with the Six Nations save through him. In writing to Governor Morris of Pennsylvania, Governor Shirley said: "I am persuaded that we shall never entrust the care of any of our interests with the commission of Indian affairs at Albany."[2]

The new Governor in New York wrote to Pennsylvania just previous to the great treaty of Albany, 1754, saying: "Where I shall find an able interpreter in this country I do not know, nor have I been able to learn; the one we have is very unequal to the service. I must therefore beg the favor of you to let Mr. Weiser accompany your commissioners to Albany, that we may have his assistance or else we may be at some difficulty to understand the Indians or they us."[3]

This opinion of Colonel Johnson was similar to that entertained by Conrad Weiser. It was not so well understood, however, that Colonel Johnson's inability was the cause of the division among the Six Nations, thus forcing them to lose control over the Western Indians.

Already the Delawares were petitioning the Iroquois "that their petticoats might be removed." Since 1742 the Six Nations had proclaimed the Delawares to be women, but now with the danger of impending war on all sides, the Delawares insist that they may be made men and allowed to fight like men. The growing disorganization among the Six Nations and the absence of Conrad Weiser from their Council Fires conspired to weaken the Iroquois influence upon the Delawares. And before the summer of 1755 was over, they had

---

1. *Penna. Colonial Records*, vol. V., p. 716.
2. *Penna. Archives*, vol. II., p. 181.
3. *Penna. Colonial Records*, vol. VI., p. 15.

declared themselves no longer subjects of the Six Nations, no longer women but men. When they were women, Pennsylvania lived in peace with the Indians; when they became men, the tomahawk and scalping knife stained with blood the peaceful soil of the province.

The Albany treaty of 1754, because of two very singular land purchases made at that time, had a marked influence on the alienation of the Western Indians. When the Ohio tribes learned that the Six Nations at the Lancaster treaty of 1744 deeded to Virginia land bounded by the setting sun, they remonstrated with their masters for using such metaphors to fix a boundary line. The wise men of the Six Nations replied that the setting sun only meant the hills of the Allegheny behind which the sun was lost. Conrad Weiser was appealed to, and this undisputed authority insisted that no land was sold to Virginia in 1744 beyond the summits of the Alleghanies. Nevertheless, Virginia pushed her claims out beyond and along the Ohio River. The Delawares protested, and late in 1753, their Shawanese allies, doubtless feeling that their own title to land southeast of the Ohio River was precarious, sent a paper to the governor of Pennsylvania in which they offered to resign all their right to land east of the Ohio River in the liquidation of their debts to the traders. This offer was considered by many to be but a mere fabrication of the traders themselves. Lewis Montour, Andrew's brother, brought this paper and was reported to be a spy in the French interest. The governor evaded a direct answer to these Indians, but their offer stimulated the appetites of the proprietors to buy land and thereby deprived Virginia of any foundation to her claim along the Ohio River.

The Six Nations had always insisted that these Western Indians had no right to sell land and were merely hunting Indians, living in that region by permission. The proprietors determined then to attend the Albany treaty and see if southwestern Pennsylvania could not be bought. They had two reasons for this: (1) To settle the difficulty about the squatters on the Juniata; (2) to hold an Indian deed for land which Virginia might soon claim. Governor Hamilton appointed John Penn, Richard Peters, Isaac Norris, and Benjamin Franklin, commissioners from Pennsylvania, to attend the Albany treaty. John Penn and Richard Peters were to represent the proprietaries in the land purchase, and all four were to represent the province in the treaty, Norris and Franklin representing the Assembly.

Conrad Weiser accompanied them as an interpreter on condition that he should not be used as the principal interpreter because from lack of practice, he was losing his former fluency, "and," wrote Governor Hamilton, "finding himself at a loss for proper terms to express himself is frequently obliged to make

THE OHIO INDIANS GO OVER TO THE FRENCH

use of circumlocution, which would pique his pride in view of so considerable an audience. He said he understands the language perfectly when he hears it spoken and will at all times attend and use his endeavor that whatever is said by the Indians be truly interpreted to the gentlemen; and in this respect, I really think you may securely rely on his good sense and integrity."[4]

That Conrad Weiser should have withdrawn from the position as the chief interpreter is a significant fact. How much he was losing his fluency in the Maqua tongue is uncertain. It had scarcely been a year since he had been in Albany negotiating with the mayor of that city and the New York Indian commissioners for the return of some Pennsylvania traders held as prisoners among the French. While there, in disguise, he served the New York commissioners as an interpreter.

"It was thought fit," he wrote, "that my name should not be mentioned for fear that the expectations of the Indians would rise too high." The leading Indian in this affair was a woman. "A very intelligent and noted woman," said Weiser, "the wife of a chief." After Weiser had finished interpreting, she "asked me," wrote Weiser, "where I lived because I could talk their language so well. She wondered that I was never heard of. I told her that I lived at Shohary (Schoharie) and traveled up and down among the Indians."[5]

It is highly improbable that Weiser's tongue had lost its cunning by July 1754. Indeed, it is more probable that Weiser was still ruminating over the insults he had received at Albany the previous year when not only the governor but Colonel Johnson desired him not to have any dealings with the Indians and made it impossible for him to proceed to Onondaga as directed.[6] Weiser's desire to withdraw from the responsibility was not granted at Albany.

The Indians at the treaty frequently made charges that the commissioners could not answer, then Conrad Weiser was called to make the explanation. At one place, the Indians were pressed for a reason why they allowed their councils to be divided, and they retorted as follows:

> You [meaning New York] have neglected us for these three years past. [Then, taking a stick and throwing it behind his back.] You have thus thrown us behind your backs and disregarded us, whereas the French are a subtle and vigilant people, ever using their utmost endeavors to seduce and bring our people over to them. You ask us if the French

---

4. *Penna. Colonial Records*, vol. VI., p. 49.
5. *Penna. Colonial Records*, vol. V., p. 644.
6. *Penna. Colonial Records*, vol. V., p. 646.

have built their forts and invaded our land with our permission. I tell you, no. The governor of Virginia and the governor of Canada are both quarreling about lands which belong to us, and such a quarrel as this may end in our destruction. They fight who shall have the land. The governors of Virginia and Pennsylvania have made paths through our country to trade and built houses without acquainting us with it. They should first have asked our consent to build there, as was done when Oswego was built. For three years past, your council fires have not burned for us. You have invited us to no treaties at Albany. You have not strengthened your cause by conquest. We would have gone and taken Crown Point, but you hindered us. We had concluded to go and take it, but we were told that it was too late and that the ice would not bear us. Instead of this, you burnt your own fort at Saratoga and ran away from it, which was a shame and a scandal to you. Look about your country and see, you have no fortifications about you; no, not even this city. Look at the French; they are men; they are fortifying everywhere.' But we are ashamed to say it, you are all like women, bare and open without any fortifications.[7]

The commissioners from the New England States and New York and Pennsylvania had some difficulty agreeing upon a suitable reply to these charges, which were made by Plendricks, the Mohawk, a warm friend of Colonel Johnson. It was finally agreed that these allegations should be denied, and then it was left to Conrad Weiser to explain these things in his own way. Said the commissioners,

What you say is a great surprise to us; we know that for five years past, in the face of all the Six Nations, in open daylight, the French have been marching troops into that country, which we ever did and do still acknowledge to belong to you, tho' within your Father, the King of Great Britain's Dominions, and under his protection. The French published their plans. They drove away the English traders that they did not capture and imprison. Last year they built two forts in that country, and notwithstanding this act, we have never heard that either Virginia or Pennsylvania sent one soldier or built one house for their and your protection till this present year.

---

7. Penna. Colonial Records, vol. VI., pp. 80, 81.

THE OHIO INDIANS GO OVER TO THE FRENCH

It is fortunate that Mr. Weiser, who transacts the public business of Virginia and Pennsylvania with your nation and is one of your council and knows this matter well, is now present. Hear the account he gives, and that will set this matter in a true light.

Weiser spoke as follows:

The road to Ohio is no new road; it is an old and frequented road; the Shawanese and Delawares removed thither above thirty years ago from Pennsylvania, ever since which, that road has been traveled by our traders at their invitation, and always with safety, until within these few years that the French with their usual faithlessness sent armies there, threatened the Indians, and obstructed our trade with them. The governor of Virginia, observing these hostilities in time of full peace, sent his Majesty an account of them. The King directed the governor to hold a conference with the Six Nations at some point near where the troubles were and also sent a present to the Six Nations. Accordingly, in 1750, I was sent to Onondaga by the governor of Virginia to invite you to come to Fredericksburg to receive the King's present, but you would not come. Thereupon the present was sent the following year to the Ohio Indians, and when the governor proposed building a fort near the mouth of the Monongahela, the Indians in that region appeared to be well pleased. They sent a belt of wampum to the Onondaga Council for advice, but nothing was ever heard from the belt. Last year the French invaded that country, and the Indians there, your flesh and blood, sent repeated messages to the governor of Virginia to send his young men to their assistance. The governor of Virginia, being a man of great forethought and prudence, hesitated and sent two messages by Andrew Montour to Onondaga for your advice how to act. It happened that no council could be called at either time. The chiefs at Onondaga desired Mr. Montour to tell their brother, the governor of Virginia, to act cautiously, and let the French strike the first blow. The French continued to come nearer when the Half King, on behalf of the Delawares and Shawanese and of the United Nations at Ohio, was sent to warn them off. In the meantime, the chiefs of these nations came to Virginia and Pennsylvania asking us to call back our people and keep them east of the Alleghanies in order to prevent bloodshed between the French and the English. But when these Indians returned and found that the French had disregarded their warning, had refused to withdraw their people, and had positively declared that they would hold that region even if they were forced to fight the Indians; then these chiefs sent a hurried message to Virginia and Pennsylvania, saying that nothing would be left of them but the ashes of their houses and bones, unless their white brethren immediately sent soldiers to aid them and built a strong house to protect them.

Moved by this request, the governor of Virginia sent people to build a house at the mouth of the Monongahela, but before they had finished it, the French came down the river with a thousand men and eighteen cannon and told the people who were building it, and were but forty- four in number, that they must either fight or give up possession, which last they were obliged to do on account of the superior force of the French. Brethren, this is the truth which we have thought proper to relate so, particularly that the prudent and cautious conduct of Virginia might be known to the Six Nations. As to Pennsylvania, they have never sent a warrior or built a fort at Ohio.[8]

The Six Nation deputies did not see fit to answer Conrad Weiser. They found other things of which to complain. They found themselves between the upper and nether millstones of the French and English, and the grinding commenced when the Six Nations discovered that they could not control the Western Indians, who were now throwing off their allegiance to the Iroquois, and beginning to fight for themselves. The united opinion of the commissioners at Albany relative to Indian affairs was (1) that the French were determined to absorb all the fur trade of North America ; (2) that the colonies being in a divided and disunited state, were unable to defeat the measures of the French; (3) that the affairs of the Six Nations, their friendship and alliance, had been sadly neglected, and great injury done by private enterprise seeking to absorb trade and acquire land; (4) that the unrestrained traffic in rum had caused a great amount of trouble. As a remedy, the commissioners recommended that in the future, no private purchases of land be legal, that all trade be regulated, that forts be built, and war vessels provided for the lakes. Before the cumbersome machinery of excessive localism in government affairs could get these suggestions into operation, the Indians were with the French, and actual war was in progress.

---

8. *Penna. Colonial Records*, vol. VI., pp. 84, 85.

During the latter part of the sessions at Albany, efforts were made to secure a tract of land in Pennsylvania from the Six Nations. Since the Shawanese offer of 1753, the proprietors realized such a purchase might be possible. The increase of squatters on the Juniata, and the inability of the governor to remove them, made it imperative that something be done. The entire Juniata difficulty grew out of a reluctant and parsimonious proprietary policy. In contrast to William Penn's method, it bought land only from the Indians under strong pressure and after it had actually been settled. Now the portentous threats of war brought the proprietors into a condition of willingness to buy land. Early in the spring of 1754, Governor Hamilton, by the advice of Conrad Weiser, sent John Shikellamy to the councils of the Six Nations to put them into the humor of selling their claim upon southwestern Pennsylvania. We are not told how successful John Shikellamy was, but when the commissioners reached Albany, they found the Indians exceedingly adverse to selling any land in Pennsylvania. Preparing the Six Nation chiefs for such a transaction was put into Conrad Weiser's hands. The old interpreter found a surprisingly complicated condition. The conference affairs were largely under the direction of the Mohawks, and during all the previous purchases made by Pennsylvania, these Indians received no share of the purchase money. Although it was generally understood that the Mohawks had no conquest rights to the Susquehanna lands, they were, nevertheless, jealous of what the other nations had received.

Conrad Weiser further learned, to his dismay, that there were several men in Albany from Connecticut, and they were secretly negotiating with the Mohawks for a large tract of land in Pennsylvania. This was for the Susquehanna Company and was to include the Wyoming Valley and the east branch of the Susquehanna. It appears that the sober judgment of the Six Nations was emphatically against selling more land on the Susquehanna. The Connecticut agents, however, strongly influenced the Mohawks, and while they could not buy the Wyoming lands, they could prevent Weiser from accomplishing his purpose.

About this time, John Shikellamy arrived in Albany and brought Gagradoda, a Cayuga chief, who had aided in persuading the Cayugas and Oneidas into a willingness to sell. Weiser took Gagradoda to his lodgings, where, for a liberal reward, he engaged him to serve as a private counselor and to direct what measures should be taken to secure the cooperation of the Indians. This kind of lobbying was quite common among the Six Nations. After a few days spent sounding the opinions of the most influential Indians, Gagradoda reported to Weiser that all the nations except the Oneidas were quite favorable to selling all southwestern Pennsylvania. The objecting nation insisted that the affair should be deferred until the arrival of the Mohawks. This movement put the control of the affair into the hands of Hendricks, who persuaded the Indians not to sell further west than the sources of the streams which emptied into the west branch of the Susquehanna. One day during the public treaty, Hendricks held up two belts of wampum, saying that the proprietaries of Pennsylvania had sent them to purchase a large tract in southwestern Pennsylvania.

The governor of New York immediately wished to know how far north this purchase was intended to extend. He was told it would include all the west branch of the Susquehanna, none of which was further north than forty-one degrees and thirty minutes.

Governor De Lancey replied that since this matter concerned only Pennsylvania, it might be transacted privately, and no record thereof should appear in the conference minutes.

The Pennsylvania commission insisted that all their land purchases had ever been conducted in the most public manner, and they desired that this one might be recorded. In this, they were overruled by the joint commission, and it was decided that the clerk should take notice in the minutes of what Hendricks had said. This ruling of the joint commission threw all land negotiations out of the general conference and made them private, thus aiding the plans of the Connecticut agents and sowing the seeds of distrust and suspicion among the Indians.

The next day in a private conference, the Pennsylvania commission offered four hundred pounds for all of southwestern Pennsylvania. The Indians withdrew and formed a circle at one end of the room, where they spent more than an hour in a private consultation. They grew "very warm and earnest in their debates and seemed to differ much in opinion. Hendricks spoke a great deal and, turning around, observed Mr. Weiser near them and desired him to withdraw, which he did, and after some little time, they sent for him and took him into their councils and asked his opinion on divers matters."

The Indians then returned to their seats when Hendricks spoke as follows:

> We have several times desired the governor of Pennsylvania to remove his people from our lands, and we understand that he has done his utmost endeavors for that purpose except using force, which we do not desire he should. We are now, therefore, willing to part with them and expect to be paid for them. Brother Onas, what we are now going to say is a matter of great moment, which we desire you to

remember as long as the sun and moon last. We are willing to sell you this large tract of land for your people to live upon, but we desire that it may be considered as a part of our agreement that when we are all dead and gone, your grandchildren may not say to our grandchildren that your forefathers sold the land to our forefathers, and therefore begone off of them. This is wrong. Let us be all as brothers as well after as before of giving you deeds for land. After we have sold our land, we, in a little time, have nothing to show for it, but it is not so with you; your grandchildren will get something for it as long as the world stands. Our grandchildren will have no advantage from it. They will say we are fools for selling so much land for so small a matter and curse us. Therefore, let it be a part of the present agreement that we shall treat one another as brethren to the latest generation, even after we shall not have left a foot of land.[9]

This was an effort on the part of the Indians to get a reservation in the deed similar to the one the Delawares had in the Walking Purchase, to the effect that owning the land would not be sufficient reason for driving the Indians away. And it was, therefore, thoroughly understood by all the Indians that while the Albany purchase gave the white man permission to settle on those lands, it in no manner was understood to mean the removal of the Indians so long as they desired to remain.

During the afternoon of the same day Hendricks made the above proposals, Conrad Weiser reported that the Indians were having a heated discussion among themselves. Their sentiments were poisoned, and he believed it was done by Mr. Woodbridge and Mr. Lydius, the men negotiating the purchase for the Susquehanna Company. Weiser was ordered by the commission not to yield but to leave the Indians to themselves. In the evening, the Indians offered to sell all the land east of the Alleghanies and south of the west branch of the Susquehanna River and no more.

Weiser told them this was a plain confirmation of the rumor that the Six Nations were secretly in league with the French and intended to sell them the land west of the mountains. Weiser knew Hendricks and the Mohawks had no conquest rights to western Pennsylvania. He knew that the proposed purchase was Cayuga and Oneida land. Therefore, he told Hendricks that the Pennsylvania commissioners were highly incensed at this last offer and would have nothing to do with the land, especially since it was evident that the Indians were

---

9. *Penna. Colonial Records*, vol. VI., pp. 115, 116.

entertaining some dark and hidden projects injurious to Pennsylvania. When Hendricks, who it is supposed was anxious to negotiate the Connecticut sale, realized that he could not limit the Oneidas to the Alleghanies, he went before the Indians and, in "a pathetic speech," recounted the ancient friendship of the sons of Onas and their constant generosity to the Red man. This removed the frowns from the Indian faces. Weiser was called in, and the boundaries were fixed. A line was to be run westward from the mouth of Kayarondinagh Creek, now Penn's Creek, which was four or five miles south of the mouth of the west branch of the Susquehanna River. The Indians were desirous of selling all the land drained by the Juniata but none drained by the west branch of the Susquehanna. With Lewis Evans' map spread before them, the Indians were shown the possibility of the Juniata being at some points further north than the mouth of Penn's Creek. Hence, the Indians consented to have the line run to the northwest to clear all the Juniata lands, even if they extended to Lake Erie. For this tract, the proprietors paid four hundred pounds in coin. The Indians then spoke to the Pennsylvania commissioners, saying:

> The north line shall go to the north of west as far as your province extends; let it reach beyond the Ohio and to Lake Erie, wherever it will. This will convince the world and you that we have no connection with Onontio [Governor of Canada] since these lands from this time will belong by our title to King George and to Onas. Make out your deed, and do not be long about it.
>
> As to Wyoming and Shamokin and the land contiguous thereto on Susquehanna, we reserve them for our hunting ground and for the residence of such, as at this time of war shall remove from among the French and choose to live there, and we have appointed John Shikellamy to take care of them. He is our representative and agent there and has our orders not to suffer either Onas' people nor the New Englanders to settle any of those lands, and if any shall presume to do it, we have directed him to complain to Onas, whether it shall be his own people or from other provinces, and to insist on their being turned off, and if he shall fail in this application we will come ourselves and turn them off. Nobody shall have this land. Get your deed ready as fast as you can.[10]

---

10. *Penna. Colonial Records*, vol. VI., p. 119.

WASHINGTON MEETING THE WESTERN INDIANS

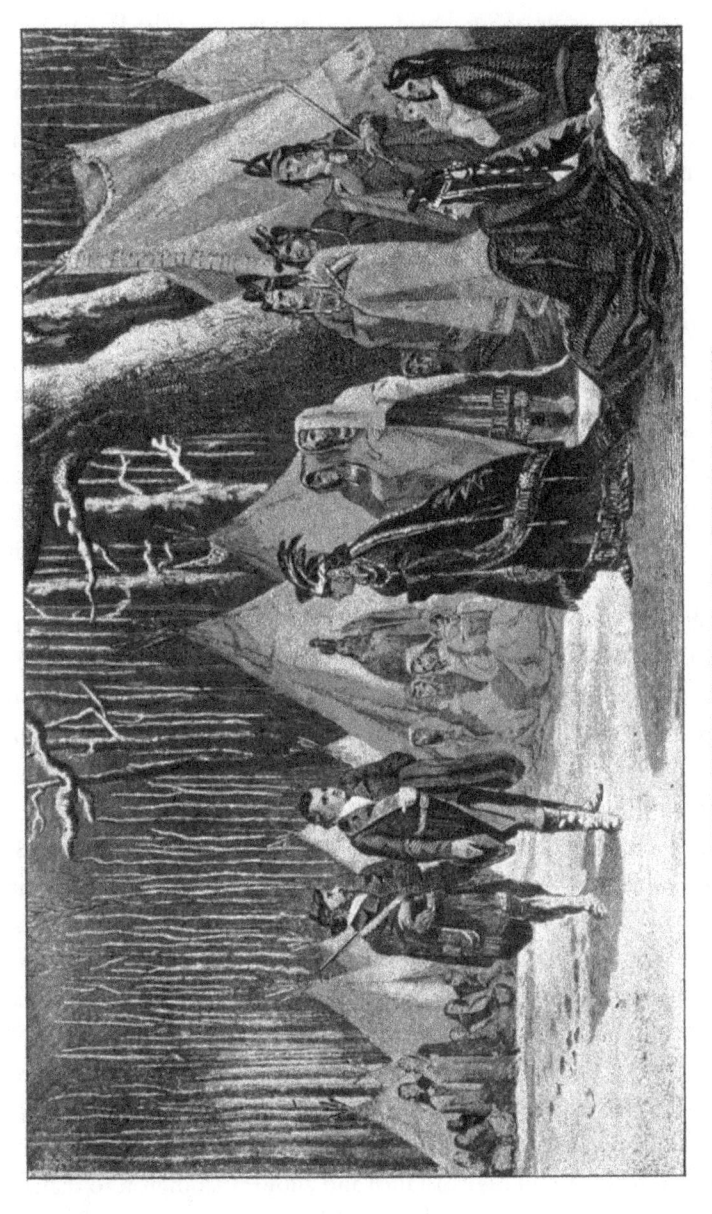

Upon the basis of these opinions, the Pennsylvania proprietaries employed Conrad Weiser to use every effort to prevent the Mohawk Indians from selling Susquehanna land to the Connecticut agents. Weiser then went to Mr. Woodbridge, the schoolmaster of Stockbridge, and showed him the Indian deeds and titles held for land by the proprietors. Woodbridge said that he was perfectly satisfied and would cause no further trouble on behalf of Connecticut. Lydius, however, made no such promises, and before the Indians had all returned home from this treaty, the Connecticut agents held Mohawk deeds for the eastern part of the Wyoming Valley and the east branch of the Susquehanna River.

In the meantime, events were transpiring on the Ohio, which caused the Albany land purchases to embarrass the governor's policy towards the Western Indians seriously. In May 1754, the Half King, still faithful to the English, sent word to Washington of the location of Jumonville, the French captain, who was supposed to be coming from Fort Duquesne to attack Washington. During the previous winter, the Half King's loyalty was severely strained by the treatment he received while acting as the guide for Washington and Gist to Venango. This, however, the old Indian overlooked. But when the attack upon Jumonville was planned, one Davison, who was present, said, "Washington and the Half King differed much in judgment, and on the Colonel's refusing to take his advice, the English and the Indians separated. After which, the Indians discovered the French in a hollow and hid themselves, lying on their bellies behind a hill; afterward, they discovered Colonel Washington on the opposite side of the hollow in the gray of the morning, and when the English fired, which they did in great confusion, the Indians came out of their cover and closed with the French and killed them with their tomahawks, on which the French surrendered."[11]

Virginia speaking of this action, said that Washington fired the first gun. The French called it a massacre, declaring that Jumonville was sent out from Fort Duquesne with a message. The Indians insisted that Jumonville was killed and scalped by one of their number. Whatever the facts were in the case, the Indians certainly secured many French scalps, which they sent with some belts of black wampum to the more Western Indians who were wavering and uncertain where to throw their alliance. Previous to the attack upon Fort Necessity, the Indians of that section were all loyal to the English. The growing coolness between Washington and the Half King caused the latter, just before the fight at Fort Necessity, to withhold his assistance and allow Washington to manage it in his own way. The defeat so stung the Virginians that they charged the friendly

---

11. *Penna. Colonial Records*, vol. VI., p. 195.

THE OHIO INDIANS GO OVER TO THE FRENCH

Indians with treachery, saying they had secretly aided the French. These charges angered the Half King and his men.

In August, the old chief came to John Harris' Ferry to meet Conrad Weiser and accompany him to Aughwick. On the way the Half King "complained very much," wrote Weiser, "of the behavior of Colonel Washington, (tho' in a very moderate way, saying the Colonel was a good-natured man, but had no experience), that he took upon him to command the Indians as his slaves, and would have them every day upon the Out Scout and attack the Enemy by themselves, and that he would by no means take advice from the Indians, that he lay at one place from one full moon to another and made no fortifications at all, but that little thing upon the meadow, where he thought the French would come up to him in open field; that had he taken the Half King's advice and made such fortifications as the Half King advised him to make, he would certainly have beat the French off; that the French had acted as great cowards and the English as fools in that engagement; that he (the Half King) had carried off his wife and children, so did other Indians before the battle begun, because Colonel Washington would never listen to them, but was always driving them on to fight by his directions."[12]

This alienation of the Indians was only temporary. At heart, the Half King was in sympathy with the English, and at the Aughwick Conference, held in August, and September 1754, Conrad Weiser, with the assistance of Pennsylvania presents, won the old warrior and his people back to the English cause. Beaver, a Delaware chief, in speaking to the deputies of the Six Nations at Aughwick, said: "Uncle, I still remember the time when you first conquered us, and made women of us, and told us that you took us under your protection and that we must not meddle with wars, but stay in the house and mind council affairs. We have hitherto followed your directions and lived very easy under your protection, and no high wind did blow to make us uneasy, but now things seem to take another turn, and a high wind is rising. We desire you, therefore, Uncle, to have your eyes open and be watchful over us, your cousins, as you have always been heretofore."

Then turning to Conrad Weiser, Beaver said:

> Brother, . . . by your speech just now made to us, you comforted our hearts and removed all doubts and jealousy. It is what you said to us, like the morning sun. We see how clear your kindness and goodwill to us and our allies. We will make it known to all . . . Brother, when

---

12. *Penna. Colonial Records*, vol. VI., pp. 151, 152.

William Penn first appeared, we looked into his face and judged him to be our brother . . . we then erected an everlasting friendship with William Penn and his people, which we on our side, as well as you, have observed as much as possible to this day. We always looked upon you to be one flesh and blood with us. We desire you will look upon us in the same light and let that treaty of friendship made by our forefathers on both sides subsist and be in force from generation to generation; both our lives, our wives' and children's lives, and those as yet unborn, depend upon it. Pray, brother, consider well what we say and let it be so.[13]

At this conference, Weiser learned that the Shawanese and Delaware tribes had formed an alliance and that the French had offered them presents to join them or remain neutral. The Indians made no reply but immediately sent their deputies to Aughwick for the purpose, as Weiser thought, of learning the attitude of the English and renewing their bond of friendship. In this conference, Weiser thoroughly secured the goodwill and alliance of those Western Indians. At the close of the treaty, the Indians pressed him to tell what happened at Albany. He accordingly told them all about the purchase.

"They seemed not to be very well pleased," wrote Weiser, "because the Six Nations had sold such a large tract." When, however, Weiser explained that it was done to frustrate the land schemes of the Connecticut men on the Susquehanna and the French on the Ohio, they appeared satisfied. The Indians did not then know that the purchase included most of the west branch of the Susquehanna. For the time being, they were content. With a child-like simplicity, they were pleased that the new Governor, Robert Hunter Morris, should have come to Aughwick to see them. They were pleased with his speech, which Conrad Weiser had carefully prepared.[14] They went back to Ohio, into danger and temptation to learn from the lips of the French that their cherished hunting grounds on the west branch of the Susquehanna had all been sold.

In the meantime, John Shikellamy reported that the Connecticut men were settling on the east branch of the Susquehanna. Weiser declared that the Indians would go to war if these men were not removed. He suggested that Hendricks, the Mohawk chief, be invited to Philadelphia and measures be taken to invalidate the Connecticut deed.

---

13. *Penna. Colonial Records*, vol. VI., pp. 155, 156.
14. *Penna. Colonial Records*, vol. VI., p. 158.

"If Hendricks should not come, then," said Weiser, "that would be evidence that he was a party to this secret business."

But Hendricks did come in January 1755. He acknowledged that the deed had been obtained by fraud. Indians are always slow to censure their own people. Yet Hendricks acknowledged that Lydius was the agent who, secretly, by getting the Indians intoxicated, obtained the deed from persons acting in a private and not in a public capacity. Hendricks was inclined to say very little on the subject. It would be wrong to destroy the deed, he said, but if the governor of Pennsylvania would kindle a council fire at Albany and invite there two deputies from each of the Six Nations, then it might be possible to oblige the government of Connecticut to give up the deed. It is not within the province of this work to examine the voluminous discussion between Pennsylvania and Connecticut upon the merits of this claim. It is only necessary here to show that the Connecticut purchase on the Susquehanna and the determination to settle there against the will of the Indians brought down on Pennsylvania the ruthless vengeance of the Indians and exposed the northeastern part of the province to their unrestrained fury.

On other matters, Hendricks became very confiding during his visit to Philadelphia. Weiser finally declined to interpret any further "because," he said, "Hendricks was complaining so vigorously of a sister colony that it might be construed as treason to interpret it."

Governor Morris authorized the council to be made public, and the complaints of Hendricks were put upon record. The Mohawk said,

> I will hide nothing from you. The Six Nations are divided. The French party is larger than the English party. Onontio [Governor of Canada] has found a way to divide our people. He gives large rewards. He builds strong houses wherever the situation is advantageous, and it can serve either to curb us or to intercept you in your commerce with us . . . He gives fine clothes. He employs artful men who live as Indians, whereas you are weak. You build no strong houses. You send persons only to trade amongst us, who consult their own interest and often impose on us . . . We are Mohawks and boast that we are on the English side and therefore have a right to speak things, tho' they may be disagreeable to you. We mean it well, however, and now shall take the freedom to tell you an affair that will always do hurt to the English till it be remedied. The government of New York does not use us well unless they can be brought to make us satisfaction; we can

never be as good friends as we were formerly. They have taken our lands from us. They carry on a clandestine trade with French Indians. This is disgusting to us and corrupting to our young men.[15]

The governor of Pennsylvania, following Weiser's advice, condoled with these Indians and promised to lay the matter before the King. But the Indians liked prompt reparation, and when they had been home for some months and heard nothing about redress of their wrongs, they lost the zeal for the English cause, and the French party grew larger among the Iroquois. This division among the Six Nations weakened their control over their tributary tribes on the Ohio and the Wyoming Valley.

To add to the embarrassment continually gathering around the English, the Pennsylvania proprietors employed Conrad Weiser in October 1754 to run the northwest line of the Albany purchase. As soon as the Indians realized that this line must necessarily cross the west branch of the Susquehanna and that the Six Nations had sold that river basin, they compelled Weiser to stop.

"They said," wrote Weiser, "that a northwest line was not according to the agreement. They insisted that it had been expressly stipulated by the chiefs of the Six Nations and the commissioners of Pennsylvania that the line should stand, provided it did not touch the lands on Zinachsa River (the west branch of the Susquehanna) or come near the Big Island, other ways the purchase must only include the land then settled by the white people (meaning the Juniata and Buffalo Creek settlers)."

Weiser then stoutly supported the cause of the Indians, saying to Peters, "You know, sir, that the Indians actually said so, and we took L. Evans' map before us, and we assured the Indians that that line would never touch the river Zinachsa below the Big Island, and so the Indians consented, but I saw plain that that course would cross Zinachsa River about Canasorgu. I should be very sorry if their Honors, the proprietors, should insist upon that line to be run against the Indians' mind, but would rather advise to make a line in presence of the Indians or some of them, to take all the settlers aforesaid and give no offence to the Indians. We would find advantage in the next purchase and save a deal of trouble now."

The Indians told Weiser that if this line was run, or if the white people attempted to settle on this land, they would kill their cattle first, and if they persisted, then the white people themselves should be killed.[16]

---

15. *Penna. Colonial Records*, vol. VI., pp. 280, 284.
16. Manuscript letters of Conrad Weiser, in collections of the Pennsylvania Historical Society.

This Albany purchase was a powerful factor in alienating the Indians. Half of the four hundred pounds purchase money was paid at the time of the contract; the remainder was not to be paid until the settlers had actually crossed the Allegheny Mountains. In 1755, the Indians declared they would not receive the second installment. Hendricks persuaded them to stand by the deed. This was in July 1755. With Braddock's defeat, this entire body of dissatisfied Indians arose to seek vengeance on Pennsylvania soil. Three years of bloodshed and outrage induced the proprietaries, persuaded by Conrad Weiser, to deed back to the Indians all of the Albany purchase, which lay west of the Allegheny Mountains. Conrad Weiser and Richard Peters accomplished this in the year 1758.

After the surrender at Fort Necessity, the Juniata and Ohio Indians were greatly excited. Swarms of them came to Aughwick and clamored for food. George Croghan petitioned the governor and the Assembly for an order to feed them. The bills which Croghan had been sending to Philadelphia had grown into uncomfortable dimensions. Suspicion had been afloat that George Croghan was unreliable, and the Assembly accordingly cut his bills. Finally, when it was hinted that Croghan was secretly in league with the French, this prince of traders became disgusted and decided to leave Aughwick.

The Assembly then approved his accounts and recommended that the Indians be invited further east where they could be supplied at less expense. While these things were uncertain, the Half King, who was still loyal to the English and the only man who could hold together the Ohio Indians, came with his family to John Harris' Ferry on the Susquehanna. Why he should have been induced to travel so far east when his councils were so necessary on the Ohio is a mystery. On the night of October 4th, he died. John Harris asked the party of about twenty Indians who accompanied him how they wished the Half King buried. The Indians replied that they looked upon their chief as one of the white people and that John Harris might bury him. They would not.

Harris managed the funeral with considerable pomp and display, which pleased the Indians very much. The Half King's family remained at Harris' for nearly a month at the province's expense.

Governor Dinwiddie, writing of this circumstance, remarked: "I am very sorry for the death of the Half King."

George Croghan said, "The Half King's death has been much lamented by all the Indians."

Conrad Weiser wrote, "The Half King died about a week ago at Paxton; I suppose by his hard drinking, most everybody treated him. He brought the sickness upon him that carried him off."[17]

---

17. Manuscript letters of October 12, 1754, in the collections of the Pennsylvania Historical Society.

Governor Morris, in a letter to the governor of New York, observed: "I have accounts from Paxton of ye death of ye Half King, a chief of ye Indians, his friends, it seems, attribute his death to French witchcraft, and threaten revenge, but this being only the opinion of an Indian trader is not to be depended on."[18]

The Indian trader was John Harris himself, who wrote, "Those Indians that were here blame the French for his death, by bewitching him, as they had a conjurer to inquire into the cause a few days before he died, and it is his opinion, together with his relations, that the French have been the cause of their great man's death, by reason of his striking them lately,[19] for which they seem to threaten immediate revenge, and desired me to let it be known. All Indians that are here are in great trouble, especially his relations. I have sent an account to Conrad Weiser at Shamokin this day, who, I expect, will be down upon notice. I humbly presume that his death is a very great loss, especially at this critical time."[20]

The mystery which hung around the Half King's death only aggravated the bitterness of the Indians' sorrow and resentment. His loss severed the last tie which bound these people to the government of Pennsylvania.

The Indians, from that time until Braddock's defeat, either remained neutral or secretly went over to the French. When Pennsylvania refused any longer to trust Croghan to distribute supplies among the Indians, Conrad Weiser was sent to do it. Weiser's letter from Aughwick, September 13th, reveals the beginning of the last influence which alienated the Delawares from the province. The Indians were very reluctant to take up the hatchet against the white men of Pennsylvania. The traditions of William Penn and his people lay close to their hearts, but starvation and ill-treatment drove them to it.

"Mr. Croghan must either be trusted," wrote Weiser, "to buy and distribute provisions, or the government must keep a man there. Lewis Montour, Andrew's brother, disturbs them often by bringing strong liquor to them. They cannot help buying and drinking it when it is so near, and Lewis[21] sells it very dear to them and pretends that his wife, who is an ugly Indian squaw, does it. He sends to the inhabitants to fetch it for him, and Mr. Croghan can by no means prevent it because they keep it in the woods about or within a mile from his house, and there the Indians will go (after having notice) and drink away their clothing, and so come back to George Croghan's drunk and naked."

---

18. *Penna. Archives*, vol. II., p. 179.
19. Attack upon Jumonville.
20. *Penna. Archives*, vol. II., p. 178.
21. Lewis Montour was thought to be a secret agent of the French.

Weiser was the first man who ever dared to inform the provincial government of the treatment the Indians received from the early settlers of Cumberland County. "It is a surprising thing," he wrote, "that no means can be found to prevent the inhabitants in Cumberland County from selling strong liquor to the Indians. I am creditably informed that some of the magistrates of that county sell the most,"

Weiser told one of these justices that the best thing for the Indians would be for the governor to discharge him and all others of his kind and "put in commission those who were not whiskey traders, men who would exercise their authority."[22]

While things were in this troubling condition, the governor of Pennsylvania sent Weiser to distribute supplies among the Indians. He distributed two hundred bushels of cornmeal in early July at John Harris' Ferry. The Indians were very grateful and begged Weiser to lead them to Wills Creek, where they could do scouting for Braddock. At Aughwick, Weiser found only women and children, who insisted they must be fed if their husbands and young men were to fight for the English. Weiser gave them five hundred weight of flour and appointed two of the Shikellamys to preside there until the pleasure of the government was learned. Weiser complained again of the white men in that county. "Our people," he said, "are very malicious against the Indians. They curse and damn them to their faces and say, 'must we feed you, and your husbands fight in the meantime for the French.'"[23]

At the time of writing this letter, Weiser and the people in and around Aughwick were ignorant of Braddock's defeat near Fort Duquesne. The Indian disaffection had spread over all of western Pennsylvania. Weiser met only the families of the Indians who yet remained loyal to the English. The unfortunate land purchases at Albany, the unrestrained traffic in rum, and the neglect and ill-treatment shown to the Indians gave the French every advantage. Their dark-skinned allies increased every day. The daring blow by a few French and Indians against Braddock and the destruction of an English army by so few men filled the Indians with amazement and admiration. The hesitating remnant of the Delawares was alienated, and the dogs of war turned loose upon defenseless Pennsylvania.

---

22. *Penna. Colonial Records*, vol. VI., p. 149.
23. *Penna. Colonial Records*, vol. VI., p. 495.

XVI

Weiser and the Pennsylvania Efforts for Defense

DUNBAR'S RETREAT DISGUSTS THE INDIANS—A MONEY BILL FRAMED—THE GOVERNOR HESITATES AND WILL NOT SIGN—THE ASSEMBLY'S POSITION—THE GOVERNOR'S POSITION—THE ASSEMBLY OPPOSES ANY AMENDMENTS—THE GERMANS FEAR CATHOLIC TREACHERY—THE FRIENDLY INDIANS CANNOT BE HELD—THE INDIANS' OPINION OF GENERAL BRAD- DOCK—WEISER'S ADVICE—THE INDIAN OUTBREAK—THE GOVERNOR SUPPRESSES THE NEWS—WEISER NOT DRAWN INTO THE FIRST POLITICAL QUARREL—THOMAS PENN'S LETTER TO WEISER—WEISER OPPOSED TO QUAKER ASSEMBLYMEN—THE INDIANS ATTACK JOHN HARRIS—WEISER ALARMS THE COUNTRY—WEISER ORGANIZES THE GERMANS FOR DEFENCE—LOCAL JEALOUSIES—THE GOVERNOR APPROVES WEISER'S ACTIONS—WEISER SURROUNDED WITH DIFFICULTIES—MOBS THREATEN TO GO TO PHILADELPHIA—THE PROPRIETORS MAKE A DONATION—THE ASSEMBLY DISTRUSTS THE GOVERNOR—BERKS COUNTY POLITICS—THE ANTI-WEISER FACTION IN BERKS COUNTY—WEISER DENIES ALL CHARGES AGAINST HIM—WEISER'S ACCOUNTS DIFFICULT TO SETTLE—THE ATTACK UPON THE MORAVIANS—THE INDIANS PLAN TO ATTACK CONRAD WEISER—JAMES HAMILTON'S SUGGESTIONS—PLANS FOR DEFENSE—THE GOVERNOR COMPLAINS OF THE PEOPLE—WAR DECLARED AGAINST THE DELAWARE INDIANS—JAMES LOGAN OPPOSED TO THE DECLARATION—WEISER'S OPOOSITION TO THE SCALP ACT—COLONEL JOHNSON OPPOSED TO THE DECLARATION OF WAR—THE FRIENDLY INDIANS TURN AWAY FROM PENNSYLVANIA.

DURING Braddock's slow and painful march towards Fort Duquesne, the Western Indians remained in suspense and expectation. When, however, a handful of French and Indians sallied out and defeated the advanced portion of Braddock's army, the Indians were astonished. They became loud in their criticisms of English inability. When General Dunbar began his inglorious retreat towards Philadelphia, destroying his magazine and his supplies, ignoring the protests of the governors of Pennsylvania, Virginia, New York, and Massachusetts, the friendly Indians lost all confidence, and there was a general stampede to the French.

Immediately upon the receipt of this disastrous news in Philadelphia, Governor Morris convened his council, and the Assembly sent for Conrad Weiser. Unfortunately, the old interpreter was confined to his house with illness, and the Assembly was deprived of his counsels; though he sent his son "Sammie," the province experienced a loss.

The Assembly was, however, in no uncertain frame of mind. Benjamin Franklin had become a leading figure in whom the Friends and the Germans reposed a large measure of confidence. The Assembly promptly framed a money bill and presented it to the governor on August 1st, 1755, for approval. No colony among the thirteen was more prompt and generous in voting money for the King's use than Pennsylvania. This money bill provided a tax of fifty thousand pounds on all personal property and real estate.

Before the governor had decided upon his defense plan or solicited any funds from the Assembly, this bill was laid before him for his signature. Ever since the death of William Penn, there had been a growing desire among the people to have proprietary estates taxed the same as any other real estate. The "Walking Purchase" from the Delawares and the "Albany Purchase" from the Iroquois had aroused popular suspicion about the sincerity of the proprietors in Indian affairs.

The Assembly had for many years insisted that Penn's heirs should share the expense of Indian treaties. Their petitions to this effect received no recognition. Now when it was evident to everyone that an Indian war was about to burst upon the province, the Assembly was determined to force the proprietary estates to bear their share of the expense.

On the other hand, the governor had explicit instructions from the proprietors to permit no legislation that would jeopardize the proprietary estates. To permit the local assessors to place values upon the manors and the unseated lands would, wrote Governor Morris to Thomas Penn, be used

> without mercy. One very good argument against your being taxed at all is the great expense you are at in administering the government, especially since the Assembly have refused the governor's salary,

which you will be obliged to pay. Since Mr. Franklin has put himself at the head of the Assembly, they have gone greater lengths than ever and have not only discovered (revealed) the warmth of their resentment against your family, but are using every means in their power, even while their country is invaded, to wrest the government out of your hands, and to take the whole power of it into their own The Quakers, indeed, do not wish you to part with the government, because they will have much less power under the Crown, but would willingly throw as much weight as possible into the Assembly. Franklin has views that they know nothing of, and tho' they submit to him in the Assembly, the more sensible part of them are not heartily satisfied with his attachment to them. The truth, I believe, is that he is courting them in order to distress you and, at the same time, leading them into measures that will, in the end, deprive them of any share in the administration.[1]

The governor amended this money bill by excluding the proprietary estates from taxation. The Assembly very promptly denied the right of any executive to amend a supply bill; they insisted that he should either accept or reject it. They said,

The proprietary instructions are secrets to us, and we may spend much time and much of the public money in preparing and framing bills for supply, which, after all, must from these instructions prove abortive. If we are thus to be driven from bill to bill without one solid reason afforded us and can raise no money for the King's service, and relief and security of our country till we, fortunately, hit on the only bill the governor is allowed to pass, or till we consent to make such as the governor or proprietaries direct us to make, we see little use of Assemblies in this particular, and think we might as well leave it to the governor or proprietaries to make for us what supply laws they please, and save ourselves and the country the expense and trouble. We are left in the dark to grope around for the right bill. All debates and all reasonings are vain, where proprietary instructions, just or unjust, right or wrong, must inviolably be observed.

Every citizen is astonished at this conduct of the proprietors, who refuse to bear any share of the increasing expense of Indian affairs,

---

1. *Penna. Colonial Records*, vol. VI., pp. 739, 740.

tho' they reap such immense advantages by their friendship; but they now, by their lieutenant (the governor), refuse to contribute any part toward resisting an invasion of the King's colony committed to their care, or to submit their claim of exemption to the decision of their sovereign. I11 fine, we have the most sensible concern for the poor, distressed inhabitants of the frontiers. We have taken every step in our power consistent with the just rights of the Freemen of Pennsylvania for their relief, and we have reason to believe that in the midst of their distresses, they themselves do not wish us to go further. *Those who would give up essential liberty to purchase a little temporary safety deserve neither liberty nor safety.*[2]

Amid this heated discussion between the governor and the Assembly, an Indian war had broken out all along the frontier. The news of Braddock's defeat and Dunbar's ignominious retreat toward Philadelphia filled the Pennsylvania pioneers with consternation and fear. The woods were full of rumors and the wildest stories. The Germans of Tulpehocken, led by Conrad Weiser and other magistrates, petition the governor, begging that all arms and ammunition be taken away from the Catholics who were settled in that vicinity. The petitioners were positive that the Catholics were in secret league with the French and were plotting against the lives of the Germans[3] The Assembly replied to these petitioners, saying: "The Plouse has, this afternoon, examined Conrad Weiser and some other gentlemen from Berks County, and we apprehend there is very little foundation for the report."[4]

Indeed, it must be said in this connection that the cool deliberation of the Assembly prevented, more than once, the outbreak of civil-religious quarrels which were fomented to the highest pitch during these exciting times.

By the middle of August, the Indians who had fought under Braddock came to Philadelphia, bringing Conrad Weiser with them. They were kindly received, and suitable rewards were given for their fidelity.

While these Indians were in Philadelphia, Conrad Weiser used every effort to retain their friendship with the English. Scaroyady, their chief, came to Weiser several times, saying that if the governor neglected this opportunity to engage these Indians as allies for the English, they would all go over to the French. It was impossible, he said, to remain neutral and live in the woods.

---

2. *Penna. Colonial Records*, vol. VI., pp. 693, 695.
3. *Penna. Colonial Records*, vol. VI., p. 503.
4. *Penna. Colonial Records*, vol. VI., p. 534.

Sir
          I arrived Just now in this
place and prevailed on the bearer
Adam Torrance who Came with the
Indians from beyond Carlile to Carry
this, in order to be Informed where
I must bring the Indians I Shall wait
for him Just a little a this Side the
town of Philad[elphi]a under the Green trees
with your orders   who am
                                        Sir
                                Your h[um]ble Servant
Germantown at
10 of the Clock
August the 7. 1755   Conrad Weiser
at peter Smiths

THE INDIANS WHO FOUGHT UNDER BRADDOCK BROUGHT TO
PHILADELPHIA BY CONRAD WEISER

He claimed to represent an extensive influence among the Delawares on the Susquehanna and the Wyandots in Ohio. The governor was at a loss to know what to do. Weiser insisted that these Indians should be made allies and given the hatchet against the French and their Indians. Governor Morris wavered and finally sent Weiser and Scaroyady to the Speaker of the Assembly for a decision in the matter. This action of the governor's seemed to provoke the Assembly, which replied that it had no knowledge of these Indians having been invited to Philadelphia. Wrote the Speaker,

It is some surprise to us," wrote the Speaker, "to find the Indians should have reason to importune him (the governor) or that he should be at any loss to know what he has to impart to them on this occasion. Our conduct towards the Indians in our alliance has always been candid and free from any subterfuge whatever so that we do not understand what the governor would mean by telling us 'that the matter cannot be now minced neither with them nor the other nations.' And we are likewise at a loss to conceive why they should expect great presents from us who are wholly ignorant of the intention of their coming. The governor has been pleased to refuse his assent to our bills which had provided for Indian and other expenses; and as our treasury is exhausted by the very heavy charges for the King's service, these Indians are coming among us at a very unfortunate time when it is not in our power to supply them in the manner we are inclined to do; however, we will do all that can reasonably be expected from us, and must leave the rest to be supplied by the proprietors, whose interest is at least, as much concerned as ours in engaging the affection of the Indians at this time.[5]

> The governor was highly incensed at this reply and declared that both the proprietors and himself had been treated unbecomingly. The Indians were given presents of fifty-seven pounds and urged to remain in friendship with the English. The governor, not feeling sure of the support of the Assembly, declined to put the hatchet in the hands of these Indians. A feeling of disappointment was felt among the natives. They expressed their thanks for the presents, saying:

It is now well-known to you how unhappily we have been defeated by the French near Minongelo (Braddock's Defeat); we must let you know that it was the pride and ignorance of that great general that came from England. He is now dead, but he was a bad man when he was alive; he looked upon us as dogs

---

5. *Penna. Colonial Records*, vol. VI., pp. 536, 537.

and would never hear anything what was said to him. We often endeavored to advise him and to tell him of the danger he was in with his soldiers, but he never appeared pleased with us, and that was the reason that a great many of our warriors left him and would not be under his command. Brethren, we would advise you not to give up the point, though we have in a manner been chastised from above; but let us unite our strength. You are very numerous, and all the English governors along the seashore can raise men enough; don't let those that come from over the great seas be concerned anymore; they are unfit to fight in the woods. Let us go ourselves, we that came out of the ground, we may be assured to conquer the French. The Delawares and the Nanticokes have told me that the French never asked them to go on the late expedition against Braddock, one word of yours will bring the Delawares to join you.

> The governor was at a loss to know how to reply. He could not afford to take the Delawares into an alliance. Not having declared war, the King of England did not feel at liberty to give them the hatchet. As usual, when seriously embarrassed, the governor consulted Conrad Weiser. The old interpreter had been a man of action for over forty years. Right or wrong, he was always ready with a clear-cut purpose. He advised the governor to give a general answer, to thank the Indians for their advice, to solicit their lasting friendship, and to beg them to wait until the decision of the Six Nations could be learned.
>
> The Indians then returned to their people, and Conrad Weiser was sent to Flams' Ferry, where in the early part of September 1755, he distributed a wagon load of flour and many other necessaries among the Indians. Scaroyady's wife, one of the recipients of this generosity, told Weiser how she had aroused her brothers to go to Ohio and bring her French scalps to avenge Braddock's death.
>
> When "The Belt," a chief of considerable importance, realized that Weiser was displeased with this act of Indian loyalty to the English, he said, "I must let you know that the Six Nations have told the Delawares to lay aside their petticoats, to take up the hatchet against the French and become men."
>
> It is unknown to what extent "The Belt's" information was correct. The Six Nations were divided. The majority were with the French. Weiser had scarcely returned from his expedition of distributing supplies until the wild war-whoop of the Indians was heard along the Blue Ridge from Maryland to Easton. The first attack was

on Patterson's Creek in Maryland, where forty white people were reportedly killed.

"The Indians destroy all before them," wrote Trent, the trader. "Firing houses, barns, stockyards, and everything that will burn."

Croghan reported one hundred and sixty Indians in the passes of the Alleghanies. A friendly Indian had advised Croghan to fly because the French had a large reward on his scalp. Croghan wrote to Charles Swain at Shippensburg. "I feared it would come to this, for I see all our great Directors of Indian affairs are very shortsighted, and glad I am that I have no hand in Indian affairs at this critical time when no fault can be thrown on my shoulders."

The first attack within the present limits of Pennsylvania occurred on Penn's Creek on the west side of the Susquehanna River on territory the Indians claimed had been fraudulently purchased at Albany a year before. The report of these outrages, promptly dispatched to the governor, was suppressed by that official. The governor desired explicit instructions from the proprietors before he acted and hesitated to advise the Assembly of the actual state of affairs on the frontier. By this means, he forfeited the confidence of the people. Even his private secretary, in a letter to Conrad Weiser, said (October 18, 1755):

> This is a private letter to tell you that we all blame the governor very much for not laying: before the Assembly all the Indian news. Your letter of the 4th of October and Croghan's information to Charles Swaine.[6] But as he is determined not to say anything more to the Assembly till he hears from the King's _____,[7] I am put under intolerable difficulties. By advice of Mr. Allen, I showed the Speaker, in confidence, George Croghan's letter to Charles Swaine, and likewise your letter of the 4th of October, 'tis last I did as I told him, to be informed of what _____* and _____* was come to respecting the Indians, but _____* said I had no orders from the governor to show to him. This is certainly (?) disagreeable work, but I could not rest until (the) contents of your letter and Swaine's was somehow made known to them, that they may take _____* measures _____* out of the governor _____* for the lives of people are not to be played with, not thrown away because the two parts of the Legislature differ, at least I am determined not to be accessory to such a step. I moved (?) [leave it?] to you whether in this

---

6. *Penna. Colonial Records*, vol. VI., pp. 640, 642.
7. Obliterated.

unhappy difference you should not write to the Speaker as well as to the governor, a least all your news. Pity me, dear Conrad, and take off from my mind all that you can. Give full accounts, give clear and full advice, say everything you shall judge proper, and notwithstanding public differences, make known to both sides all the particulars that are absolutely necessary.

I am your ft.
This is private.[8]
R. Peters.

During all this heated controversy between the Assembly, led by Benjamin Franklin, and the proprietors led by the governor, Conrad Weiser appears to be the only man holding a public position who did not warmly advocate one side or the other. He retained not only the confidence of the governor and the Assembly but also of the proprietors in England. He wrote plainly and with force to all of them and was probably important in bringing the proprietors to something like temporary terms.

It would be interesting to know what Weiser wrote to Thomas Penn. A fragment of the reply has been found. Wrote Penn to Conrad Weiser:

It gives me great concern that the situation of our country should oblige you to write in the manner you have done to me. The accounts I have received made very deep impressions on me, and tho' I and my family have been treated with so much injustice by the Representatives (of) the people, I would willingly undertake any hazards to . . . peace and good order among the people in general, but in the . . . have given the strictest orders to the governors represented them to everyone here as people not only useful but unless [except?] this debauched crew of Shawanoes and Delawares, faithful to their engagements.

Weiser had doubtless written asking that a law be issued forbidding Quakers from holding seats in the Assembly. Thomas Penn replied, "I was not thought wright here to exclude Quakers by law from the Assembly, yet as they have been told they will be excluded in case they do not withdraw at the next session."[9]

---

8. In the MS. collections of Conrad Weiser's correspondence. Pennsylvania Historical Society.
9. Fragment in MS. collection of Conrad Weiser's correspondence in Pennsylvania Historical collections.

JOHN HARRIS' FERRY [HARRISBURG], PA.

Weiser shared with the governor's party a widespread belief that the Quakers were responsible for the attitude of the Assembly, that they urged the taxation of the proprietary estates as a clog to the passing of a supply bill. As the Indian outrages increased, the indignation of the people grew warmer. These Delawares were once the petted friends of the Quakers. Now the land is steeped in blood, and these same Quakers must somehow be the cause of it all. Others placed all censure upon the proprietors and the governor; if they would yield the point about taxing the proprietary estates, the frontier could be defended. The people and the Assembly were ready and willing to furnish the money. The governor alone blocked the way. From certain quarters threats of vengeance went out against the governor.

The Assembly passed another bill on November 8, providing an issue of sixty thousand pounds in "Bills of Credit." A fund to sink the same was to be raised by a tax of sixpence to the pound on all real estate and eighty shillings per head annually for four years. This the governor amended by making an exception for all proprietary estates. Then the war between the legislature and the executive was renewed with greater vigor.

In the meantime, the Indians were burning and scalping on the frontier. The settlements in the "Big and Little Coves" were destroyed. All settlers north and west of the Blue Ridge became targets of Indian wrath.* John Harris, while returning from Shamokin, where he went to deliver a message, was attacked by a party of Indians in ambush and lost over half of his men. The old trader came home and cut loopholes in his house, thus producing the first attempt toward a fort ever made in Eastern Pennsylvania. He immediately wrote to the governor, urging that a bounty be offered for Indian scalps.

When Conrad Weiser heard of this attack, he sent his servants in the night to alarm the neighborhood. At daybreak, the people were gathered around his house, a mass of sturdy Germans armed with guns, old swords, pitchforks, and axes. Weiser told them of the Indian outrages along the Susquehanna. With one voice, the men declared they would stand by each other if Weiser were their leader. Two hundred men representing two townships assembled at two o'clock that afternoon; each was carrying provisions for three days. Weiser volunteered to join them as a private soldier. The men elected him their commander-in-chief.

Weiser divided them into companies of thirty men each and allowed them to elect their captains, with three subordinate officers, each of whom was to have charge of ten men. In the meantime, he had secretly sent a messenger some miles or more after a Lutheran minister, who preached a sermon and offered prayer to this hastily improvised and democratically organized little army. Fifty men were at once detailed to hold the "Swartaro Pass," and Weiser set out for the Susquehanna River with the remainder.

After marching ten miles that evening, he found, when he went into camp, that his citizens' army had received over one hundred recruits. A hurried inspection showed that his men were all well-armed except about twenty, who were supplied with axes and pitchforks. With characteristic instinct and practiced forethought, Weiser had ordered a supply of powder and lead from Reading early that morning. This arrived while the inspection was progressing. In writing to Governor Morris, he said we all "unanimously agreed to die together and to engage the enemy wherever we should meet with them, never to inquire the number, but fight them, and so obstruct their progress further into the inhabited parts, till others of our brethren should come up and so do the same, and so save the lives of our wives and children."[10]

Weiser led his men over into Hanover township, Lancaster County, where a consultation was held with Adam Read, Esq. This gentleman reported the attack on John Harris' party, which went up the river to bury the dead at Penn's Creek. Just what occurred at this consultation, we are not told. Local jealousies were strong. Weiser merely said: "We had a consultation, and as we did not come up to serve as guards to Paxton people but to fight the enemy if they were come so far as we first heard, we thought best to return and take care of our townships."

Weiser, therefore, preserved the organization but disbanded his men, who numbered nearly five hundred. He believed the friendly Indians had all gone over to the French and that the enemy was determined to build a fort on the Susquehanna River, probably at Shamokin. He declared that the people in that vicinity were willing to fight. "I had two or three long beards[11] in my command, one a Menonist, who declared he would live and die with his neighbors; he had a gun with him."

Governor Morris was well pleased with this prompt action of Weiser's and immediately sent him a colonel's commission, saying, "I have not time to give you any instructions, but leave it to your judgment and discretion, which I know are great, to do what is most for the safety of the people and service of the Crown . . . You may, on behalf of this government, make such offers of rewards to the Indians or others that you employ in this service as you shall judge best, and I will remit you the money or other things you shall agree for as soon as you please."[12]

---

10. *Penna. Colonial Records*, vol. VI., p. 657.
11. Germans who opposed war.
12. *Pennsylvania Colonial Records*, vol VI., p. 660.

This *carte blanche* of the governor's led Weiser into interminable difficulties. The trust and responsibility imposed, the continued and ruthless assaults of the Indians, the disorganized condition of the defense, and the paralysis of industries caused by such numbers of people being driven from the frontiers all these things made it imperative that someone should act, and in this Conrad Weiser was prompt and emphatic. He did things in his own way. Supplies were purchased with his or his son's money, and the items were charged to the province. There were no complaints as long as the war whoop was heard in the mountains.

Weiser had, at first, general control of the forts and defenses between the Susquehanna and Delaware Rivers. He was held responsible for all disasters. When the Indians stole around the forts and fell upon the inhabitants, Weiser received the censure. When there was a lull in the butcheries, the soldiers, who were not well disciplined, not infrequently committed outrages upon the settlers. Indeed, in some communities, the soldiers were as much feared as the Indians. For all these things, Conrad Weiser was held accountable. A strong local hatred grew toward him.

While this was waxing stronger, the Assembly had succeeded in bringing down upon the governor and the proprietors such a storm of indignation that mobs from Lancaster and Berks counties were only prevented from going to Philadelphia by the earnest appeals of the magistrates. The governor became thoroughly frightened and wrote to England for help. He insinuated that if these mobs came to Philadelphia, the Assembly would find some means to poison their minds and make the governor the victim of their anger.

This desperate condition of things brought the proprietors to their senses, and they directed their land agent to donate five thousand pounds from uncollected quitrents and fees to go towards the expenses of the war. This donation induced the Assembly to yield their long-contested point about taxing proprietary estates. A bill for sixty thousand pounds in bills of credit was then presented, and the tax to sink the same was not to apply to the proprietary estates. While this matter was pending, a committee of the Assembly had been distributing military supplies on the frontier without the knowledge or permission of the governor.

Now when the sixty thousand pounds was placed at the King's service, the Assembly was unwilling to place the disposition of it entirely in the governor's hands. Accordingly, a commission was appointed, which largely gained control of the finances. Before these commissioners, complaints were laid against Conrad Weiser's expenditures and his conduct as commander-in-chief. Nothing is surprising about this action of some of the Berks County people. Conrad Weiser had never been without bitter enemies, and all they had wanted for many years was a place to strike.

Next to the Indian war, the Berks County election of 1755 was the most exciting thing in that locality. It had been customary for the Freemen to elect two men for sheriff and leave it to the governor to select and commission one of them. Conrad Weiser joined the governor's party and supported Jonas Seely for sheriff. The Assembly's party was strong in Berks County, and Seely they declared was a governor's man. He belonged to the ring in Reading. He was a war man and, if elected, would force a musket into the hands of those whose religious convictions were against the war. Our foolish people believed all these things, wrote Weiser to Richard Peters, "and elected William Boone and John Hughes."

Weiser was very much incensed at this "foolish action of the Germans" and wrote to R. Peters to persuade the governor to appoint John Hughes "in order to bring that spiteful fellow W. B. to some disappointment."[13]

Such and similar actions led to the appearance of an anti-Weiser faction, not only in Berks County but also in Philadelphia. A complaint was sent to the governor in 1757 that Weiser frequently ordered his soldiers to be quartered at farmhouses, and there was no security from their outrages; that he enlisted more men than were needed and refused to discharge men when their time was expired; that he was a "lover of money," trying to rob the province. The last complaint insisted that Weiser's own company was the worst disciplined.

Weiser flatly denied all charges and called the people who instigated them, liars. "If my own company was so worthless, he retorts, why did they want it in Cumberland County, in Shamokin, and on Susquehanna."

Then with characteristic energy, he declared that he would resign rather than rest under such charges.

However, Weiser's greatest difficulty was settling his accounts against the province. The commissioners of the Assembly considered his bills excessive and hesitated to pay them. Weiser wrote to Richard Peters, saying,

I hope by this time my accounts against the gentlemen, the provincial commissioners, are settled, some way or other, and I don't expect much good or favor, nay, even doubt their doing me justice, which they have refused me before; now, I don't intend to wait their pleasure any longer if I can help it. I have his honor, the governor's order for my late service done, and his promise to see me paid for the balance of my accounts, which you will be so good as to send to me

---

13. Manuscript letters of Conrad Weiser, in the collection of the Pennsylvania Historical Society.

THE BEGINNINGS OF BETHLEHEM

by my son Peter, the bearer thereof before it grows an old debt. I have found by experience that new debts are suffered to grow old ones, and old ones are never paid, which is but poor encouragement for faithful servants to the government. I have served the government of pensilvania as provincial interpreter since the year 1731 to the satisfaction of the governors and Assemblies as much as I know. I never heard nothing to the contrary till three years ago (1755)—when a certain set of gentlemen got the Administration or the purse into their hands, then I could no more please, having been a little too free when the blood of the back inhabitants was spilled like water, and they (Assembly's commissioners), in a manner unconcerned, did let me suffer prodigeously and showed their spite openly to me for what reason well-known to them, to you, and to me, but I won't give up the point, truth will prevail at last. If even I should not live so long. I perhaps went a little too far, but what signifies writing, if not one's mind.

Richard Peters promised Weiser that his accounts should be settled. When General Forbes was lying at the point of death, Weiser was again summoned to Philadelphia for council. The old man hesitated and again pressed the governor for a settlement of his accounts. A short time after this, we find Weiser in Philadelphia as of yore, giving advice freely, and from that, we suppose that his bills were paid.

For a time, Weiser's prompt and decided actions during the autumn of 1755 stayed the Indian invasion. Other localities, however, were attacked. All the settlements in the Big and Little Coves were destroyed, and a portion of the people only escaped with their lives. The Moravian missionary stations were destroyed, and these godly people were slaughtered in great numbers.

The Delaware Indians from Ohio met their Eastern brethren on the Big Island in the west branch of the Susquehanna River and endeavored to arouse them against the English. These Western Indians danced the war dance and then addressed themselves to the Delawares on the Susquehanna. "When Washington was defeated, we, the Delawares, were blamed without a cause. We make up three parties of Delawares. One party will go against Carlisle, one down the Susquehanna, and I, myself with another party, will go against Tulpehocken to Conrad Weiser. And we shall be followed by a thousand French and Indians."[14]

The French undoubtedly inspired this plan to attack Conrad Weiser. Furthermore, the Delawares on the Ohio were not without cause of complaint against the great champion of the Six Nations. In some way, they secured the impression that Conrad Weiser had been the means of persuading the Iroquois

---

14. *Penna. Colonial Records*, vol. VI., p. 683.

to sell the west branch of the Susquehanna. Weiser soon found that it was impossible to protect the Tulpehocken people. When John Harris returned home from the massacre on Penn's Creek, he wrote to Edward Shippen, insisting that scalping parties should be sent into the woods or the Indians would soon overrun the settlements.

Not only John Harris, the trader, but James Hamilton, the lawyer, favored a scalp act. The latter, writing to the governor from Easton, said,

> I heartily wish you were at liberty to declare war against them and offer large reward for scalps, which appears the only way to clear our frontier of those savages, and will, I am persuaded, be infinitely cheaper in the end. For I clearly foresee the expense of defending ourselves in the way we are in will ruin the province and be far from effectual at last, principally for want of a good militia law by which men might be subjected to discipline, for at present, they enter themselves and then leave their captains at their own humor, without a person in the officers to punish them for that or any other misbehavior.

The general opinion along the frontier was that a chain of forts and block houses along the Blue Mountains from Easton to Maryland would be the only effectual means of defense. John Potter, sheriff of Cumberland County, declared that the only way to prevent slaughter and destruction on the frontier was to send a strong force into the center of the Indians' strongholds rather than supply a chain of forts. However, Governor Morris and the council considered a system of forts the best possible means of defense; Hamilton on the Delaware, Franklin on the Lehigh, Weiser on the Schuylkill and Susquehanna, and Potter in Cumberland County directed and controlled the erection and maintenance of these forts. The governor, in person, during December 1755, and January 1756, directed this movement.

Writing from Reading in January, he said, "The commissioners have done everything that was proper in the County of Northampton, but the people are not satisfied, nor by what I can learn from the commissioners would they be, unless every man's house was protected by a fort and a company of soldiers, and themselves paid for staying at home and doing nothing. There are in that county at this time three hundred men in pay of the government, and yet from the disposition of the inhabitants, the want of conduct in the officers, and of courage and discipline in the men, I am fearful that whole country will fall into the enemy's hands."[15]

---

15. *Penna. Colonial Records*, vol. VI., pp. 771, 772.

The governor's fears were not without foundation since the Indians laid waste the frontier for two years and scalped the settlers under the very shadow of the forts.

After the quarrel between the governor and the Legislature over the supply bill, the Assembly lost confidence in the Executive, and a secret committee was appointed to distribute arms and ammunition among the settlers. This movement led to appointing a board of commissioners, which assumed executive control of the provincial defenses and paid out all the money.

During the winter of 1755–1756, the commissioners urged the governor to declare war with the Delaware Indians. Scaroyady, the leader of the friendly Indians, favored such a course and ventured the opinion that the Six Nations would approve such action. Accordingly, the governor declared war against the Delaware Indians in April 1756 and offered one hundred and thirty Spanish dollars for every male Indian scalp over twelve years of age. For every female Indian scalp, fifty Spanish dollars were to be paid. Indian prisoners were valued at one hundred and fifty dollars for men and one hundred and thirty dollars for women.

James Logan, a council member, vigorously opposed this declaration of war. It will be remembered that James Logan was a prominent member of The Society of Friends but a stout advocate of defensive warfare. Yet this declaration of war he declared to be fraught with evil and ruin for the province. He further showed that it was issued just at a time when Conrad Weiser, Colonel Johnson, and the Six Nations were endeavoring to unite the councils of the Delawares and win back the alienated friendship of the Western tribes. James Logan then insisted upon a full council and urged that the Assembly be consulted before the declaration was issued. The governor and council decided that they would declare war first and consult the Assembly afterward. Doubtless, this attitude of the executive grew out of some very poignant criticisms made during the winter by the Assembly, in which it was hinted that the alienation of the Shawanese Indians was due to the refusal of the proprietors to pay them for certain land claims in Cumberland County, and the surveying of certain proprietary Manors on land which the Shawanese Indians claimed. This was denied by the governor, who insisted on behalf of the proprietors that the Shawanese were squatters and never had any land claims in Pennsylvania.

Conrad Weiser was summoned to Philadelphia at the time of this declaration of war. He came with reluctance. Weiser was loath to speak his mind. He said that he was in favor of a declaration of war but opposed to offering a reward for scalps. The government, he said, might offer rewards for Indian prisoners, but a bounty on scalps would only aggravate existing evils. Since anyone could bring in these scalps, there was no means of distinguishing between the scalps of an enemy and a friendly Indian. Indeed, this was the core of the whole difficulty. Scalps of friendly Indians were taken, and the peace negotiations with the Eastern Indians were frustrated. The members of the Society of Friends and many others in Philadelphia united in a petition to the governor against the declaration of war and the bounty on scalps. They urged that such action was hasty and premature; that full time had not been allowed "for those Indians who still remain well affected towards us, to use and report the effect of their endeavors to reconcile our enemies." They claimed that by such conduct, even our allies might become alienated and urged that a fuller opportunity be given to make peace with these Indians.[16]

Col. Johnson, in writing to Governor Shirley on April 24, 1756, said:

> I am surprised that Mr. Morris, whose province was so much interested in the results of the Six Nations' Embassy, who was a principal in it, and to whom I sent a copy of my late proceedings, would not want to bear the effects of this embassy before he entered into this consequential measure. What will the Delawares and Shawonese think of such opposition and contradiction in our conduct? How shall I behave at the approaching meeting at Onondaga, not only to those Indians but to the Six Nations; these hostile measures which Mr. Morris has entered into is throwing all our Schemes into confusion and must naturally give the Six Nations such impressions and the French such advantage to work against us that I tremble for the consequences. I think without consulting your Excellency, without the concurrence of the other neighboring provinces, without my receiving previous notice of it, this is a very unadvised and unaccountable proceeding of Governor Morris; I cannot but be of opinion if terms of good accommodation can be brought about, that in the present critical situation of affairs it will be far more eligible than to enter into hostilities against these Indians, especially as a few days will determine what part we have to choose.[17]

The friendly Indians in Pennsylvania were numerous and could easily have been increased until their number would have been a far more effectual barrier

---
16. *Penna. Colonial Records*, vol. VII., pp. 85, 86.
17. *Penna. Colonial Records*, vol. VII., p. 117.

against the French and their allies than any chain of forts. The old "Belt," a friendly chief on the Susquehanna near Harris' Ferry, was very much disappointed, and his affection for the English cooled by the action of the "Paxton people." Early in this struggle, Weiser, in a letter to the governor of Pennsylvania, said:

> Your Honor will have heard by this time that Paxton people took an enemy Indian on the other side of the Narrows above Samuel Hunters and brought him down to Carson's house, where they examined him. The Indian begged his life and promised to tell all what he knew tomorrow morning, but (shocking to me) they shot him in the midst of them, scalped him, and threw his body into the river. The old 'Belt' told me that as a child of Onontio, he deserved to be killed, but he would have been very glad if they had delivered him up to the governor in order to be examined stricter and better.[18]

The "old Belt" was disappointed that his white brothers should resort to lynching. He felt that no mob of citizens had a right to take even an enemy's life. Such actions as these cooled the ardor of the friendly Indians and seriously embarrassed peace negotiations. The plan of defense by a line of forts, the expenditure of over 50,000 pounds, the arming of over one thousand men, the bounty on Indian scalps, all these things were of no avail in protecting the frontier. The stealthy savage, in the dead hours of the night or at high noon, fell upon the inhabitants in the least suspected quarter. Pennsylvania was saturated in blood. Whole settlements were destroyed. Fire and plunder, death, and murder flourished in the teeth of all opposition. For over seventy-five years, Pennsylvania had lived in peace with the Indians. Now when war raged along her border, it was not so much her defenses as her peace negotiations that won protection for her people.

On the one hand, Weiser maintained resistance but negotiated for peace with the other. The Wyoming Indians and most of the Eastern Indians, during the darkest periods of the war, 1756-'57 and '58, refrained from joining the French and the Ohio Indians. The greatest victories which Pennsylvania ever won in this French and Indian war were victories of peace.

---

18. *Penna. Colonial Records*, vol. VI., p. 763.

XVII

Reconciliation

THE SOCIETY OF FRIENDS ENDEAVORS TO MAKE PEACE WITH THE INDIANS—CONRAD WEISER AND ISRAEL PEMBERTON HAVE AN INTERVIEW WITH THE INDIANS—THE GOVERNOR CONSULTS HIS COUNCIL—WEISER NOW SUPPORTS THE DECLARATION OF WAR AGAINST THE DELAWARES—THE FRIENDS FAVOR THE DELAWARES—THE WRONGS OF THE DELAWARES—THE PEACE MESSAGE—COL. JOHNSON'S PEACE CONFERENCE—TEEDYUSCUNG BURIES THE HATCHET—THE FIRST EASTON CONFERENCE—TEEDYUSCUNG'S SPEECH—"THE BIG PEACE HALLOO"—"THE PEACE BELTS"—TEEDYUSCUNG LOSES HIS TEMPER—THE GOVERNOR ISSUES THE PEACE MESSAGE—THE CAUSE OF PEACE IN DANGER—PENNSYLVANIA FORBIDDEN FROM MAKING FURTHER PEACE NEGOTIATIONS—THE INDIANS SUSPICIOUS OF CONRAD WEISER—THE SECOND EASTON TREATY—GOVERNOR DENNY REFUSES TO GO TO EASTON—THE CONFERENCES OPENED AT EASTON—TEEDYUSCUNG CLAIMS TO HAVE BEEN DEFRAUDED OF HIS LANDS—WEISER DEFENDS THE WALKING PURCHASE—AN INVESTIGATING COMMITTEE APPOINTED—CONDITIONS OF PEACE SUGGESTED—WEISER CONDUCTS TEEDYUSCUNG AWAY FROM EASTON—THE ANTI-PROPRIETARY PARTY TAKE UP THE CAUSE OF TEEDYUSCUNG—WEISER DEFENDS THE PROPRIETARY FACTION—THE LANCASTER CONFERENCE—THE COMING OF TEEDYUSCUNG—TEEDYUSCUNG DEMANDS A PRIVATE SECRETARY—WEISER SUSPECTS ISRAEL PEMBERTON—THE GOVERNOR ANGRY WITH THE COMMISSIONERS—RICHARD PETERS OFFENDED—TEEDYUSCUNG SECURES CHARLES THOMSON AS CLERK—CHARLES THOMSON CHARGES WEISER WITH GETTING TEEDYUSCUNG INTOXICATED—TEEDYUSCUNG'S FEAR OF THE SIX NATIONS—EFFORTS TO SECURE A RETRACTION OF TEEDYUSCUNG'S CHARGES OF FRAUD—THE OLD DEEDS TO BE SHOWN TO TEEDYUSCUNG—AN INDIAN PEACE SECURED.

RECONCILIATION

GOVERNOR Morris's declaration of war against the Delaware Indians, and the scalp bounty offered, aroused the active members of The Society of Friends. They felt that the entire Indian policy of Pennsylvania was reversed, that the Indians would not have fallen upon the frontier without a grievance, and that adequate efforts had not been made toward reconciliation. Accordingly, in April 1756, while some friendly Indians were in Philadelphia, Israel Pemberton waited upon the governor on behalf of numerous Friends and asked permission to invite the chiefs to dine with a committee of Quakers so that the Indian grievances might be learned and efforts made to bring about peace.

The Friends offered to bear all the expenses, conduct the negotiations as a private affair, and do nothing without the governor's approval. The provincial finances were, at that time, in such an embarrassing condition that the governor seemed entirely willing to place the peace negotiations in the hands of the Friends on condition that Conrad Weiser should be advised of everything said to the Indians as all information received from them. Weiser entered into this affair with hearty zeal. When Israel Pemberton set forth the peace principles of the Friends at dinner, the Indians were greatly pleased, and Scaroyady, their speaker, was delighted. He declared that the Six Nations would eagerly join in such a project. The governor told Israel Pemberton that when these negotiations were sufficiently ripened, he would lay the affair before the council.

That afternoon Conrad Weiser and Israel Pemberton had a long conference with Scaroyady, in which it was deemed wise to send messengers to the councils of the Six Nations,

> setting forth their conference with the Quakers, their religious Professions and their Characters, and the influence they had as well with the government as the people, their desiring to bring about a peace, and their offer to become mediators between them and the government; that he (Scaroyady) and the other Six Nations had heard what they said with pleasure and desired that they would hearken to it, cease their hostilities and accept this mediation, and least they (the Indians) might be afraid that they had done too much mischief and taken too many lives, even more than could possibly be forgiven, he assured them these peaceable People would, notwithstanding this, obtain their pardon if they would immediately desist, send the English prisoners to some place, there deliver them up to the governor, and request peace of him and forgiveness for what was past.

When Israel Pemberton and Conrad Weiser laid this report before the governor, he called his council together and asked (1) if it were proper to permit Friends to act as mediators; (2) should peace be proposed on conditions of forgiveness and return of prisoners; (3) would such a message in any way obstruct establishing a fort at Shamokin; (4) would it not be better to invite the friendly Indians such as Paxinosa to come near the settlements and thus be out of danger.[1]

The council was a long-time deliberating, and they finally advised the governor to leave it entirely with the Quakers. They were opposed to the government's assuming any responsibility. Scaroyady, Newcastle, and several friendly Indians agreed to carry this peace message among the hostile Delawares and even into the haunts of the Six Nations, where the deputies were instructed to solicit Sir William Johnson's influence in persuading Pennsylvania to recall her declaration of war and "scalp bounty act."

Conrad Weiser, however, advised the governor to leave the war declaration stand. It would, he thought, influence the hostile Delawares to sue for peace. Conrad Weiser was called in to assist the council, unable to decide what message to send to the Indians. He urged that the Declaration was absolutely necessary to bring the Delawares to their senses and that it would be agreeable to the Six Nations. Then Weiser quoted from former interviews with their chiefs, who insisted that the English were cowards sitting with their heads between their knees while the Delawares struck and begging the Six Nations to chastise their subjects for breaking the peace. Weiser went further and insisted that Scaroyady, as the representative of the Six Nations, was not offended at the bounty offered for scalps. In these matters, Weiser revealed his inbred admiration for the Iroquois and undying contempt for the Delawares.

The Friends, on the other hand, sympathized with the Delawares and their wrongs. They believed that the Six Nations had been oppressive in their policy. Scarcely anyone at that time knew to what extent the Delawares had thrown off the yoke of the Iroquois. It was only after long years of bloody warfare, after the entire frontier of the State had been plundered and burned, and settlers had been scalped and butchered again and again, under the very shadows of the forts, that the authorities of Pennsylvania awoke to the fact that the Delawares were an independent people, and able to manage their affairs.

Had the Indian policy of Pennsylvania, since the coming of Conrad Weiser, recognized the rights of the Delaware Indians to land on the Delaware River, and confined the Six Nations to their land claims on the Susquehanna, as William

---

1. *Penna. Colonial Records*, vol. VII., pp. 103, 104.

Penn himself did, this dark chapter in colonial history might have read differently today. It will be remembered that in 1736 when the Iroquois gave a deed for all their Susquehanna lands south of the Blue Mountains, a second deed was procured for the Delaware lands. This was done at the suggestion of the provincial authorities and revealed to the Delaware Indians in 1742 that they had not only lost their fathers' rights on that river but that they had become outcasts in the wilderness without a hunting ground. They swallowed their insult from the Six Nations and removed to Wyoming, with the wrongs of the "Walking Purchase" still rankling in their bosoms. Indians have long memories. They brooded over these things, and finally, when the French promised to aid them in getting back their lost lands, many of their young men, and most of the Ohio tribes, put on the war paint. Although the Indians had long memories, they had faithful hearts, and many of the old men remembered William Penn and the kind treatment of former years. Old Paxinosa, the Shawanese chief at Wyoming, poured forth his eloquence for peace. Newcastle declared that he would die for the sons of Onas. Hundreds of brave warriors were undecided until they heard of the Declaration of War and the Scalp Act, "then a mighty shout arose which shook the very mountains, and all the Delawares and Shawanese, except a few old sachems, danced the war dance." Those who felt it wrong to use the war paint were heartbroken. Paxinosa took his family and moved up toward Tioga, away from the scenes of war. He sat for days at a time, meditating over the waywardness of his people. The sons of Teedyuscung, the "King of the Delawares," dragged Paxinosa for a brief time into their war parties. Such was the condition of affairs when the Friends offered to act as peacemakers.

The Delaware chiefs, Newcastle, Jonathan, and Andrew Montour, grasped at these overtures as drowning men would at a straw. They would risk their lives carrying messages of peace for the governor. So strong, however, was the hatred of these Delawares for their former masters, the Iroquois, that they declared they would do nothing for Scarovady and the Six Nations.[2]

The governor was about to issue passes for these Indian messengers when he suddenly changed his mind and determined to have no official connection with the affair. The next day a message arrived from New York containing Sir William Johnson's criticisms of Governor Morris' declaration of war and his scalp bounty. The governor immediately changed his mind again and decided to send forth the messengers of peace in his name.

While these messengers were penetrating the mountain paths leading to Wyoming, with their lives in continual jeopardy, Sir William Johnson was

---

2. *Penna. Colonial Records*, vol. VII., p. 105.

holding a peace conference with the chiefs of the Six Nations at Otsaningo, where it was decided that the Delaware Indians were acting like drunken men, and deputies were sent to order them to get sober and leave off striking their friends the English. Since this conference was composed of only a portion of the Iroquois, the Delawares replied in a very haughty manner, saying, we are no longer women; we are men. "We are determined to cut off all the English except those that make their escape from us in ships."[3]

While Newcastle was spreading the "Quaker peace doctrine" among the Indians at Diago (Tioga), another message was sent to Sir William Johnson, in which the Delawares promised to make peace with their white brothers in Pennsylvania and to obey their uncles, the Iroquois. In July 1756, Newcastle was again in Philadelphia.

Teedyuscung, the great war chief of the united Delaware Nations, had been persuaded by Newcastle to bury the hatchet. This was a remarkable victory. The backbone of the Indian outrages was broken. Newcastle pleaded with Governor Denny to be prompt, or all would be lost. The Indians could not give up their prisoners, he said, until peace was completed. For this reason, Newcastle urged that the governor refrain from pushing this demand until a firm peace was established. With much reluctance, the governor yielded to this faithful and intelligent Indian.

Arrangements were made for a conference at Easton. Conrad Weiser was ordered to concentrate his soldiers in that vicinity and furnish a guard for the governor, who, with his council, reached Easton on July 24, 1756. But nothing important could be done until the 27th because Conrad Weiser had not arrived. Teedyuscung insisted upon having his own interpreter. After some hesitation, this was allowed. After a long conference with the council, Weiser determined the course to be pursued. The treaty was then formally opened on the 28th.

The governor welcomed Teedyuscung, who replied:

> The first messages you sent me came in the spring; they touched my heart, they gave me abundance of joy. You have kindled a council fire at Easton. I have been here several days smoking my pipe in patience, waiting to hear your good words. Abundant confusion has of late years been rife among the Indians because of their loose ways of doing business. False leaders have deceived the people. It has bred quarrels and heart-burnings among my people. The Delaware is no longer the slave of the Six Nations. I, Teedyuscung, have been

---

3. *Penna. Colonial Records*, vol. VII., p. 522.

TEEDYUSCUNG, CHIEF OF THE DELAWARE INDIANS

appointed King over the Five United Nations and representative of the five Iroquois Nations. What I do here will be approved by all. This is a good day; whoever will make peace let him lay hold of this belt, and the nations around shall see and know it. I desire to conduct myself according to your words, which I will perform to the utmost of my power. I wish the same good that possessed the good old man William Penn, who was a friend to the Indian, may inspire the people of this province at this time.[4]

The governor responded warmly to Teedyuscung's overtures, and the preliminaries of peace were arranged. Since only a few Indians had accompanied Teedyuscung to Easton, it was argued that "the King"[5] and Newcastle should go back among the Indians and give the "Big Peace Halloo" and gather their people together for another larger peace conference. The governor then gave Teedyuscung a small present, saying:

I think it necessary to inform you that a part of this present was given by the people called Quakers (who are descendants of those who first came over to this country with your old friend William Penn) as a particular testimony of their regard and affection for the Indians, and their earnest desire to promote the good work of peace in which we are now engaged.[6]

Teedyuscung and his followers were given grand entertainment. The old chief was highly pleased with such hospitality, declaring again and again that he would go forth and do all in his power for peace. After dinner, when the Philadelphia Friends came to bid him "farewell, he parted with them in a very affectionate manner." He pleaded for peace and insisted that he and his people were not responsible for the actions of the Ohio Indians. He repeatedly urged that the white people hold fast to that peace belt until he could persuade his people to bury the hatchet.

This peace belt contained a "square in the middle, meaning the lands of the Indians, and at one end the figure of a man, indicating the English and at the other end another" man "meaning the French." "Our uncles, the Iroquois," said Teedyuscung, "told us that both these coveted our lands" and invited us to join

---

4. *Penna. Colonial Records*, vol. VII., p. 213.
5. Teedyuscung.
6. *Penna. Colonial Records*, vol. VII., p. 214.

them in defending our lands against both the English and the French, promising that we should share the land with them.[7]

This explanation excited the governor's suspicion. He called together his council secretly and invited Conrad Weiser, asking him if it would be wise or proper for the governor to keep that belt. Weiser replied that he had entertained some doubts upon that subject himself and therefore sought advice from Newcastle. This faithful Indian disciple of Quakerism told him that the Six Nations had sent the belt to the Delawares, who in turn had sent it to the governor of Pennsylvania. This of itself was an act introductory of peace. It was a belt of much consequence and should be preserved among the council wampum, and another bigger belt nearly a fathom long should be given to the Indians at the council tomorrow. Newcastle further advised that Teedyuscung be liberally supplied with wampum if the cause of peace was expected to prosper. Conrad Weiser immediately emphasized Newcastle's advice and observed that the French gave quantities of wampum to their Indians, and if we hoped to draw the Indians away from the French, we must outbid them in the length of our wampum belts. These arguments were convincing to the council. A messenger was immediately sent to Bethlehem to bring the material, and the Indian women were called in and set to work making belts. One for Teedyuscung was to be a fathom long and sixteen beads wide. In the center was the figure of a man typifying the governor of Pennsylvania. On each side were five other figures emblematic of the ten nations that Teedyuscung professed to represent.

While this work was going on, Teedyuscung, suspicious and fearful of treachery, grew angry because, as he supposed, the governor had invited Indian women into his councils. He rushed into the room unannounced and, in a loud voice, said: "Why do you council in the dark? Why do you consult with women? Why do you not talk in the light?"

The governor replied: "My councils are set on a hill; I have no secrets. The governor never sits in swamps but speaks his mind openly. The squaws are here making belts, not holding a council."

This explanation, which was doubtless the words of Weiser in the mouth of the governor, appeased the anger of Teedyuscung, and he withdrew.

The next day the governor "taking two belts" of wampum "joined together in his hands, and addressing Newcastle and Teedyuscung, declared" them to be messengers of peace for the province of Pennsylvania, to go abroad among the hostile tribes persuading them by eloquence and reason to bury the hatchet, to desert the French and unite again with the English. The governor gave each

---

7. *Penna. Colonial Records*, vol. VII., p. 213.

messenger an armload of wampum and bid them Godspeed. This was no slight mission that these two Indians undertook. The savage heart was moved not so much by bribes but by plausible arguments and fervid eloquence. The secret embassies of the French were everywhere, using every conceivable device to thwart the designs of the peacemakers. French rewards were upon the scalps of these faithful Indians, and danger surrounded them on every side.

But the greatest danger to the cause of peace lay with some soldiers sent to defend the frontiers. After the Easton Conference, Teedyuscung lingered at Fort Allen. The captain was in Philadelphia, and Lieutenant Miller was in charge. Teedyuscung had sixteen deer skins which he said he would present to "the governor to make him a pair of gloves." Miller probably well knew that this was the figurative language of the Indian to express his appreciation of the governor's kind treatment, yet he insisted that one skin was enough to make the governor a pair of gloves, and after liberal use of rum secured the entire sixteen deer skins for three pounds. Teedyuscung could not, like the Iroquois counselors of a generation earlier, withstand the temptation of strong drink. While intoxicated, he sold the deer skins and then tarried at the Fort demanding rum, which Miller freely gave since it belonged to the provincial supply. Newcastle went off in disgust. The authorities at Philadelphia were apprehensive that Teedyuscung was not sincere in his peace professions. Indians on the border insinuated that the Easton Conference was but a ruse to gain time and that Teedyuscung was a traitor, working in the French interest.

Finally, when William Parson's letter to the governor was received (August 14, 1756) setting forth the true cause of Teedyuscung's detention at Fort Allen, Conrad Weiser was ordered to look into the affair and punish the offending lieutenant.

This was promptly done, but the mischief Miller caused nearly destroyed all that had been done for peace. Miller was discharged, and Teedyuscung went to Wyoming and up the North Branch of the Susquehanna, persuading the Indians to bury the hatchet and to send deputies to a second conference at Easton to be held in October. In the meantime, when he became suspicious of Teedyuscung's delay at Fort Allen, the governor sent Newcastle secretly to New York to learn from the Six Nations if they had ever deputized Teedyuscung to represent them in public treaties. Newcastle returned with the report that the Six Nations denied the authority of Teedyuscung.

The prospects of peace were growing more and more embarrassing. Now that war was declared with France (April 1756), England sent Lord Loudon to America to take charge. Indian affairs were under the control of two men, Sir

William Johnson for the Northern and Mr. Atkins for the Southern colonies. Loudon's policy was to secure as many Indians as possible for allies and strike the French with them. To this end, Mr. Atkins secured the alliance of the Cherokee and other Southern tribes. These were immediately added to the armies of Virginia and Western Pennsylvania. This act stirred the Northern Indians. The Iroquois and the Delawares declared they could never fight on the same side as the despised Cherokees. This Southern alliance meant a Northern revolt and threatened to crush the peace negotiations at Easton.

At this critical juncture, Lord Loudon, whose ignorance of the problem before him was equaled only by his contempt for provincialism, ordered the governor of Pennsylvania to have nothing to do with Indian affairs. Sir William Johnson only, should control these things. Moreover, all efforts towards peace were advantages given to the enemy. However, Johnson was inclined towards peace, but he seriously complicated affairs in Pennsylvania by appointing George Croghan as his sole deputy in the province. Croghan and Weiser had quite different views on Indian affairs. The Indians were quick to notice these changes.

In conversation with Conrad Weiser, Jonathan, an old Mohawk chief, said: "Is it true that you are become a fallen tree, that you must no more engage in Indian affairs, neither as counselor nor interpreter? What is the reason?"

Weiser replied, "It is all too true. The King of Great Britain has appointed Warruychyockon (Col. William Johnson) to be manager of all Indian affairs that concern treaties of friendship, war, etc. And that accordingly the Great General (Lord Loudon) that came over the Great Waters had in the name of the King ordered the government of Pennsylvania to desist from holding treaties with the Indians, and the government of Pennsylvania will obey the King's command, and consequently I, as the government's servant, have nothing more to do with Indian affairs."

Jonathan and his companion replied in concert, "Ha! Ha!" meaning "Oh, sad." The two Indians then whispered together for a few minutes, during which Weiser politely withdrew into another room.

When he returned, Jonathan said, "Comrade, I hear you have engaged on another bottom. You are made a captain of warriors and laid aside council affairs and turned soldier."

To this, Weiser replied with some spirit, setting forth his reasons for self-defense, the bloody outrages of the Indians, and the reception of the first peace messengers. "You know," said Weiser, "their lives were threatened. You know the insolent answer which came back that caused us to declare war. I was at Easton working for peace. I love peace more than war. I am a man for peace, and if I had my wish, there would be no war at all . . . So, comrade, do not charge me with such a thing as that."

The Indians thanked Weiser for the explanation and went away satisfied. But at the same time, Weiser was shorn of his power among the Indians. Making him commander of the provincial forces robbed Pennsylvania of her most powerful advocate at the council fires of the Indians.

Peace negotiations were further encumbered by a change of governors in Pennsylvania. Morris was recalled, and Denny was sent out in his stead. In the latter part of October 1756, Teedyuscung returned to Easton. He had over one hundred Indians with him, all for peace. He left one hundred beyond Fort Allen and came to Easton with thirty, his purpose being to see what his reception would be before bringing in the others.

Denny read Lord Loudon's instructions and declared he would not go to Easton. If Teedyuscung would come to Philadelphia, the governor was willing to act for Sir William Johnson. The friends of peace compared Loudon's orders with the charter granted Pennsylvania by the King, in which sole control of Indian affairs was placed in the hands of the proprietary. Accordingly, they reasoned that by no subsequent act could the King or the King's servants deprive the proprietary of that privilege.

Denny sent an invitation to Teedyuscung to come to Philadelphia. The chief replied, "Brother, you remember very well that in time of darkness and danger, I came in here at your invitation. At Easton, we kindled a small council fire . . . If you should put out this little fire, our enemies will call it only a Jack Lantern, kindled on purpose to deceive those who approach it. Brother, I think it by no means advisable to put out this little fire but rather to put more sticks upon it, and I desire that you will come to it as soon as possible, bringing your old and wise men along with you and shall be very glad to see you here."[8]

The governor was highly incensed over Teedyuscung's attitude and declared to his council that it was ridiculous to humor the Indians and that no treaty should be held outside of Philadelphia. Weiser's confidential letters about this time were in no way complimentary to the governor.

The Friends sent a memorial to Denny, begging him to finish the peace that Governor Morris had commenced, offering to furnish a liberal present and asking permission to attend the treaty. The governor, on condition that a heavy guard attended him and be constantly around him at Easton, concluded to go.

---

8. *Penna. Colonial Records*, vol. VII., p. 310.

He accepted the Indian present from the Friends and permitted them to attend the treaty.

Just before the governor reached Easton, it was rumored that the Indians that Teedyuscung left near Fort Allen were bent on some treachery. Israel Pemberton, the leader of the Quaker delegation at Easton, went out immediately to investigate the report and allay the governor's fears. Weiser informed the governor that this was a false rumor. When this news reached Governor Denny, he proceeded on his journey. When he arrived, Teedyuscung and the two Iroquois chiefs met him, Weiser and some other Indians having missed him by going out another road. When the treaty opened, at three o'clock in the afternoon, "the governor marched from his lodging to the place of conference guarded by a party of Royal Americans in the front and on the flanks and a detachment of Colonel Weiser's provincials in sub-divisions in the rear, with colors flying, drums beating and music playing, which order was always observed in going to the place of conference."[9]

Teedyuscung opened the conference with the customary ceremonies, telling the governor to take no cognizance of the numerous Indian massacres around them. These things, he said, were instigated by the French and should not mar the negotiations for peace. These idle reports should "no more be regarded than the chirping of birds in the woods. I remember well the leagues and covenants of our forefathers. We are but children in comparison to them. What William Penn said to the Indians is fresh in our minds and memory, and I believe it is in yours. The Indians and Governor Penn agreed well together; this we all remember, and it is not a small matter that would then have separated us, and now you fill the same station he did in this province; it is in your power to act the same part. I am sorry for what our foolish people have done. I have gone among my people pleading for peace. If it cost me my life, I would do it."

The governor asked Teedyuscung why his people went to war with their brothers, the English. In the chief's lengthy reply, he hinted that injustice had been done to the Indians in land affairs. The governor and commissioners immediately pressed him for an explanation. Teedyuscung replied with great reluctance and only after he had been repeatedly urged to it. The Delaware Indians still feared the Iroquois. They remembered the chastisement given to them in 1742. Teedyuscung knew that if he mentioned land, it would offend the Six Nations. Therefore he hesitated. His counselors had evidently urged him to make peace without mentioning land. But after he was urged to it, he stamped

---

9. *Penna. Colonial Records*, vol. VII., p. 314.

upon the earth, saying: "This very ground was my land and inheritance and is taken from me by fraud."

The governor then asked Teedyuscung what he meant by fraud. The chief replied, after William Penn's death, his "children forge a deed like the true one with the same Indians' names to it and thereby take lands from the Indians they never sold. This is fraud." Also, when "the proprietaries greedy to purchase lands buy of one King (Indian Confederation) what belongs to the other, this is fraud."[10]

When the governor asked him if he had ever been treated in this manner, he replied that he had. The young proprietaries, by the Walking Purchase, had, by the use of a compass, taken more than double the quantity of land intended to be sold. "I did not intend to speak this," he said, "but I have done it at your request; not that I desire now that you should purchase these lands, but that you should look into your own hearts and consider what is right, and that do."

The next day the governor asked Conrad Weiser if there was any foundation for Teedyuscung's complaint about the Walking Purchase and the Six Nations' right to sell land on the Delaware River. Weiser was never in sympathy with the Delaware Indians. His reply was worthy of an Iroquois sachem. He said that none of the Delawares present could remember when they had held original claims to land. If any injustice was done, the Indians were either dead or gone to the Ohio country. That the land mentioned was first bought by William Penn (1686). His sons John and Thomas renewed this agreement and adjusted the limits, "and a line (Walking Purchase) was soon after run by Indians and surveyors." The Indians complained in 1742, and the deeds were then examined by the chiefs of the Six Nations, who told the Delawares that no injustice had been done to them. Both Weiser and Peters insisted that if this matter were thoroughly investigated, it would be found that the proprietaries had done no wrong.

The governor then told the Indians that the matter would be thoroughly investigated. Some days later, the governor denied that any injustice had been done but offered the Indians a handsome present to make satisfaction for their injuries. This Teedyuscung refused to receive. The matter was then placed in charge of an investigating committee.

It was decided that a general peace should be proclaimed, provided that the Indians deliver all their prisoners and that the governor's declaration of war and scalp act should not apply to the Indians who would promise to bury the hatchet. Presents were then delivered to the value of four hundred pounds, the

---

10. *Penna. Colonial Records*, vol. VIII., p. 324, 325.

governor announcing that the larger part of this present was furnished "by the people called Quakers . . . as a particular testimony of their regard and affection for the Indians and their earnest desire to promote this good work of peace."[11]

Teedyuscung, in reply, desired that everyone apply himself to the good cause of peace. "The corn that is planted," he said, "must be tended, or it will come to nothing. Though we have done well in the cause of peace, we must be prudent, or our success will not meet our expectations. God that is above hath furnished us both with powers and abilities. I am aware that I have not done my part. I must confess to my shame. But let us all do our part. Let us complete this good work for the sake of our children. It is our duty to act for their good."[12]

Weiser accompanied Teedyuscung and the Indians to Fort Allen. It was determined that the disgrace and loss which followed the first conference should not be repeated. "We reached Bethlehem after dark," wrote Weiser, "and after the soldiers and Indians were quartered at the public inn this side of the creek, I gave Deedjoskon (Teedyuscung) the slip in the dark, and he went along with the rest to the said inn."

The next morning Teedyuscung could not get his wife away from Bethlehem, where she had been staying in the care of the Moravian brethren. She declared she would not live with him because of his debauched habits. The chief then took all the children from her but one, whereupon the Moravian brothers induced Conrad Weiser to use his influence in persuading the woman to live with her husband. Weiser succeeded and started for Fort Allen by ten o'clock.

At Hesse's Inn, the Indians dined on cider and beef, which cost the province fifteen shillings. A ten-gallon keg of rum had been sent along for the Indians to drink after they were beyond Fort Allen. When the party came near the fort, several Indians came to meet Teedyuscung and receive their share of the presents. They were constantly importuning Teedyuscung to be treated with rum. Despite Weiser's vigilance, five gallons were consumed before they reached the fort. Then Teedyuscung demanded the remainder that he might have a frolic with the Indians. Weiser finally surrendered the keg on condition that all the Indians stay away from the fort or suffer the consequences. Teedyuscung agreed to the terms, and Weiser wrote,

> I ordered a soldier to carry it (the rum) down to the fire; about midnight, he came back and desired to be let in, and it was found that he was alone; orders were given to let him in because his wife and

---

11. *Penna. Colonial Records*, vol. VIII., p. 332.
12. *Penna. Colonial Records*, vol. VII., p. 332, 333.

children were in the fort; he behaved well. After a while, we were alarmed by one of the drunken Indians that offered to climb over the stoccadoes. I got on the platform and looked out of the porthole, and saw the Indian, and told him to be gone; else the sentry should fire upon him; he ran off as fast as he could and cried, 'Damn you all, I value you not,' but he got out of sight immediately, and we heard no more of it.[13]

After the rum was all gone and Weiser had furnished a sick Indian with a horse and settled the case of a stolen gun, Teedyuscung, who was quite sober, parted from Weiser with tears in his eyes. He desired me, said Weiser, "to stand a friend to the Indians and give good advice till everything that was desired was brought about. Though he is a drunkard and a very irregular man, yet he is a man that can think well, and I believe him to be sincere in what he said."

Teedyuscung went out among his people to hunt the prisoners and arouse a more widespread peace sentiment. Newcastle, the warm friend of the English, had died of smallpox at Philadelphia. The great peace apostle among the Indians was dead. Teedyuscung alone remained. The charge of fraud by the great chief was the tocsin for civil strife. The anti-proprietary party took up the issue. Dark suspicions had hung over the "Walking Purchase." Now the governor had promised that all would be investigated. The Assembly and the Quakers determined that the committee should investigate.

At about this time, Sir William Johnson selected George Croghan as his deputy and gave him entire control of Indian affairs in Pennsylvania. Croghan desired that the coming treaty, which included a large number of Susquehanna Indians, should be held at Lancaster. During May 1757, a great concourse of Indians gathered there. But Teedyuscung was still among the Iroquois pleading for peace. Sir William Johnson and Croghan desired that all friendly Indians take up the hatchet in the English cause. Teedyuscung opposed this and advocated the Quaker view of peace and neutrality for the Indians. While the chiefs were waiting near Lancaster for Teedyuscung, the governor received imperative orders again from Lord Loudon to keep clear from all Indian treaties and to forbid the Quakers from either attending those treaties or in any manner contributing thereto.

For these reasons, Governor Denny declined to go to Lancaster. Letters and petitions now poured in upon the governor. William Masters and Joseph Galloway of Lancaster voiced the sentiment of that vicinity in a letter urging

---

13. *Penna. Archives*, vol. III., p. 67.

the governor to come to Lancaster immediately and use every possible means to ascertain the truth or falsity of Teedyuscung's charges. "The Indians now present have plainly intimated that they are acquainted with the true cause of our Indian war."

The Friendly Society for the Promotion of Peace among the Indians asked permission from the governor to examine the minutes of the provincial council and the proprietary deeds to "assist the proprietary in proving their innocence of Teedyuscung's charges."

The governor positively refused to show them any papers. The commissioners in charge of Indian affairs were also refused the same request. The governor then lost his temper and charged the Quakers of Pennsylvania with meddling in affairs that did not concern them. The Assembly then sent a message to the governor, denying that the province's people ever "interfered with his Majesties prerogative of making peace and war. Their known duty and loyalty to his Majesty, notwithstanding the pains taken to misrepresent their actions, forbid such an attempt. It is now clear by the inquiries made by your Honor that the cause of the present Indian incursions on this province, and the dreadful calamities many of the inhabitants have suffered, have arisen in a great measure from the exorbitant and unreasonable purchases made or supposed to be made of the Indians, that the natives complain they have not a country left to hunt or subsist in."[14]

This view which was entertained by the people as well as the Assembly, was contradicted by Conrad Weiser, who the proprietors requested to furnish them something in writing. "I can never agree," he said, "that the Indians came to complain about their land or some of it being fraudulently got from them, but they were pressed for reasons why they struck us and gave that as one of their reasons, but I am satisfied that it was put into their mouth sometime before. Witness Sauer's News after the treaty in July, in Easton, upon that head we want no treaty, without they, the Indians, require it. We want no mediator between the proprietors and the Indians about land affairs."[15]

The pressure of the people compelled Governor Denny to go to the Lancaster Conference. Croghan was desirous that the consultation be held at Lancaster and that the Western Indians be drawn into a treaty there. Croghan and Weiser could not agree upon the policy to be employed. Finally, Weiser yielded to his superior in office.

---

14. *Penna. Colonial Records*, vol. VII., p. 577.
15. C. Z. Weiser's *Life of Conrad Weiser*, p. 386.

The Cherokee Indians serving in the army near Fort Loudon and Fort Cumberland were stoutly opposed to any peace with the Delaware Indians. Consequently, while the conference was in progress at Lancaster, many Indian outrages took place within a few miles of that town. This exasperated the people to such an extent that, in one instance, they brought the mutilated body of a woman whom the Indians had scalped and left it on the courthouse steps, a silent witness as they said of the fruits of an Indian peace. These things, with the absence of Teedyuscung, made it impossible to accomplish anything at Lancaster. Presents were given, and the principles of peace were expounded among the Indians. This was done by the Friends who attended in large numbers.

The governor, writing to the proprietaries, said:

> In case the Quakers should again apply for liberty to give presents and attend the treaty, I have prepared an answer agreeable to the Proprietor's letter of the 12th of March, in which I shall give them in writing, considering how fully and openly I had censured their numbers and behavior at Easton. I did not expect such a body of Friends would have attended at Lancaster, where the Secretary counted above one hundred in the Court House at one of the conferences, and some told me there were one hundred and forty; all as I am creditably informed deputed by the several meetings for that purpose. Four members of the Quaker meeting applied to me before I went to Lancaster for leave to join their presents as usual to the provincial presents. I consented it should be done exactly as it was agreed on by Governor Morris. On this answer, they have given out that I consented to their going, which I did no otherwise than as I have related.[16]

To what extent the interference of the Friends embarrassed the governor's conferences is unclear. His correspondence with the proprietaries would indicate that he was under instructions to exclude them from public treaties if possible. Yet the governor seems to have been unwilling to refuse their offers of Indian presents, and in winking at their presence, an influence potent for peace was permitted to circulate among the Indians. Therefore, the question of peace with the Ohio Indians was postponed until Teedyuscung should arrive.

In June 1757, a message came from the "King," as he was called, asking that "four or five horse loads of provisions" be sent to Wyoming, "not by white people, but by Indians I desire you would be careful," said Teedyuscung, "I

---

16. *Penna. Archives*, vol. III., pp. 196, 197.

have heard and have reason to think it will grieve both you and me to the heart. There are many nations belonging to the French who go around me, and as I have heard and have reason to believe, they know and have understood that I have taken hold of your hand, and their aim is to break us a peace and to separate us. When I visited the Indians over the Great Swamp and told them my message of peace, they said it was a bait and that the English would kill us all; however, when they saw me come back safe the first time, they dropt their tomahawks, and said, 'If the English are true to you they will be true to us.'"[17]

When the third Easton Conference opened in July 1757, Teedyuscung was very much incensed at Conrad Weiser. The chief wanted to go out and meet Governor Denny, which he claimed was the Indian custom of complimenting a great man. Weiser had promised to give Teedyuscung notice of the governor's arrival. The chief now complained that Weiser deceived him, and if he did it in one instance, he would do it again. The old Indian never knew that the governor had no desire to be a recipient of the Indian's compliments, shown in this manner and that Weiser was under instructions to keep the Indians from coming to meet him.

Teedyuscung declared that he would do no business until he could have his own clerk. He considered that it was proper to have a copy of the proceedings which should be kept among the Indians' wampum. The governor consulted his council and had a lengthy interview with Conrad Weiser when it was decided that Teedyuscung didn't need to have a clerk. That evening a meeting was held, and the governor explained why Teedyuscung didn't need to have a private secretary. The chief seemed satisfied.

The next morning "the governor and council were surprised at Teedyuscung's applying again with so much warmth for a clerk after he had expressed himself so well satisfied the evening before with the speech made them by the governor, assigning reasons why he could not comply with his request, and suspected that the Indians had been tampered with on this occasion by some evil-disposed persons and put on renewing this demand."[18]

Croghan insisted that Teedyuscung had no such intention when he came to Wyoming a few weeks previous but, on the contrary, expressed his entire approval of the clerk that Croghan had selected.

Weiser was positive that Israel Pemberton, the Friends' peace association leader, had seduced Teedyuscung into such a demand. He said,

---

17. *Penna. Colonial Records*, vol. VII., p. 590.
18. *Penna. Colonial Records*, vol. VII., p. 657.

I was sitting alone in my room at the tavern when Israel Pemberton suddenly opened my door but noticing that I was alone, he asked my pardon and withdrew. Sometime later, I joined Captains Orndt and Busse, who were sitting together in another room; in a few minutes, Teedyuscung and Pumpshire, his interpreter, joined the company. The chief, in an abrupt and rough manner, complained that the governor had not used him well in reference to the clerk. As the King of Ten Nations, he had a right to a clerk. He would have one. He would no longer be led by the nose, and the governor might be told so. I told him he could tell the governor himself. After the Indian withdrew, Captain Orndt said that Teedyuscung had been in his room before that evening, but a Quaker gentleman, known to be Israel Pemberton, had taken him out scarcely a half hour before.

From this, Weiser and Orndt concluded that Pemberton was the cause of Teedyuscung's unusual demand. The governor was very much disturbed by this request. With the advice of all the council except James Logan, it was thought best to leave it all with George Croghan. The old trader endeavored to persuade the "King" away from such "an infatuation, but to no purpose." The crafty chief broke off the conversation abruptly and, pulling out a belt of wampum, gave it to Croghan, declaring that he would either have a clerk or break up the treaty and leave the town. Croghan, thereupon, recommended the governor to grant Teedyuscung's request.

The governor then grew angry with the Assembly's Indian commissioners and charged them with bringing all this trouble upon him, saying:

> Your presumption on this occasion, either as commissioners or private subjects, to receive any complaint or application from the Indians, and taking upon you to remonstrate in their behalf to me, is illegal, unconstitutional, introductive of the greatest confusion and mischiefs, and the highest invasion of the just rights of the Crown By what means Teedyuscung came to demand a clerk, I am at a loss to determine; nor is it less surprising to me that you should undertake to give him your opinion of the matter (as you acknowledged you did), and pronounce his demand so very reasonable and just before he had advised with me upon it.[19]

---

19. *Penna. Colonial Records*, vol. VII., pp. 661, 662.

CHARLES THOMSON

Denny's vigorous defense of the proprietary privilege to keep all the records was finally overruled. The next day the governor, in open treaty, said to Teedyuscung,

> No Indian chief before you ever demanded to have a clerk, and none has ever been appointed for Indians in former treaties, nay I have not even nominated one on the part of the province; therefore, I cannot help declaring it against my judgment. I am afraid by your showing so little confidence in me and the King's deputy agent that you have hearkened to idle stories or the singing of birds, tho' you advised me against it; however, to give you fresh proof of my friendship and regard, if you insist upon having a clerk, I shall no longer oppose it.

Teedyuscung thanked the governor and apologized for any rudeness he may have shown, desiring that the past might be forgotten, and with cheerfulness, he said, "Let us proceed with all our power in the great work of peace."

Richard Peters was very much incensed over the attitude of the Assembly, the Friends, and the commissioners in urging that Teedyuscung's demands were proper. He took it as a reflection upon the honesty and sincerity of his own actions as clerk. He accordingly declared that he would have nothing to do with the records. In a private letter to Conrad Weiser, he said:

> I enclose you the Indian Conference (treaties of 1756), published without the governor's leave or knowledge by the Assembly. You will observe the reports tagged to the Conference; it is one other specimen of Mr. Franklin's disingenuity and baseness. You observe justly that it is not a time to provoke the Delawares, and therefore it will be difficult how to act, but nevertheless, the proprietors and other folks must be under their infamous misrepresentations.[20]

Peters, on behalf of the proprietors, held the council records. He even refused to allow the Indian commissioners appointed by the Assembly to examine them.

When the treaty opened, Mr. Trent, a former trader, took Mr. Peters' place as the clerk for the province. He recorded the following opening minute:

---

20. Manuscript letters of Conrad Weiser, in the collection of the Pennsylvania Historical Society.

RECONCILIATION

As soon as the governor and council and Indians had taken their seats, Teedyuscung, by his interpreter, John Pumpshire, called for Charles Thomson, master of the Quaker school in the city of Philadelphia; placed him by Mr. Trent at the table, and said he had chosen him for his clerk; whereupon he sat down and began taking minutes, without asking permission of the governor, who took no further notice of it.[21]

In writing about this affair to his friend Samuel Rhodes, Charles Thomson said:

> I need not mention the importance of the business we are come about. The welfare of the province and the lives of thousands depend upon it. That an affair of such weight should be transacted with soberness, all will allow; how, then, must it shock you to hear that pains seem to have been taken to make the King[22] drunk every night since the business began. The first two or three days were spent in deliberating whether the King should be allowed the privilege of a clerk. When he was resolute in asserting his right and would enter into no business without having a secretary of his own, they, at last, gave it up and seem to have fallen on another scheme which is to unfit him to say anything worthy of being inscribed (?) by his secretary. On Saturday, under pretense of rejoicing for the victory gained by the King of Prussia and the arrival of the fleet, a bonfire was ordered to be made and liquor given to the Indians to induce them to dance. For fear they should get sober on Sunday and be fit next day to enter on business under pretense that the Mohawks had requested it, another bonfire was ordered to be made and more liquor given them. On Monday night, the King was made drunk by Conrad Weiser, on Tuesday by G. Croghan; last night, he was very drunk at Vernon's, and Vernon lays the blame on Comin and G. Croghan. He did not go to sleep last night. This morning he lay down under a shed about the break of day and slept a few hours. He is to speak this afternoon. He is to be sure in a fine capacity to do business. But thus, we go on. I leave you to make reflections. I, for my part, wish myself at home.[23]

---

21. *Penna. Colonial Records*, vol. VII., p. 665.
22. Teedyuscung.
23. From *Pennsylvania Magazine*, vol. XX., p. 422.

That Teedyuscung, with his inordinate appetite for rum, should have succeeded in guiding his public affairs between the two conflicting parties is a subject of some moment. The old chief had a clear mind and was unswerving in his purpose. He placed large confidence in Charles Thomson and doubtless accepted his guidance in many things. The governor and his party were quick to charge Charles Thomson with all of Teedyuscung's whims and obstinate rulings, especially his attitude on the old land dispute. Weiser and Croghan each declared that Teedyuscung himself was ready to drop all land controversies and would have done so had it not been for Thomson and his crowd. But in this, Croghan and Weiser were either mistaken, or their advice was rendered merely to please the ear of the governor and their employers, the proprietors.

The real reason Teedyuscung and his Indians were reticent about the fraud perpetrated by the "Walking Purchase" was fear of the Six Nations. This was a transition period with the Delaware Indians. They were asserting their independence from the Six Nations and were content with accomplishing that, feeling that they could afford to wait until after peace was fully established before they asserted their ancient rights to the lands drained by the Delaware River.

Teedyuscung's advisers urged him not to push the land dispute: The governor, however, on behalf of the proprietors, was determined to make Teedyuscung deny that any fraud had been used in land purchases. His object in this was to exonerate the proprietors from any suspicions. The Assembly's party, which was in league with the Friends, knowing that the "Walking Purchase" was a flagrant fraud, was determined to use this opportunity to have all the proceedings of that purchase thoroughly examined.

When pressed for the cause of the Indian alienation, Teedyuscung declared that it was the land.

> The complaint I made last fall I yet continue. I think some lands have been bought by the proprietors or his agents from Indians who had not a right to sell . . . I think, also, when some lands have been sold to the proprietors by Indians who had a right to sell to a certain place,[24] whether that purchase was to be measured by miles or hours walk, that the proprietors have contrary to agreement or bargain, taken in more lands than they ought to have done; anti lands that belonged to others. I therefore now desire that you will produce the writings and deeds by which you hold the land and let them be read in public and examined, that it may be fully known from what Indians you have

---

24. The water shed between the Delaware and the east branch of the Susquehanna Rivers.

bought the lands you hold; and how far your purchases extend; that copies of the whole may be laid before King George, and published to all the provinces under his government. What is fairly bought and paid for, I make no further demands about. But if any lands have been bought of Indians to whom these lands did not belong and who had no right to sell them, I expect a satisfaction for those lands; and if the proprietors have taken in more lands than they bought of true owners, I expect likewise to be paid for that.[25]

Teedyuscung then asked that the territory of Wyoming be reserved for the Indians forever—that it might be surveyed and a deed given to the Indians—that they might have something to show when it became necessary to drive the white men away. After these charges were again made, the governor called Croghan and Weiser together to know what was the best thing to do. With his large share of experience in Indian affairs, each of these men agreed that some outside influence had induced Teedyuscung to revive these charges. They also united in the opinion that the Indians merely wanted a glimpse of the old deeds, and would be satisfied with a cursory examination of the signatures.

Upon these assertions, the governor and council were induced to grant Teedyuscung's request and show him the deeds of 1686 and 1737 from the Delawares and 1749 from the Iroquois. When the governor applied to Mr. Peters for the papers and deeds, they were again refused. Peters declared that he held them as a sacred trust from the proprietors and would neither surrender them nor permit himself to be placed under oath and give testimony. He insisted that these two things could only be done in the presence of Sir William Johnson, before whom, as a final arbitrator, the proprietors desired that these charges be laid.

James Logan immediately opposed Richard Peters. He insisted that all deeds relating to lands the Indians claimed were fraudulently purchased should be shown. To refuse this would be unjust to the Indians and dangerous to the cause of peace. Logan explained that the proprietary instructions should not be too literally construed and obeyed. The Indians were opposed to having their case settled before Sir William Johnson. After an animated discussion in council, it was reluctantly agreed that the deeds should be shown. The council only consented to this after Conrad Weiser had assured them that Teedyuscung did not insist upon seeing all the deeds but only those pertaining to the backlands.

---

25. *Penna. Colonial Records*, vol. VII., p. 681.

R. Peters again protested but was overruled. The deeds were laid on the table on August 3, 1757.

Charles Thomson, at Teedyuscung's request, copied these deeds. The chief said he would have preferred to have seen the deeds of confirmation given to Governor Keith in 1718. Still, the great work of peace was superior to the land dispute. If the proprietors made satisfaction for the lands which had been fraudulently secured, he would return the English prisoners held captive among the Indians. The governor and Teedyuscung then grasped the peace belt, and the two years of struggle for peace were crowned with victory. After much feasting, dancing, drinking, and burning of bonfires, the treaty closed.

Teedyuscung promised to fight for the English on condition that white captains should not command his men. The governor and his party returned to Philadelphia, deeply worried over the publicity of the Indian fraud charges at the Easton Conference. Peace to the proprietors was dearly purchased if the people of the province were confirmed in their belief that the Indian outrages had been caused by fraud in land purchases. Two things, therefore, must be done, peace must be extended to the Western Indians, and the charges of Teedyuscung must be revoked.

XVIII

Peace

PEACE DESIRED WITH THE WESTERN INDIANS—POST'S JOURNEY—WEISER'S WANING POWER—WEISER'S LOYALTY TO THE SIX NATIONS—WEISER'S ADVICE ABOUT THE WYOMING FORT—HOUSES BUILT FOR THE INDIANS AT WYOMING—TEEDYUSCUNG AND HIS BAND WANT TO SHARE THE WHITE MAN'S BOUNTY ON SCALPS—TEEDYUSCUNG IN PHILADELPHIA—THE INFLUENCE OF THE FRIENDLY ASSOCIATION FOR THE PROMOTION OF PEACE—THE QUAKERS CLOSELY WATCHED—THE CHEROKEE ALLIES CAUSE DISAFFECTION—FREDERICK CHRISTIAN POST'S FIRST MISSION—POST WINS A VICTORY—POST'S OHIO MISSION—PREPARING FOR THE GREAT CONFERENCE THE FOURTH EASTON CONFERENCE—SOUTHWESTERN PENNSYLVANIA DEEDED BACK TO THE INDIANS—THE MUNSEY LAND CLAIM IN NEW JERSEY—THE MOHAWKS TRY TO BREAK DOWN TEEDYUSCUNG'S INFLUENCE—GOVERNORS BERNARD AND DENNY APOLOGIZE FOR TEEDYUSCUNG—TEEDYUSCUNG'S DEFENSE—THOMAS KING TEMPORARILY SETTLES THE DIFFICULTY—TEEDYUSCUNG'S CHARGE OF FRAUD—THE GOVERNOR LOATH TO INVESTIGATE—FOR FOUR HUNDRED POUNDS STERLING TEEDYUSCUNG WITHDRAWS HIS CHARGES OF FRAUD IN THE WALKING PURCHASE.

THE Work of peace would not be complete until the Western Indians were secured and the approbation and approval of the Six Nations were obtained. To this end, the Friendly Association and the Indian commissioners strained every effort. The removal of Lord Loudon and the accession of William Pitt favored the Pennsylvania projects. While the Forbes Expedition was forming and slowly chopping its way into Western Pennsylvania, while Montgomery was planning to subdue Quebec, the peace element in Pennsylvania robbed the French of their Indian allies on the Ohio. Pennsylvania accomplished this through two influences. First, the embargo laid on breadstuffs by the greatest exporting center among the Colonies seriously embarrassed the French, who could no longer feed their allies. Second, the peace sentiment of the Friendly Association worked through Teedyuscung and finally through Frederick Christian Post, the great Moravian peacemaker.

Post journeyed several times to the Ohio country, persuading the Shawanese and the Delawares to bury the hatchet and desert the French. He did this with a heavy reward upon his scalp while his every footstep was surrounded by danger. Post worked with unshaken faith in the cause of peace and its final triumph.

The Easton Conference of 1758 completed the work among the Indians in the Delaware and Susquehanna. It secured the friendship of the Six Nations and consummated the efforts of Christian Post among the Western Indians. Conrad Weiser saw his former influence shorn of its power. By the King's authority, Colonel Johnson was now Sir William Johnson and had exclusive control of Iroquois affairs. Croghan, his deputy, managed Western Indian matters. The Delawares had thrown off their allegiance to the Six Nations and declared themselves independent and able to treat for themselves.

Charles Thomson now became the chosen adviser of the Indians on the Delaware. Teedyuscung and his followers were not admirers of Conrad Weiser. The Moravians found their champion in Frederick Christian Post, and through his zeal and warm friendship for the Delawares, they turned away from Weiser, whose love for a Delaware was not remarkable. The old interpreter, who had once been the leader in the Indian policy of six provinces, now found himself despised by the Delawares because he took up arms against them, suspected by the Iroquois who had opened their ears to Sir William Johnson. Nor was Weiser's standing better among his white brethren. The Germans distrusted him, and all the Quakers turned from him because he adhered to the cause of the proprietors. Weiser's enemies declared that money was the sole motive for all his actions and that he engaged in Indian affairs for profit.

Conrad Weiser was a staunch supporter of the proprietors and their interests, but he had a deep sense of justice for the Indians. Whenever the province's policy threatened to injure the natives, Weiser quickly rallied to their aid. This is especially noticeable with the Iroquois Indians. For them, Weiser had a genuine friendship. When some of the Six Nation deputies were in Philadelphia in June 1758, the governor not receiving them in person as promptly as Weiser considered best. He, therefore, wrote the following letter to Richard Peters:

> Sir:—If the governor won't meet the Indians this Evening only to shake hands with them, and signify his satisfaction to see them in

Town, and leave business to other days when they are recovered from their fatigue, I will say that he does not act the part of a well-wisher to his Majesties people and interest, at this critical times. You may let him know, so here is my hand to my saying so. I am, Sir, a loyal subject and a well-wisher to my Country.
Conrad Weiser.
Philadelphia, July the 6th,
at half an hour after five.[1]

No one but Conrad Weiser would have dared to have spoken in that manner to the governor. But the old interpreter had imbibed the fearless Indian spirit, which brooked no overawing aristocracy when the truth must be spoken.

After the Conference of 1757, the Pennsylvania Assembly offered to enact a law that would permanently settle the Wyoming lands upon Teedyuscung and his people. This was per the chief's wishes expressed at Easton. The governor was prompt and eager in his desire to secure such legislation but insisted that the Six Nations had never given the proprietors a deed for that region. For this reason, he advised delay until the Six Nations and the proprietors sanctioned and provided for such a disposition.

Teedyuscung and his warriors were unable to understand any reason for this delay. They insisted that the houses and a fort should be built for them at Wyoming. The governor and council immediately consulted Weiser upon the advisability of doing this and desired that he undertake the affair. He replied:

> I am in a very low state of health and cannot, without great hazard, undertake any journey; besides, if the Six Nations should not be pleased with the building of a fort at Wyoming, they would blame me more than anybody else because they would have it to say that I knew their rights, etc., tho' I believe if the building a fort at Wyoming is cautiously carried on, merely for the use of the Indians, and left to them when finished, all will be well. A trading house at Fort Augusta (Shamokin) should immediately be erected, else our Indian Interests, what little we may yet have, will be entirely lost. If the government cannot agree about the condition, some well-disposed men should be appointed to keep stores at Fort Augusta and furnish the Indians with what they want; clothing especially, as they must be, for the most part, naked at this time. This article requires all possible

---
1. *Penna. Archives*, vol. III., p. 439.

care and speed. Rum should not be allowed to be sold or given by any licensed trader. A little, or just a dram, might be given by the commanding officer of Fort Augusta, and he to deny obstinately and absolutely a second, and the Indians will like it better when they judge of the thing coolly and by themselves.[2]

This unsolicited prohibitive advice offered by Weiser reflects his genuine sentiments. The man who staved the rum casks at Logstown at the risk of his life knew full well that this was a never-failing cause of Indian dissatisfaction. The charges made by Charles Thomson while at Easton in 1757 were doubtless obtained from Teedyuscung himself, and the old chief never lost an opportunity to injure Weiser, whom he despised. That the proprietary interests at Easton in 1757 used quantities of liquor to confuse Teedyuscung is only too true; that Weiser was a party to it is extremely doubtful.

After Weiser refused to go to Wyoming to build the houses, the council reluctantly appointed one of their number, who, during the following spring, with a force of fifty to sixty carpenters and masons, built at the provincial expense ten wooden houses at Wyoming. These houses were on stone foundations and were sixteen by twenty-four feet. During the process of erection, one of the masons was scalped by a party of French and Indians, who, with a jealous eye, were lurking in the vicinity.

After the peace of 1757, Teedyuscung could not remain neutral; he desired to send his young men against the French. He accordingly petitioned the governor for a reward on scalps. If the white men of the province could enjoy the profits of such a bounty, Teedyuscung saw no reason why the recently acquired Indian allies might not come in for their share. The governor was seriously embarrassed over this demand. To thwart the desire of this self-willed chief was a matter of great danger to the province. The Assembly promptly opposed such a measure. Then in proportion to the Assembly's opposition, the governor favored the project. Since no conclusion could in this manner be reached, Conrad Weiser was again summoned, and his advice solicited.

"It is my humble opinion," he said, "that no encouragement should be given to the Indians for scalps for fear we must pay for our own scalps and those of our fellow subjects, as will certainly be the case. Allow as much for prisoners as you please, rather more than was intended."

This advice settled the dispute, and the Indians were not allowed any bounty for French and French Indian scalps.

---

2. *Penna. Colonial Records*, vol. VII., pp. 735, 736.

CONRAD WEISER'S HOUSE IN READING

Early in the spring of 1758, Teedyuscung came to Philadelphia and demanded a private conference with the governor and his council, with permission to bring his clerk, Charles Thomson, with him. The governor and council refused to have the clerk meet with them and, in this matter, overruled Teedyuscung but promised him that he could have his clerk at all future public conferences. After the chief had gotten over his anger, he renewed his request for a settlement at Wyoming, asking for schoolmasters, counselors, and two ministers, saying: "You must consider that I have a soul as well as another."[3]

After smoking the calumet pipe of peace sent from the Western Indians, he asked that his peace belts be sent to the Ohio country, saying: "I have received encouragement from the Indian Nations. Now Brothers, press on with all your might in promoting the good work we are engaged in; let us beg the God that made us to bless our endeavor, and I am sure that if you exert yourselves, God will grant a blessing, we shall live."[4]

This appeal for peace with the Western Indians, coming from the lips of Teedyuscung, was the initial move toward Christian Post's daring mission into the heart of the French territory. It is probable that Teedyuscung's plea for peace was inspired by the members of "the Friendly Association for the Promotion of Peace." For two years, the Friends had treated Teedyuscung and his people in the most considerate manner. At one time, his savage nature would appear on the surface and demand a bounty on scalps for his young men; at another time, the instincts of peace reinforced by numerous Quaker sermons would be in the ascendency, and Teedyuscung would plead for a general peace with all the subdued fervor so characteristic of this remarkable Indian. The influence of the Society of Friends upon these Indians, and through them upon the peace negotiations on the Ohio, is probably not overdrawn by the enemies of the Friends.

The proprietary party generally believed that the Friends were bent upon injuring the reputation of the proprietors since they had spread the report among the people that the Indians had been defrauded of their lands. The governor's party could not comprehend why the Friends spent so much on the Indians and attended treaties in such numbers unless it was to harm the governor's authority and blacken the character of the proprietors. That they could do such a thing purely from a love of peace was at that time incomprehensible.

The governor's party at the Easton Treaty of 1757, therefore, had William Peters and Jacob Duche appointed to watch the Quakers carefully and, if possible, discover what purpose they had in attending the treaty in such large

---

3. *Penna. Colonial Records*, vol. VIII., p. 47.
4. *Penna. Colonial Records*, vol. VIII., p. 34.

numbers, especially after the governor had told them plainly that such actions would be distasteful to him. These two gentlemen, acting as spies and full of suspicion, reported that "the Quakers distributed a number of presents privately among the Indians, greatly to the injury of the governor's influence, so much so that when we met any of the Indians on the streets or in our evening walks after business, they would generally accost us with this question in their broken English, 'Are you a Quaker, a Quaker?'—and if we answered no, they would frown and look very stern and ill-natured upon us, and say we were bad man—bad man, governor's man; but if we answer in the affirmative (as we did sometimes to try them) that we were Quakers, they would smile and caress us, and call us brothers, and sav we were good men—Quaker good men—governor's men bad men—good for nothing."

One afternoon the governor decided not to confer with the Indians. In the journals of the conference, he assigned a reason that Teedyuscung was drunk. Charles Thomson, in his report, said Teedyuscung was not drunk. This action of the governor inflamed the Indians until they put on the war paint and loaded the guns. Peters and Duche report this revolt among the Indians, alarming Easton's white people.

> Many of them went to the riotous Indians and endeavored to quiet and disarm them, but they would suffer nobody to do it till the Quakers came, and to them, they immediately submitted and delivered up their arms as readily and submissively as common soldiers would to their officers. At another time, when the detectives were taking an evening walk, they met an Indian dressed in a remarkably plain manner, with a broad flat hat, like a Quaker. We asked him if he was a Quaker, and he smiling, answered, "Yes, yes, I a Quaker now—but when I go away, I—Indian again."[5]

From this, it would appear that Teedyuscung was supported, if not moved to peace by the Friends. He persisted in asking the governor to send his peace belts to Ohio. The province acting slowly in this matter, Teedyuscung himself decided to send two brave and trustworthy Indians to Ohio with the peace belts.

While these efforts were progressing, numerous outrages were occurring along the border. The French Indians again fell upon the inhabitants in Berks County and alarmed the citizens of Reading. Teedyuscung's two messengers were still at Fort Allen. Having a bad dream, one of them immediately decided not

---

5. *Penna. Archives*, vol. III., pp. 275, 276.

to go. Reports came in that old Paxinosa, the faithful Shawanese chief, who had been true to the English since the war began, had turned against the men of Pennsylvania. A general uprising seemed to be among the Indians. The French appeared to be gaining ground. General Forbes was quick to see this and urged Governor Denny to accede to all of Teedyuscung's demands. At this critical juncture, those intimate with the secrets of the Delaware Indians discovered that the cause of this sudden disaffection was due to the presence of the Cherokee Indians in the province. The men of Cumberland County, joining with Virginia, and Mr. Atkin, the Southern Superintendent of Indian affairs for the Crown, secured the alliance of the Cherokee and Southern Indians. Their presence at Carlisle and Cumberland excited the Six Nations and the Delawares. If their old enemies were friends to the English, the Northern Indians would go over to the French. Old Paxinosa arose and said he would take his people and go to Ohio.

Governor Denny and General Forbes at once sent Christian Post and Charles Thomson to Wyoming to persuade the Indians from their purpose and, if possible, to call all the friendly Indians east of the mountains while Forbes should complete his expedition towards Fort Duquesne. Thomson and Post met Teedyuscung on the mountains some fourteen or fifteen miles from the Wyoming Valley. When they told him their mission, he said, "Go back; I will not answer for your lives if you go on."

They then reminded him that the road to Wyoming had been opened by a belt of wampum and that it was his business to keep it open from Fort Allen to his town, just as the governor kept it open for the Indians from Fort Allen to Easton. Post said that it was the custom of all nations to allow peace messengers to go to and fro. Teedyuscung replied that this was true and that the Six Nations, not Teedyuscung, had blocked the road. They would not listen to his plea for peace that the woods were full of their war parties but declared that the Cherokee alliance and the murder of Seneca Indians in Virginia stirred them to war. Post and Thomson couldn't go further against Teedyuscung's advice. The cause of peace was growing dark. The messengers returned with their ears full of complaints.

In this dark hour, Frederick Christian Post gathered the Cherokee messages and offers of peace with the Delaware Indians and took them to Teedyuscung. He convinced the chief and his people that there was nothing to fear from the Cherokees and the Southern Indians.

When Teedyuscung realized this, he immediately renewed his efforts to send his peace belts to the Ohio. Since no Indians who were willing to take their lives in their hands and carry these messages could be found, Christian

Post agreed to go on behalf of both Teedyuscung and Governor Denny. Several Indians now offered to accompany Post. He accepted their offer but applied to the council as a white man and companion. The council approved this request.

Post then said that since Charles Thomson had offered to go with him, he would ask to have him appointed. The governor objected and told Post "he might take any other person."[6]

As a result, Post went to Ohio with a few Indians, one of whom proved a traitor to the cause. His first journey prepared the Shawanese and Delaware Indians for peace. His second mission robbed the French of their entire Indian alliance on the Ohio, enabling General Forbes to occupy Fort Duquesne without opposition.

While Post was performing this remarkable work on the Ohio, Teedyuscung was stirring the Six Nations to send their deputies to a great peace conference at Easton. By this means, the old chief hoped to draw all the Indians into an English alliance and secure a general peace. As a preliminary to this movement, Teedyuscung induced the Minisink Indians and some Seneca chiefs to go to Philadelphia in August 1758. Teedyuscung's son and a Seneca chief preceded these Indians and waited upon the governor, saying that they had a matter of great moment to present and desired that Conrad Weiser be sent for at once. The governor replied that Conrad Weiser was not at home and could not come to Philadelphia in time. The Indians said they did not choose to deliver their messages without his assistance. Some time was lost in waiting for the arrival of the other Indians. A council was held to determine what to do.

> The Indians seemed in great confusion and desired to be alone. They were an hour in consultation, keeping the governor and council waiting. At length, they came into council, and John Hudson acquainted the governor that he was much disappointed in Conrad Weiser's not coming but believed his message could be interpreted by Moses Tetemy and Sam, and therefore he inclined to give it; and as all he should say was very good and related to all his brethren, he desired the governor would sit in the State House and that the people might hear his good news.[7]

This reluctance among the Indians to have their most valued messages translated by someone who used poor English or failed to grasp their full

---
6. *Colonial Records*, vol. VIII., p. 147.
7. *Colonial Records*, vol. VIII., p. 150.

meaning reveals the unlimited confidence they had in the ability and honesty of Conrad Weiser.

The fourth Easton treaty convened on October 8, 1758. The Six Nations, the Minisinks, and the Delawares were there, and Christian Post came to speak for the Ohio Indians before the treaty was over. The Friends were there with their presents and Charles Thomson as clerk for Teedyuscung. So great was the assemblage that all the ancient rites and ceremonies of the Indian nations were performed with scrupulous care.

Conrad Weiser apologized, saying that his memory did not serve him. Therefore, he requested that Nichas, the Mohawk chief, perform these ceremonies for him. After the usual preliminaries and considerable delay in discussing the return of prisoners, the principal business of the treaty was entered upon. There were three old land disputes. The Iroquois sale at Albany in 1754 had been the source of trouble, if not of war. The Walking Purchase was complained of so often by Teedyuscung, and the Minisink or Munsey Indians complained that their lands in Jersey had never been bought. And now, as the price of peace these three disputes were to be settled, let it cost what it would. The Assemblies of New Jersey and Pennsylvania had decreed it so. The people had asserted their prerogative in government, and governors and proprietors were forced to submit.

Conrad Weiser had since 1754 insisted that the Albany purchase was not just, that the Indians were deceived, and the running of the lines had been misrepresented. Weiser's zeal, however, in this cause seems to have been weakened by the fact that the proprietors gave him two thousand (?) acres of land in Cumberland County. The Six Nations complained to Sir William Johnson in 1755 and told him they would never consent to this sale. That the west branch of the Susquehanna was held in trust as a hunting ground for their cousins, the Delawares. Sir William immediately took measures to compel the proprietors to cede back the land west of the Alleghanies. Three years were consumed in accomplishing this. The delay was a costly one to the people on the Pennsylvania frontier. The Delawares, who had lost their hunting grounds, joined the French and sought revenge in scalps and fire. At the Easton treaty of 1758, the governor, on behalf of the proprietors, told the Six Nation Indians that Conrad Weiser and Richard Peters would deed back to them all of the Albany Purchase west of the summits of the Alleghany Mountains.

"The Proprietors," said the governor, "have on all occasions manifested their particular regard for you. They prefer your friendship and the public good to their own private interest. Their former conduct gives you no room to doubt price."

The Munseys turned to the Iroquois, saying they would be glad for the opinion of their uncles.

The Six Nations, who excelled all the Indians of America in diplomacy, replied: "that it was a fair and honorable offer, and if it were their own case they would cheerfully accept it; but as there were a great many persons to share in the purchase money, they recommended it to his Excellency to add two hundred dollars more; and if that was complied with the report of it would be carried to all the nations and would be a proof of the affection and generosity of their brethren, the English."[8]

Governor Bernard found there was nothing else he could do. The great number of the Munseys reported by the Iroquois was a sufficient reason for an increase in the price.

The third subject of land dispute was the old complaints made by Teedyuscung, i. e., (1) Was the Walking Purchase just? (2) Had the Six Nations any right to sell land on the Delaware? Since 1742 the Delawares and the Six Nations had not met in a public land treaty with Pennsylvania. The question now brewing was whether the Delaware Indians were women or men. Were they subjects of the Iroquois, or were they independent? Teedyuscung was much more humble at Easton in 1758 than in 1756 and 1757. This was due to the presence of the Iroquois. The Mohawks were his enemy.

The Six Nations concluded that the first thing for them to do was to break down the influence and standing of Teedyuscung. One day, when the governor was about to close that conference session, Nichas, a Mohawk, arose and, pointing to Teedyuscung, spoke with great warmth and vigor. Weiser was ordered to interpret it but declined and desired that Mr. Montour should do it. Then after a pause, the old man's fertile brain saw how the approaching storm might be averted. He advised that this matter be interpreted at a private conference. The governor asked Weiser to consult the Indians. Nothing daunted, the old man did so, asking if they chose to have this matter interpreted now or at a private conference.

"Now," the Indians replied.

Then finally, since Conrad Weiser requested it, they consented to attend a private conference in the morning.

The next day, October 14, there was no conference. Doubtless, Weiser took means to prevent a conference until the anger of the Iroquois had somewhat abated.

---

8. *Penna. Colonial Records*, vol. VIII., p. 209.

On the morning of the 15th, in a private conference, Nichas, the Mohawk, arose, saying, "Who made Teedyuscung the chief of the Nations? If he be such a great man, we desire to know who made him so. Perhaps you have, and if this be the case, tell us so. It may be the French have made him so. We want to inquire and know whence his greatness arose."

Then Tagashata, on behalf of the Senecas, spoke: "We do not know who made Teedyuscung this great man over Ten Nations, and I want to know who made him so."

Then Assarandonquas, on behalf of the Onondagas, said: "I never heard before now that Teedyuscung was such a great man, and much less can I tell who made him so. No such thing was ever said in our towns."

Then spoke Thomas King on behalf of the Oneidas, Cayugas, Tuscaroras, Nanticokes, and Conoys, saying: "I now tell you we none of us know who has made Teedyuscung such a great man. Perhaps the French have, or perhaps you have, or some among you, as you have different governments and are different people. We, for our parts, entirely disown that he has any authority over us, and we desire to know from whence he derives his authority."[9]

The next day Governor Denny acknowledged Teedyuscung's claims at previous treaties but denied making him a great Chief. "At our former public treaties," said Denny, "Teedyuscung never assumed any such power; but on many occasions when he spoke of you, called you his uncles and superiors. I never shall attempt to nominate or impose a chief on any Indian tribe or nation, but on all occasions will pay due regard to those who are chosen by their countrymen ... I shall be greatly concerned that any uneasiness should arise among you and hope you will guard against it, and preserve this harmony which ought to subsist between friends and relations."

Governor Bernard also denied making Teedyuscung a King and, with great skill, apologized for the Chief's actions, saying: "In the Pennsylvania treaties which I have read since our last meeting (October 15), I have observed that Teedyuscung said he was a woman till you made him a man by putting a tomahawk in his hand, and through all these treaties, especially at the last one held in this town, he calls you his uncles and professes that he is dependent on you, and I know not that anything has since happened to alter his relation to you. I, therefore, consider him to be still your nephew."[10]

Thus, under the skillful guidance of Conrad Weiser, who delayed this outburst of Iroquois anger and put words into the mouths of the governors present,

---

9. *Penna. Colonial Records*, vol. VIII., pp. 190, 191.
10. *Colonial Records*, vol. VIII., pp. 193, 194.

things were smoothed over, and the cause of peace was not hindered. It was not until after Weiser's death that the Mohawks, in secret, destroyed the life of Teedyuscung and thus crippled the rising power of the Delawares forever.

The governors' apologies brought Teedyuscung to his feet upon his land claim and his losses. "I do not pretend," he said, "to mention any of my uncle's lands. I only mention what we, the Delawares, own, as far as the heads of the Delaware. All the lands lying on the waters that fall into the Susquehanna belong to our uncles."

Teedyuscung then took up another belt and turned to speak to the Iroquois, but the proud chiefs of that confederacy had, during his speech to Governors Denny and Bernard, noiselessly, one by one, left the room. Teedyuscung then declined to speak further, and the Indians spent the following day in private conferences.

The next day after Governor Denny had had a private interview with the Six Nations, Teedyuscung came to the governor's headquarters to say that the Delawares did not claim land high up on the Delaware River; those belonged to their uncles. The land Teedyuscung complained about was included in the Walking Purchase and included the larger part of current Monroe and Pike counties, part of Carbon, and nearly all of Northampton. Except for the latter county, this same land was purchased from the Six Nations in the deed of 1749.

The Delawares felt they were wronged in 1736 when the Iroquois gave a separate deed for land on the Delaware south of the Blue Mountains. Their wrongs became an insult when Canassatego called them women in 1742 and ordered them to Wyoming. When the war broke out, this turned the Eastern Delawares against the English. One of the conditions of peace made by Teedyuscung was that Wyoming be settled upon the Delawares and a deed be held for the same. Governor Denny declined to give such a paper, saying he had no right since the proprietors had never bought this land from the Six Nations.

Now in a public conference, Teedyuscung charged the Six Nations with selling this land to the Connecticut commissioners. "Uncles," he said, "you may remember that you placed us at Wyoming and Shamokin, places where Indians have lived before. Now I hear since that you have sold that land to our brethren, the English. Let the matter now be cleared up in the presence of our brethren, the English. I sit here as a bird on a bough. I look about and do not know where to go. Let me, therefore, come down upon the ground and make that my own by a good deed, and I shall then have a home forever; for if you, my uncles, or I die, our brethren, the English, will say they bought it from you, and so wrong my posterity out of it."

One day during Teedyuscung's absence, Thomas King replied that the Six Nation Deputies, now assembled at Easton, had "no power to convey lands to anyone. But we will take your request to the great council fire for their sentiments, as we never convey or sell lands before it be agreed in the great council of the United Nations. In the meantime, you may make use of those lands in conjunction with our people."[11]

The remaining important feature in the treaty of 1758 was the charge of fraud made by Teedyuscung, which was not yet settled. Said Teedyuscung,

> I did let you know formally what my grievance was; I told you that from Tohiccon (Lehigh?), as far as the Delawares owned, the proprietaries had wronged me. Then you and I agreed that it should be laid before the King of England, and likewise, you told me you would let me know as soon as ever he saw fit. You would lay the matter before the King, for you said he was our Father, that he might see what was our differences, for as you and I could not decide it, let him do it. Now let us not alter what you and I have agreed. Now let me know if King George has decided the matter between you and me.[12]

The governor deferred a direct reply to this until he could lay the dispute before the Six Nation Deputies. He told them they had sold land to the proprietaries their nephews, the Delawares, claim. He said,

> This is the case with regard to some part of the lands lying between Tohiccon Creek and the head of the River Delaware, which Teedyuscung in your hearing ... said the proprietaries had defrauded him of. The proprietaries are desirous to do strict justice to all Indians, but it cannot be supposed they can know in which of you the right was vested. It is a matter which must be settled among yourselves. Till this is done, there will probably remain some jealousy and discontent among you that may interrupt both your and our future quiet, which we should guard against by all means in our power.

The Six Nations replied that they did not exactly understand the governor; he "had left matters in the dark. They did not know what lands he meant. If he meant the lands on the other side of the Mountains (Blue Mountains), he knew

---

11. *Colonial Records*, vol. VIII., p. 221.
12. *Penna. Colonial Records*, vol. VIII., p. 201.

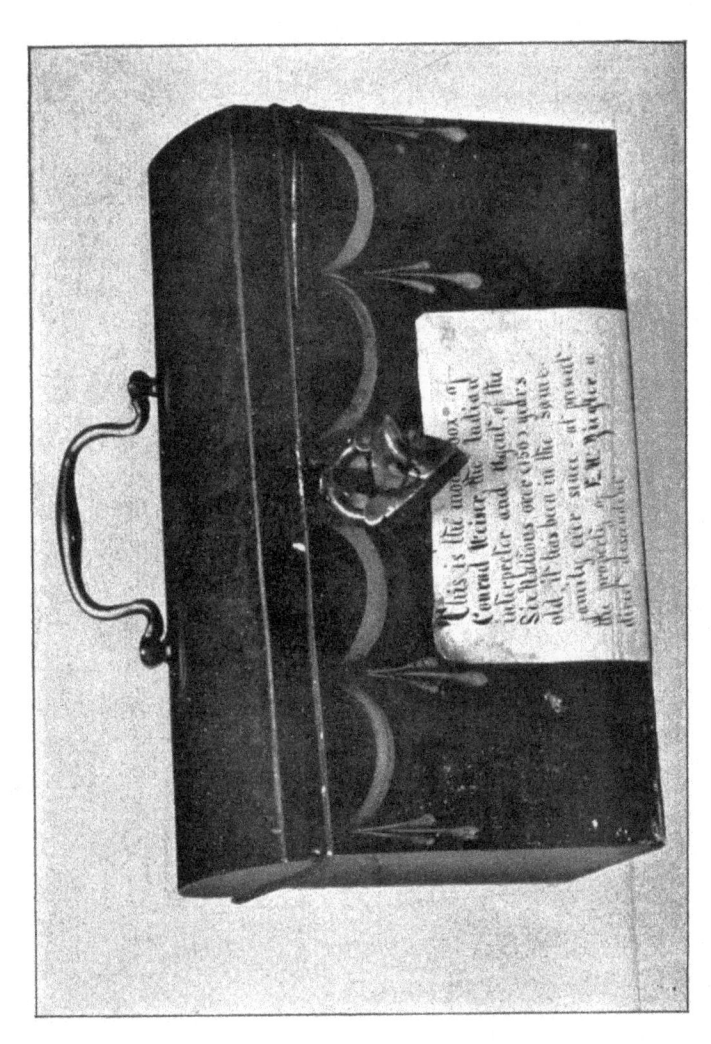

FROM A PHOTOGRAPH FURNISHED BY THE COURTESY OF E. M. ZEIGLER'

the proprietaries had their deeds (Deed of 1749) for them, which ought to be produced and shown to them. Their deeds had their marks, and when they should see them, they would know their marks again."

Conrad Weiser was sent for the deed. The Indians examined it and said, "The land was ours, and we will justify it."[13]

Teedyuscung said no more. The treaty adjourned with an apparent good feeling. Peace was secured, and the Ohio Indians had been drawn away from the French. The Meeting for Sufferings for the Philadelphia Yearly Meeting of Friends now demanded an investigation into Teedyuscung's charges to clear themselves of certain aspersions. The governor was quick to exonerate the Friends from dishonor in the affair but slow to push an investigation. A council committee had been laboring for two years to prove that the Walking Purchase was strictly an honest proceeding. This report[14] was not approved by James Logan and Benjamin Shoemaker, two council members.

In 1759 Croghan concluded a peace treaty at Pittsburgh with the Western Indians, gathering the fruit and the glory of Christian Post's efforts.

In 1761 Teedyuscung proposed to leave Wyoming since he could get no title to that country for his people. The governor, however, persuaded him not to do such a rash thing. The case to be arbitrated before Sir William Johnson was deferred and postponed until, in May 1762, Teedyuscung came to Philadelphia, when he was told if he would withdraw his charges against the proprietors of fraud in the Walking Purchase, there were four hundred pounds in it for him.

Teedyuscung then came into the conference, saying what he had been saying for five years, that he did not want Sir William Johnson to arbitrate the dispute. Teedyuscung further said that he had never charged "the proprietaries with fraud, but had only said that the French had informed them that the English had cheated them of their lands, and his young men desired him to mention it at the treaty of Easton and that he did it to please them, and was sorry it had reached their hearts."[15]

The governor told him if he would acknowledge this in public, he would make him a present, not on account of the lands which had been bought and paid for, but on account of his needy circumstances. Therefore, when Teedyuscung made his public acknowledgment, the governor made him a present of four hundred pounds. Isaac Still, the interpreter, said this was a great dispute indeed to be all about four hundred pounds. The governor then, to quiet their

---

13. *Colonial Records*, vol. VIII., p. 205.
14. See *Colonial Records*, vol. VIII., p. 246.
15. *Colonial Records*, vol. VIII., p. 708.

dissatisfaction with the smallness of the bribe, said that the dispute should go before Sir William Johnson when it was found that the proprietaries had not cheated the Indians at the Walking Purchase, the governor would not be under obligations to pay Teedyuscung one farthing. The old Peacemaker then begged the governor not to take the case before Johnson. The governor refused. In June, Sir William Johnson was at Easton,[16] and Teedyuscung acknowledged his error in charge of forgery. This was reported to the Western Indians in a conference at Lancaster in August when they also repudiated any claim they may ever have had to lands on the Delaware. Liberal presents were then given to all. Teedyuscung again received a present. This time it was two hundred Spanish dollars and the value of two hundred pounds in goods.

With these transactions, the charges of proprietary fraud were thought to be buried forever. Before this was accomplished, Conrad Weiser was no more.

---

16. *Colonial Records*, vol. VIII., pp. 739, 740.

Conclusion

THE career of Conrad Weiser in Pennsylvania marks an epoch in the Indian policy of the province. The struggle between the two rival European nations for possession of the Ohio Valley was retarded by the attitude of the Six Nations. Conrad Weiser was a powerful factor in preserving this neutrality for over thirty years.

This attitude of the Six Nations enabled the English colonies to grow strong and self-reliant, producing their own breadstuffs, and making their own powder. And when the final struggle came, they were not, like the French, compelled to rely upon Europe for supplies, nor were they forced to purchase these stores with peltry obtained from the Indians in trade. When hostilities prevented hunting and trapping, the French found themselves without the means of purchasing even the munitions of war. They were no longer able to lavish presents upon their Indian allies.

Through their peace association, the Society of Friends in Pennsylvania took advantage of the needy circumstances of the French and, utilizing the skill of a devoted Moravian missionary, Frederick Christian Post, drew the Indians of Ohio away from the French into the English interests. In the wake of the peace victories, the French strongholds from Duquesne to Quebec commenced falling. Conrad Weiser aided the Iroquois in their struggle for neutrality and often prevented open disruption with the English.

The appearance of Weiser in Pennsylvania a few years after the death of Penn marks that transition period when the Delaware Indians began to lose, and the Iroquois gained influence and power with the province's authorities.

The treaty of 1736 could not have operated as it did without the guiding force of Conrad Weiser's presence. He persuaded the province to recognize the supremacy of the Six Nations and to buy out their claims to all Susquehanna lands southeast of the Blue Mountains. Then, as an afterthought, Weiser urged the governor and proprietors to offer a present and secure a deed from these same Indians for all Iroquois claims on the Delaware River southeast of the before-mentioned Blue Mountains. The governor and proprietors may have thought that they were strengthening their titles to the land by this deed. Weiser may have believed that he was doing his friends, the Iroquois, a good turn, but the chiefs of the Six Nations knew they had gained a right to claim Delaware land and that henceforth Pennsylvania would be obliged to support them in this claim. This was the beginning of the movement which robbed the Delaware Indians of all power to sell land.

It became the policy of Conrad Weiser, with one foot on the Delawares, to caress the Iroquois and condemn the French. In a short time, the province of Pennsylvania, through its governor, pursued the same policy. After the Delawares were insulted in Philadelphia in 1742, called women, and ordered to quit the lands of their fathers and remove to Wyoming, after the Iroquois sold their hunting grounds on the Susquehanna to Penn's heirs in 1754, and their Wyoming asylum to the Connecticut agents, the Delawares arose and struck the English. Their revenge wreaked itself upon the Pennsylvania border. The policy, which held the Six Nations aloof from the French for twenty-five years, and made an English Republic possible on American shores, cost Pennsylvania the friendship of the Delawares and the best lives on the frontiers.

Weiser's Iroquois alliances, his skill in preventing Virginia and Maryland from becoming involved in an Indian war, and his ability to secure the friendship of the Six Nation allies on the Maumee and Wabash stimulated the fur trade in Pennsylvania. The exports of peltries from Philadelphia at this time excelled those of New York and Baltimore. The protection offered by Weiser's Logstown treaty of 1748 revealed to Virginia the wealth of trade in the territory she had always claimed. The Ohio Land Company was formed, and the Virginia traders pushed rapidly into this Eldorado. Bitter jealousies sprang up between the trade interests of Pennsylvania and Virginia. The keen perceptions of the French were quick to detect this condition, and their centralized system of government enabled them to take prompt advantage of this state of affairs to regain their losses in trade and territory.

Virginia and New York vied with each other in a desire to secure through the King of England entire control of Indian affairs. The Crown compromised the matter and gave Sir William Johnson control in the northern and middle and Mr. Atkins in the southern colonies. This led to a decline in Weiser's influence. Croghan became Johnson's deputy in Pennsylvania, and Weiser sank in importance to that of an ordinary interpreter. As years advanced, disappointments thickened around this iron-willed man. From his youth, Weiser had been deeply moved by his strong likes and dislikes. Yet, in his heart, there was a vigorous disposition to forgive. He became reconciled to the community at Ephrata; he forgave Montour and befriended him when he knew Andrew was false. Weiser could love his enemies and forgive those who despitefully used him. A strong sense of justice actuated all his dealings with the Indians. Even the Delawares and Shawanese, whom he despised, were again and again befriended and protected. Weiser's strong will made him a positive character. His unflinching administration of justice as a magistrate embarrassed him with many enemies. When they saw his acres increasing, many were the corruption and fraud charges flung at him. They said that he was no better than other Indian agents and traders.

About his possession of the Isle of Que, where a part of Selinsgrove now stands, his enemies floated the rumor that Shikellamy once went to Weiser, saying, "I had a dream. I dreamed that Tarachawagon (Weiser) had promised me with a rifle."

Conrad, we are told, handed over the gun. Some days later, Weiser had his dream. He took it to the old chief, saying, "I dreamed that Shikellamy presented me with the large and beautiful island nestled in the Susquehanna River."

The chief, we are told, deeded over the land and then said, "Conrad, let us never dream again."

The confidential correspondence between Weiser and Richard Peters would indicate that Weiser purchased not only the Tulpehocken plantation but his lands on the Susquehanna from the proprietors. The services he rendered John and Thomas Penn were in more cases than one paid for in land. At the Albany treaty, Weiser and Richard Peters represented the proprietors and received, for their labor in persuading the Iroquois to sell southwestern Pennsylvania, a large tract of land west of the Susquehanna River. The possession of this tract became a thorn in the flesh during his declining years. The squatters had possession and refused to permit anyone to survey them, and with some emphasis, they declared that they would fight before they were driven off.

In a letter dated April 12, 1755, Weiser said, "I will give up my claim west of the Susquehanna rather than cause bloodshed."

Four years later, the land commissioners for the proprietors asked Weiser to "fix the date of settlement" on his "western tract, that the date of quitrents might be fixed."

The events of the French and Indian war prevented Weiser from taking possession of the land. With its accumulated rents and disputes, he bequeathed

BURIAL PLACE OF CONRAD WEISER, NEAR WOMELSDORF, PA.

it to his five sons and two daughters. In less than eight months after this will was made, Weiser, who had been declining in health for several years, started out from his home in Reading to visit his farm in Womelsdorf, where he died the next day, July 13, 1760, from what was then called a violent attack of the colic. His remains still rest in the little private burying ground near the present town of Womelsdorf and are marked by a very modest stone.

Secretary Peters, writing from Philadelphia the following winter, said, "Poor Mr. Weiser is no more; he died suddenly in the summer and has not left anyone to fill his place as Provincial Interpreter. His son Samuel has almost forgotten what little he knew."

At the Indian Treaty held at Easton, August 3, 1761, Seneca George arose saying, "Brother Onas: We, the Seven Nations, and our cousins, are at a great loss and sit in darkness, as well as you, by the death of Conrad Weiser, as since his death we cannot so well understand one another. By this belt, we cover his body with bark."

While the proprietors and governors all bore testimony to Weiser's ability, his declining years were saddened by a growing distrust on all sides. His determination to see justice done to the Indians brought upon him the censure of the frontier people, especially the men of Paxtang and the Susquehanna country. These people were determined to have the scalp bounty, and during the autumn previous to the passage of that bill, they insisted that Weiser could pay them the scalp bounty if he would.

From a damaged letter of Weiser's in which he mentions going into that region to protect some friendly Indians, he recounts the difficulties of the situation. "I went with them (the Indians). When we came near B.—lys, I saw about 400 or 500 men and a loud noise. I rode before, and in riding along the road and armed men on both sides of the road, I heard some say, 'Why must we be killed by the Indians and we not kill them? Why are our hands so tied?' I got the Indians to the house with much adieu."

The people then gathered around, clamoring for a scalp bounty. Weiser told them he had no power from the governor or Assembly to do this.

> They began to curse the governor and the Assembly, called me a traitor of country, who held with the Indians, and must have known of the murder . . . beforehand. I sat in the house by a low window. Some of my friends came to pull me away from it, telling me some of the people threatened to shoot me. I offered to go out to the people and either pacify them or make the King's proclamation, but those

in the house with me would not let me go out. The cry was, the land is betrayed and sold . . . the common people from Lancaster County were the worst . . . I was in danger of being shot to death . . . In the meantime, a great smoke arose under Tulpehocken mountain.

The people all hastened toward that, and Weiser, relieved from the press of the mob, said, "I took my horse and went home, where I intend to stay and defend my own house as long as I can."[1]

Shikellamy's son John in recounting the difficulties he experienced in his efforts to remain loyal to the English, said:

I was cursed by some of the people of Pennsylvania to my face and threatened to be killed, and in order to save my life, I was obliged to make my escape and almost perished in the woods for want of food, having above two hundred miles to travel before I could reach the Indian town, and had nothing to eat but what I could pick up in the woods, having no gun with me. I thought it very hard that there was nobody that spoke in my favor among the people on the Susquehanna, tho' they all knew I was a constant friend to the people of Pennsylvania. I desired them to give me a safeguard to convey me to my uncle, C. Weiser, but they would not do it but said that C. W. was as great a rogue as myself.[2]

This contempt for Conrad Weiser was shared by Teedyuscung and the Delawares, who followed him into peace with the English. The Moravians looked with suspicion and distrust upon the old interpreter. His former friends among the Indians turned away from him when he accepted the governor's commission as commander of the colonial forces and defenses between the Susquehanna and the Delaware. The French, during the war, had a reward on the old man's scalp, and the woods were full of his enemies. During his prosperous and declining hours, Weiser never shirked a revealed duty or swerved from his conception of justice. The training of his youth and the experiences of his public life combined strengthened his loyalty to those in authority.

He was of the governor's party and served the proprietors' interests. Yet under no circumstances did he ever swerve from the right as it appeared to him.

---

1. Manuscript letter of Conrad Weiser, in the collection of the Pennsylvania Historical Society.
2. *Penna. Archives*, vol. II., pp. 777, 778.

The governor and the proprietors took his advice with what grace they could, knowing full well that this blunt-spoken interpreter meant it all for the best.

After the death of Weiser, Pennsylvania figured no longer in Indian affairs. On behalf of the English Crown, Sir William Johnson and George Croghan managed all Indian affairs and conducted all treaties. In 1768, Johnson held a conference with the Six Nations at Fort Shawnee, where a line was drawn forever separating the possessions of the Indians from those of the white man. This division line started in New York, not far from the eastern end of Lake Oneida, from which it followed the shortest route to the Chenango River, and along that stream to the Susquehanna, which it followed to Shamokin, and ascended the west branch of that river through the present Clearfield County to "Canoe Place" or "Cherry Tree," where a straight line was drawn to Kittanning, on the Alleghany River. The line then followed this stream and the Ohio River. It was agreed that all land north and west of this division line should forever belong to the Indians, and under no circumstances should it be sold to the white man. All land south and east of this line, which belonged to the Indians, was open for sale. The Pennsylvania proprietors immediately purchased all the Indian claims south and east of the division line. It included all that part of Western Pennsylvania west of the Alleghany Mountains and south of the division line. It was a part of that vast region that Weiser and Peters ceded back to the Indians in 1758. The proprietors also purchased all the land in northeastern Pennsylvania south and east of the Susquehanna River and north of all former purchases.

Later in the same year, the proprietors' agents persuaded the Indians to make an exception in the case of Pennsylvania and sell all that region north of the division line lying in the forks of the Susquehanna and bounded on the north and west by Towanda and Pine creeks. This was the last Indian purchase made by the proprietors. The province became a Commonwealth in 1776. The Iroquois and more warlike Delawares, influenced by Sir William Johnson, joined the British during the Revolutionary War. The Moravian converts and a few other Delawares remained true to the colonists. After the treaty with England in 1783, the Commonwealth of Pennsylvania dictated her own terms to the Indians still claiming land in Pennsylvania, and in 1784 and '85, all the remaining northwestern portion of the State was bought. With the birth of our Federal government, the State of Pennsylvania secured from Congress that part of the present Erie County, which lies north of the present southern boundary of New York, and with these purchases, Pennsylvania disappeared forever from the arena of Indian affairs.

Index

A

Adams County, 43
Aix-la-Chapelle, 88, 136–37, 139, 162, 171n, 174
Albany, New York, 2, 7, 26, 42, 71, 77–79, 85, 92–93, 95, 97, 100, 102, 107, 131, 160, 166–67, 170, 175, 178–79, 184, 191–96, 198–99, 201, 204, 206–209, 211, 213, 219, 266, 276
Alleghany River, 170–71, 280
Allummappees (Delaware chief), 2, 39, 57
Annapolis, Maryland, 65, 84
Armstrong, John, 64, 82–83, 113
Armstrong, Justice, 112
Aughwick, Pennsylvania, 148–49, 190, 192, 205–206, 209–11

B

Baltimore, Lord, 75, 139, 275
Beaver (Delaware chief), 205
Beissel, Conrad, 27, 29–32, 34
Berks County, Pennsylvania, 131, 212, 215, 225, 263
Bernard, Governor of New Jersey, 257, 267–69
Bethlehem, Pennsylvania, 226, 239, 245
Beverely, Col. William, Virginia commissioner, 67
Big Cove, Pennsylvania, 150
Big and Little Coves, Pennsylvania, 138, 222, 227
Bigg Island, 53–54
Black Log Sleeping Place, Pennsylvania, 130
Black Prince (Tocanontie of the Onondagas), 60, 94
Black, William, Virginia Secretary, 66n, 67
Boone, William, 225
Braddock, General Edward, 209–13, 215, 217–18
Broken Kettle (Ohio chief), 157
Burnt Cabins, Pennsylvania, 138–39, 142, 147–48, 150
Busse, Captain, 250

C

Cachiadachse (village), 61
Cajadis, 140
Canada, 35, 42, 79, 87, 94, 101–103, 108, 120, 154, 163–64, 168, 193
Canada, Governor of (aka Onontio), 9, 11, 11n, 12n, 85–86, 94, 98–99, 119, 160, 163, 171, 175, 180, 184, 190, 196, 202, 207
Canassatego (Iroquois chief), 38, 44–46, 50, 61, 66, 69, 73, 75–76, 82–83, 107, 138, 144–45, 159, 166–67, 167n, 178, 269

Canataquany (Indian town near Harris' Ferry), 59
Canoe Place, Pennsylvania, 280
Cape Breton, 99
Captain John (Delaware chief), 50
Carlisle, Pennsylvania, 137, 175, 181, 185–86, 188, 191, 227, 264
Carolina, 1, 4–5, 12, 22, 26, 40, 54, 82, 89, 126, 132–33, 156, 163, 166
Catawba Indians, 1, 4, 26, 40, 52, 64, 80–81, 85–86, 89–91, 93–94, 96, 100, 132–33, 139, 146, 156, 165–66
Catholics, 215
Cayuga Indians, 11, 42, 68, 131, 199, 201, 268
Céloron De Blainville, Captain Pierre-Joseph, 159–62, 171, 171n
Chambers, Benjamin, 147–48
Chambers, Joseph, 112
Chartiers, Peter, 10, 85, 87, 89, 94, 96, 100, 107
Chartier's Old Town, 130
Cherokee Indians, 26, 91, 241, 248, 257, 264
Cherry Tree, Pennsylvania, 280
Chesapeake Bay, 68
Chiniotta (Indian village), 54
Chonanous (Indian village), 160
Clearfield County, Pennsylvania, 280
Clinton, Governor of New York, 37, 159–60, 164–65, 171, 175, 178–80, 183, 191
Cohoon, George, 147
Conestoga Indians, 13, 16–17, 39, 68, 71
Conewago (Indian village), 137
Connecticut, 7, 97, 192, 199–200, 202, 204, 206–207, 269, 275
Conococheague Creek, 155
Conolloways, Big and Little, 139, 150
Cookson, Thomas, 73, 155
Corlear, *see New York, Governor of*
Coscosky (Indian village), 130
Crawford, Hugh, 162
Cresap, Colonel Thomas, 76, 157, 157n
Croghan, George, 106, 108–109, 115–17, 122, 124–26, 130, 133, 136–37, 147–48, 157–59, 163, 169–77, 179–83, 186, 190, 209–10, 219, 241, 246–47, 249–50, 253–55, 258, 272, 275, 280
Crown Point, New York, 104, 196
Cumberland County, Pennsylvania, 43, 137–38, 146–47, 149–51, 155, 181, 211, 225, 228–29, 248, 264, 266

D

De Lancey, James (Governor of New York), 200
Delaware Indians, 1–2, 4, 7–8, 10, 13–14, 16–17, 38–45, 45n, 46–47, 49–51, 57–58, 60, 82–83, 87, 124, 127, 134, 138–39, 144, 158, 161, 164, 169, 173, 180–81, 187, 192–94, 197, 201, 205–206, 210–13, 217–18, 220, 222, 227–30, 232–36, 239, 241, 243–44, 248, 252, 254–55, 258, 264–67, 269–70, 274–76, 279–80
Delaware River, 13, 16, 44, 46, 145–46, 162, 166, 173, 224, 244, 254, 254n, 258, 269–70, 273, 275, 279
Denny, Governor of Pennsylvania, 232, 236, 242–43, 246–47, 249, 252, 257, 264–65, 268–69
Detroit, Michigan, 100, 167n, 168
Dill, Matthew, 147
Dinwiddie, Governor of Virginia, 185, 190–91, 209
Dongan, Governor of New York, 13–14, 64, 68
Duche, Jacob, 262–63
Dunbar, General, 212–13, 215
Dunning, James, 112

E

Easton, Pennsylvania, 218, 228, 232, 236, 238, 240–43, 247–49, 256–60, 262–67, 270, 272–73, 278
Economy, Pennsylvania, 130
Ephrata, Pennsylvania, 27–34, 37
Erie County, Pennsylvania, 280
Evans, Lewis, 153–55, 202, 208

F

Fairfax, Lord, 153, 155
Finley, John, 147
Five Nations, 4, 8, 68, 77, 79, 131
Flams' Ferry, Pennsylvania, 218
Forbes, General, 227, 257, 264–65
Fort Allen, 240, 242–43, 245, 263–64
Fort Augusta, 259–60
Fort Cumberland, 248
Fort DuQuesne, 204, 211–12, 264–65
Fort LeBœuf, 186
Fort Loudon, 248
Fort Necessity, 2049, 209
Franklin, Benjamin, 185, 194, 213–14, 220, 228, 252
Franklin County, 43
Frankstown, Pennsylvania, 130
Fraser, John, 168, 184–86
French Creek, 186
Friends, Society of, 8, 97, 101, 229–30, 232–33, 262, 274
Friendly Society for the Promotion of Peace, 247
Furney, Adam, 137

G

Gagradoda (Cayuga chief), 199
Galbreath, James, 130, 147
Galloway, George, 147
Galloway, Joseph, 246
Galloway, William, 147
Girty, Simon, 148–49
Gist, Christopher, 156, 177, 188, 204
Glenn, Governor of South Carolina, 132, 156
Gooch, Governor of Virginia, 20–21, 55, 58, 60, 65, 89–91, 123, 131
Gordon, Patrick (Governor of Pennsylvania), 2, 8
Great Hominy (Shawanese chief), 57
Groeme, Dr., 140

H

Haig, Mr., 132–33
Half King (Seneca chief aka Tanacharison), 197, 204–205, 209, 210
Hamilton, James (Governor of Pennsylvania), 138–40, 142–46, 148, 152–53, 158–62, 164–65, 169, 171, 173, 175, 177–78, 182–83, 185, 190–91, 194, 199, 212, 228
Hanover Township, Lancaster County, Pennsylvania, 223
Harmony Society, 130
Harris' Ferry (aka Harrisburg), Pennsylvania, 49, 52, 59, 117, 120, 205, 209, 211, 221, 231
Harris, John, 209–10, 228
Heans family, 92
Hendricks (Mohawk chief), 192, 200–202, 206–207, 209
Henry (Mohawk chief), 166
Hiddleston, David, 147
Hopkinson, Thomas, 128n
Hudson, John, 265
Hudson River, 25, 166
Hughes, John, 225
Huntingdon, Pennsylvania, 130

I

Iroquois tribe, 1, 4–5, 7, 10, 12–14, 16–18, 20–22, 25–26, 35, 38–44, 47, 49, 51–61, 63–64, 69, 72, 76–77, 79–83, 85–87, 89–91, 93–96, 98–100, 102, 104, 106–107, 110, 116–17, 124–25, 127, 133–35, 138–39, 144, 146, 156, 159, 164–67, 170, 173–74, 179–80, 184, 191–93, 198, 208, 213, 227, 234–36, 238, 240–41, 243–44, 246, 255, 258, 266–69, 274–76, 280
Isle of Que, 276

J

Janontady Havas tribe (aka Juniata Ohios), 121, 142, 209
Jennings, Edmund, 67

INDEX

Jonathan (Delaware chief), 235, 241,
Johnson, William, 14, 42, 85–87, 101–103, 103n, 104, 151, 158, 158n, 159, 163, 166, 171, 174, 179, 191, 193, 195–96, 212, 229–30, 232, 234–36, 241–42, 246, 255, 258, 266, 272–73, 275, 280
Joncaire, 159, 169–71, 173–74, 176
Jounhaty (Indian captain), 61
Jumonville, 204, 210n
Juniata River, 44, 82, 111, 113n, 130, 138–39, 141–42, 144–47, 194, 199
Juniata Valley, 38, 43–44, 52, 58, 64, 82, 138–39, 141, 145–46, 158, 163, 181–82, 190, 199, 202, 208

K

Kanawha River, 135, 156, 190
Keith, Governor of Pennsylvania, 2–3, 256
Kilgore, Ralph, 168
Kinsey, John, 85, 97, 101–102, 104, 106, 122, 142, 151
Kiskiminitas Creek, 130
Kittanning, Pennsylvania, 280

L

Lake Erie, 106–107, 112, 115–17, 127, 129, 135, 154, 171, 175, 184, 186, 202
Lake Erie Indians, 110, 115, 117, 120
Lake Huron, 49
Lake Ontario, 111, 169
Lancaster, Pennsylvania, 32, 41, 44, 52–53, 63–86, 88–90, 93–94, 101, 106, 117, 126–30, 133, 135, 138–39, 151, 153–54, 156–68, 180–81, 185, 192, 194, 223–24, 232, 246–48, 273, 279
Lapapeton (Delaware chief), 57
Lawrence, Thomas, 115
Lee, Colonel Thomas, 67, 135, 153, 156
Lock Haven, Pennsylvania, 53n
Logan, James, 1–2, 9–10, 26, 47–48, 65, 67, 77, 115–19, 212, 229, 250, 255, 272
Logan, William, 73, 128n
Logstown, Pennsylvania, 42, 123, 126, 130, 132, 135–37, 142, 152, 154–56, 159, 161, 163, 168–73, 178, 181–82, 186–87, 190, 260, 275
Loudon, Lord, 240–42, 246, 257
Louisiana, 9, 154
Lowery, James, 169
Loyalsock Creek, 22
Lutherans, 27, 29, 222
Lycon, Andrew, 147–48
Lydius, John Henry, 101–104, 201, 204, 207
Lynching, 231

M

Mamburg, Mr., 135–36
Maryland, 13, 18, 30, 38, 47, 49, 51–52, 58, 61, 63–69, 71–73, 75–77, 82–83, 87, 106, 123, 125, 133–36, 139, 148–51, 153–55, 157, 163, 165, 218–19, 228, 275
Maryland, Governor of, 47, 49, 59, 69, 73, 123
Maqua Indians, 5, 25, 179, 192, 195
Marshe, Witham, 67, 67n, 68n, 69n, 72, 72n, 73, 73n, 75n 75n, 76, 76n
Massachusetts, 97
Masters, William, 246
Maumee River, 275
McKee, Thomas, 52–55, 57–58, 110
Miami Indians (aka Twightwee), 126, 136, 159, 162–64, 168–69, 171, 175–76, 179, 182–85
Michigan, 106, 135
Miller, Peter, 27, 29, 31, 34
Miller, Lieutenant, 240
Minisink Indians, 40n, 44–45, 265–66
Minquas Indians, 68
Mississippi River, 25, 87, 100, 107, 120, 127, 129, 135, 156
Mohawk Indians, 7, 10, 18, 34, 37, 42–43, 76, 85–87, 92, 94, 98, 101–104, 131, 164, 166, 196, 199–201, 204, 206–207, 241, 253, 257, 266–69
Monongahela River, 135, 154, 190, 197–98
Montour, Andrew, 94, 126–28, 131, 136–37, 157–59, 161, 169–70, 173, 175, 177, 180–82, 184, 186, 188, 190, 194, 197, 235, 267, 276
Montour, Lewis, 194, 210, 210n,
Montour, Madame, 22, 35, 57, 127
Montreal Conference, 99
Moravians, 27, 34–35, 37, 93, 212, 227, 245, 258, 274, 279–80
Morris, Robert Hunter, 193, 207, 213, 217, 223, 228, 230, 242–43
Munsey Indians, 257, 266–67
Muskokee Indians, 4, 20, 89
Mussemeelin, John, 82–83

N

Nanticoke Indians, 61, 144, 218, 268
New England, 82, 86–87, 97–98, 100, 104, 120, 160, 178, 196, 202
Newcastle (Delaware chief), 234–36, 238–40, 246
New York, 4, 5, 14, 27, 42, 52–53, 64, 86, 95, 97–98, 100–101, 103–104, 107, 154, 158–59, 163–67, 171, 175, 178–79, 182, 184, 186, 191–93, 195–96, 207, 235, 240, 275, 280
New York, Governor of (aka Corlear), 11n, 14, 37, 68, 71, 77, 79, 97–98, 117, 120, 131–32, 161, 163–64, 179, 184, 192–93, 200, 210, 213

Nichas (Mohawk chief), 266–68
Norris, Isaac, 185, 194
Northampton County, Pennsylvania, 228, 269

O

Ogle, Governor of Maryland, 49, 153
Ohio Company, 126, 135, 151–53, 155, 156, 158, 165, 184–85, 191
Ohio Indians, 10, 106, 117, 119–25, 128, 158–59, 169–70, 174–75, 182, 192, 197, 209, 231, 238, 248, 266, 272
Ohio River, 9, 39, 82, 112, 115–16, 130, 135, 159, 171, 184, 194, 280
Ohio Valley, 114, 117, 125, 127, 135, 152, 156, 159, 163, 175, 178, 184, 274
Oneida Indians, 7, 11, 42, 70, 73, 87, 128, 131, 186, 199, 201–202, 268, 280
Onondaga (council, village, tribe), 7, 10–11, 17, 20–21, 23–26, 35, 42, 48, 52–53, 58, 60–61, 66, 69, 71, 77, 86–87, 90–94, 131, 139, 141, 146, 156, 165–69, 174, 180–81, 184, 191, 193, 195, 197, 230, 268
Orndt, Captain, 250
Oswego (village, trading post), 86, 94, 99, 111, 160, 171, 196
Otkon (evil spirit), 20, 22
Otsaningo (village), 236

P

Palmer, Anthony, 101–102, 104, 108, 123
Palatines, 2, 79
Parson, William, 154–55, 240
Path Valley, 138, 149
Patterson's Creek, 219
Paxinosa (Shawnee chief), 234–35, 264
Paxton, Pennsylvania, 112, 122, 209, 210, 223, 231
Pemberton, Israel, 232–34, 243, 249–50
Penn's Creek, 202, 219, 223, 228
Penn, John, 116, 194
Penn, Thomas, 11–12, 45, 220, 243, 276
Penn, William, 8, 14, 16, 39, 68, 172–73, 206, 210, 235, 243–44, 276
Pennsylvania, 1–280
Peters, Richard, 11, 56n, 91, 93, 115, 117–18, 125, 127, 141, 146–50, 154–57, 166, 180–82, 185, 194, 208–209, 220, 225, 227, 232, 244, 252, 255–56, 258, 266, 276, 278, 280
Peters, William, 67, 262–63
Philadelphia, Pennsylvania, 2, 9–10, 12–14, 16–18, 35, 38–41, 43, 46–48, 52, 60, 65–66, 84, 93–94, 96, 102, 105–106, 110, 117, 124–26, 128, 139–40, 142, 144, 155, 179, 181–83, 185, 206–207, 209, 212–13, 215, 217, 224–25, 227, 229–30, 233, 236, 238, 240, 242, 246, 253, 256–59, 262, 265, 272, 275, 278

Piankaskaw (King of the Miamis), 184
Pine Creek, 280
Piquet, 167
Pitt, William, 257
Pittsburgh, Pennsylvania, 42, 187, 272,
Potomac River, 55, 72, 77, 79, 153–55
Post, Frederick Christian, 37, 257–58, 264–66
Potter, John, 150n, 228
Powle, John, 112
Pumpshire, John, 250, 253

Q

Quakers, 38, 41, 214, 220, 222, 233–34, 238, 245–46, 248, 257–58, 262–63
Quebec, 99, 129, 257, 274

R

Read, Adam, 223
Reading, Pennsylvania, 166, 223, 225, 228, 261, 263, 278,
Rigbie, Colonel, 73

S

Sachsidowa (Tuscarora chief), 57, 60
Sanderson, George, 76
Scalp Act, 212, 228, 235, 244
Scaroyady (Oneida chief), 87, 128, 215, 217–18, 229, 233–34
Schlechl, Abraham, 142
Schoharie Valley, New York, 2, 95
Scioto (trading post), 106, 158
Seely, Jonas, 225
Selinsgrove, Pennsylvania, 276
Seneca George (Ohio chief), 157, 278
Seneca Indians, 43, 68, 86–87, 97, 104, 131–32, 134, 138–40, 142, 144, 171, 264–65, 268
Seventh Day Baptists, 27, 30–31, 34, 67
Shamokin (village), 20–21, 24, 34–35, 46, 49, 52, 54, 56–58, 82, 87, 91–93, 102–103, 111, 116, 138, 140–41, 144–45, 202, 210, 222–23, 225, 234, 259, 269, 280
Shawanese Indians, 1, 7–10, 12–13, 18, 35, 37–39, 42, 47, 52–54, 57–59, 85, 87–89, 94, 96, 107, 128, 134, 161, 164, 169–71, 175–76, 182–83, 187, 194, 197, 199, 206, 229, 235, 258, 264–65, 276
Shenandoah Valley, 20, 53, 78, 135
Sherman's Creek, 139, 141, 148–49
Shikellamy (Iroquois regent), 1, 7–10, 13–14, 16, 25, 40, 54–55, 57–61, 61n, 64, 73–76, 82, 85–86, 93–94, 102–103, 106, 112–13, 116, 121, 124–25, 128, 138, 140, 141, 148, 155, 166, 276
Shikellamy, John, 192, 199, 202, 206, 211, 279
Shippen, Edward, 93, 228,
Shippensburg, Pennsylvania, 148, 219

INDEX

Shirley, Governor of Massachusetts, 102, 213
Shoemaker, Benjamin, 128n, 272
Six Nations, 1, 4, 7–14, 16, 18, 24, 26, 38, 41–43, 46–47, 49–52, 55–56, 58–59, 61, 63–64, 68–69, 72, 75, 79, 81–86, 89–92, 94–97, 99–104, 106–108, 110–11, 116–17, 121–22, 124–25, 127–28, 131–32, 138–39, 141, 144, 146, 153, 156, 162–66, 169–70, 174, 176–77, 180, 182, 184, 191, 193–94, 196–99, 201, 205–208, 218, 227, 229–30, 232–36, 239–40, 243–44, 254, 257–59, 264–67, 269–70, 274–75, 280
Spangenberg, Bishop, 34, 37n
Standing Stone (landmark), 130
Star, Frederick, 138
Stenton, 14–15
Stoddard, Col. John, 101–102, 104
Sugar Creek, 23
Susquehanna Company, 199, 201
Susquehanna Indians, 68, 71, 246
Susquehanna River, 21–22, 35, 43, 52, 53n, 60, 68, 137–38, 145–46, 181, 201–202, 204, 219, 223, 227, 254n, 276, 280
Swain, Charles, 219,
Swatara Creek, 2

T

Taming Buck (Shawanese chief), 88
Teedyuscung (King of the Delawares), 233, 235–38, 238n, 239–40, 242–53, 253n, 254–60, 262–70, 272–73, 279
The Belt (Delaware chief), 218
The Stone (Ohio chief), 157
Thomas, Governor of Pennsylvania, 27, 30, 34–35, 37, 40, 49, 52, 55–56, 60, 65–67, 73, 85, 87–90, 95, 98, 100–101, 107, 116, 132, 139
Thomas, Philip, 67
Thomas King (chief), 257, 268, 270
Thompsontown, Pennsylvania, 147
Thomson, Charles, 232, 251–54, 256, 258, 260, 262–66
Titami (Delaware chief), 50
Tocanontie (aka Black Prince), 60
Towanda, Pennsylvania, 23
Towanda Creek, 280
Trent, William, 188, 219, 252–53
Tulpehocken Valley, 1–2, 4, 7, 27, 29, 31, 49, 130, 148, 215, 227–28, 276, 279
Turner, Joseph, 128n
Turner, Morris, 168
Tuscarora Path, 130, 141, 148
Tuscarora Indians, 1, 4, 57, 60, 78, 134, 268
Twightwees (*see Miami Indians*)

U

Unhappy Jake, 93

V

Venango (trading post), 170, 175, 185, 187, 204
Virginia, 1, 4, 5, 13, 18, 20–21, 26, 30, 38, 47, 51–84, 86–87, 89–90, 93, 106, 117, 123, 125, 127, 135–36, 148, 151–61, 163, 165–66, 170, 173, 175, 177–79, 181–86, 188, 190–92, 194, 196–98, 204, 241, 264, 275
Virginia, Governor of, 21, 25–26, 40, 47, 52–84, 123, 130, 133, 165, 178, 180, 184, 187, 190, 196–98, 213

W

Wabash Indians, 164
Wabash River, 100, 106–107, 128–29, 158, 160, 162–63, 168, 180, 275
Walking Purchase, 2, 38, 40, 40n, 44–46, 57, 173, 201, 213, 232, 235, 244, 246, 254, 257, 266–67, 269, 272–73
Warren, Admiral, 103
Washington, Augustine, 135
Washington, George, 189, 191–92, 203–205, 227
Weiser, Conrad, 1–280
Weiser, Conrad Sr., 2
Weiser, Mrs., 6
Weiser, Samuel, 93, 179, 213, 278
White, William, 147
Williamsburg, Virginia, 21, 26, 84, 91, 94, 156
Wilson, James, 150n
Wilson, John, 150n
Wilson, Thomas, 147
Winchester, Virginia, 184–85
Womelsdorf, Pennsylvania, 278
Woodbridge, Mr., 201, 204
Wyandot Indians, 126, 131, 134, 164, 169, 176, 217
Wyoming Valley, 7, 35, 37, 46, 139, 192, 199, 202, 204, 208, 231, 235, 240, 248–49, 255, 257, 259–60, 262, 264, 269, 272, 275

Y

York County, Pennsylvania, 43
Youghiogheny River, 136

Z

Zeisberger, 34
Zilla Woolie (chief), 62
Zinzendorf, Count, 27, 34–37

CPSIA information can be obtained
at www.ICGtesting.com
Printed in the USA
BVHW071900231222
654914BV00004B/641